Communications
in Computer and Information Science   1559

Rationale

The CCIS series is devoted to the publication of proceedings of computer science conferences. Its aim is to efficiently disseminate original research results in informatics in printed and electronic form. While the focus is on publication of peer-reviewed full papers presenting mature work, inclusion of reviewed short papers reporting on work in progress is welcome, too. Besides globally relevant meetings with internationally representative program committees guaranteeing a strict peer-reviewing and paper selection process, conferences run by societies or of high regional or national relevance are also considered for publication.

Topics

The topical scope of CCIS spans the entire spectrum of informatics ranging from foundational topics in the theory of computing to information and communications science and technology and a broad variety of interdisciplinary application fields.

Information for Volume Editors and Authors

Publication in CCIS is free of charge. No royalties are paid, however, we offer registered conference participants temporary free access to the online version of the conference proceedings on SpringerLink (http://link.springer.com) by means of an http referrer from the conference website and/or a number of complimentary printed copies, as specified in the official acceptance email of the event.

CCIS proceedings can be published in time for distribution at conferences or as post-proceedings, and delivered in the form of printed books and/or electronically as USBs and/or e-content licenses for accessing proceedings at SpringerLink. Furthermore, CCIS proceedings are included in the CCIS electronic book series hosted in the SpringerLink digital library at http://link.springer.com/bookseries/7899. Conferences publishing in CCIS are allowed to use Online Conference Service (OCS) for managing the whole proceedings lifecycle (from submission and reviewing to preparing for publication) free of charge.

Publication process

The language of publication is exclusively English. Authors publishing in CCIS have to sign the Springer CCIS copyright transfer form, however, they are free to use their material published in CCIS for substantially changed, more elaborate subsequent publications elsewhere. For the preparation of the camera-ready papers/files, authors have to strictly adhere to the Springer CCIS Authors' Instructions and are strongly encouraged to use the CCIS LaTeX style files or templates.

Abstracting/Indexing

CCIS is abstracted/indexed in DBLP, Google Scholar, EI-Compendex, Mathematical Reviews, SCImago, Scopus. CCIS volumes are also submitted for the inclusion in ISI Proceedings.

How to start

To start the evaluation of your proposal for inclusion in the CCIS series, please send an e-mail to ccis@springer.com.

Rostislav Yavorskiy · Ana Rosa Cavalli ·
Anna Kalenkova

Editors

Tools and Methods
of Program Analysis

6th International Conference, TMPA 2021
Tomsk, Russia, November 25–27, 2021
Revised Selected Papers

 Springer

Editors
Rostislav Yavorskiy ⓘ
Tomsk Polytechnic University
Tomsk, Russia

Ana Rosa Cavalli ⓘ
Telecom SudParis
Paris, France

Anna Kalenkova ⓘ
The University of Adelaide
Adelaide, SA, Australia

ISSN 1865-0929 ISSN 1865-0937 (electronic)
Communications in Computer and Information Science
ISBN 978-3-031-50422-8 ISBN 978-3-031-50423-5 (eBook)
https://doi.org/10.1007/978-3-031-50423-5

This Springer imprint is published by the registered company Springer Nature Switzerland AG
The registered company address is: Gewerbestrasse 11, 6330 Cham, Switzerland

Paper in this product is recyclable.

Preface

The 6th TMPA International conference on Software Testing, Machine Learning and Complex Process Analysis held on 25–27 November 2021 covered various aspects of application of modern methods of data science to the analysis of software quality. The event was organized by Exactpro in cooperation with the ACM Special Interest Group on Software Engineering (ACM SIGSOFT). Due to the pandemic restrictions, the conference sessions were conducted remotely.

The conference aims to allow specialists from different fields to meet each other, present their work, and discuss both theoretical and practical aspects of their research, to stimulate scientists and people from industry to benefit from the knowledge exchange and identify possible grounds for fruitful collaboration.

The program committee of TMPA 2021 included 30 experts from leading academic institutions and industry organizations in Australia, Chile, Estonia, France, Germany, Italy, Japan, Russia, the Netherlands, the UK, and the USA.

Out of 40 submissions, only 18 papers were accepted for live online presentations. Each submission was put through single-blinded review by at least three reviewers.

The conference featured a tutorial:

- Formal Methods: Theory and Practice of Linux Verification Center, by Alexey Khoroshilov, ISP RAS;

  and the following invited talks:

- Meta-heuristic Techniques and Their Applications, by Mohamed Elsayed Ahmed Mohamed, TPU;
- Automation in Software Testing. Humans and Complex Models, by Iosif Itkin, Exactpro;
- Formal Verification of the Eth2.0 Beacon Chain, by Franck Cassez, ConsenSys.

We would like to thank the authors for submitting their papers and the members of the Program Committee for their efforts in providing their detailed and objective reviews. We would also like to express our special gratitude to all the invited speakers and industry representatives.

Ana Rosa Cavalli
Anna Kalenkova
Rostislav Yavorskiy

Organization

Program Committee Chairs

Ana Rosa Cavalli   Télécom SudParis, France
Anna Kalenkova   University of Melbourne, Australia
Rostislav Yavorskiy   Tomsk Polytechnic University, Russia

Program Committee Board

Abel Armas Cervantes	University of Melbourne, Australia
Alexander Kamkin	Russian Academy of Sciences, Russia
Alexei Lisitsa	University of Liverpool, UK
Andrea Burattin	Technical University of Denmark, Denmark
Andrey Rivkin	Free University of Bozen-Bolzano, Italy
Claude Michel	Université Côte d'Azur, CNRS, I3S, France
Dmitry Boulytchev	Saint Petersburg State University, Russia
Dmitry Tsitelov	Devexperts, Russia
Franck Cassez	ConsenSys Software Inc., USA & Macquarie University, Australia
Goran Frehse	ENSTA Paris, France
Iosif Itkin	Exactpro, Malta
Irina Lomazova	National Research University Higher School of Economics, Russia
Jorge Munoz-Gama	Pontificia Universidad Católica de Chile, Chile
Marat Akhin	Saint Petersburg Polytechnic University, Russia
Massimiliano de Leoni	University of Padua, Italy
Mikhail Belyaev	Saint Petersburg State Polytechnic University, Russia
Mikhail Moiseev	Intel, USA
Nikolaj Bjørner	Microsoft, USA
Nikolay Pakulin	Russian Academy of Sciences, Russia
Pawel Sobocinski	Tallinn University of Technology, Estonia
Peter Habermehl	Université Paris Cité, France
Roberto Giacobazzi	University of Verona, Italy
Santiago Zanella-Béguelin	Microsoft, UK
Silvio Ranise	University of Trento and Fondazione Bruno Kessler, Italy

Tachio Terauchi	Waseda University, Japan
Tim Willemse	Eindhoven University of Technology, The Netherlands
Victor Kuliamin	Institute for System Programming, Russian Academy of Sciences, Russia
Victor Zakharov	IPI Russian Academy of Sciences, Russia
Vladimir Itsykson	Saint Petersburg State Polytechnical University, Russia
Vladimir Zakharov	Lomonosov Moscow State University, Russia

Local Chair

Anna Bogdan	Tomsk Polytechnic University, Russia

Contents

Short Papers

Contributed Papers

Algorithm for Mapping Layout Grids in User Interfaces: Automating the "Squint Test"

Maxim Bakaev[✉] 🆔 and Maxim Shirokov

Novosibirsk State Technical University, Novosibirsk, Russia
bakaev@corp.nstu.ru

Abstract. Human-Computer Interaction sees increased application of AI methods, particularly for testing and assessing the characteristics of graphic user interfaces (UIs). For instance, target users' subjective perceptions of visual complexity, aesthetic impression, trust, etc. can be predicted to some extend based on UI appearance. Buttons, text blocks, images and other elements in today's UIs at all platforms are usually aligned to grids – i.e. regular vertical and horizontal lines – in order to decrease visual clutter. However, the grids are not apparent in the UI representations available for analysis (HTML/CSS, etc.), unlike in design mockups, and have to be reverse-engineered for the benefit of further UI assessment. In our paper we propose the algorithm for automated construction of layout grids on top of visual representations (screenshots) of existing UIs and demonstrate its work with various configuration parameters. The algorithm was inspired by the informal Squint Test known from Usability Engineering practice and is based on subsequent application of several computer vision techniques supported by OpenCV library. The main stages are edge detection, image pixelization, grid overlaying, and cell coding. The tuning of the algorithm's configuration parameters can be performed to match the UI perception by representative users, as demonstrated in the paper. The outcome of the algorithm is a coded representation of graphical UI as a 2D matrix, which is a convenient medium for further processing. The automation of UI layouts coding can allow obtaining large datasets needed by up-to-date user behavior models that predict the quality of interaction with UIs.

Keywords: User Interface · Visual Perception · Pattern Recognition · Computer Vision · Software Analysis

1 Introduction

It is already well established in the field of human-computer interaction (HCI) that perceived visual complexity (VC) of a user interface (UI) significantly affects not only users' cognitive load, but also aesthetic and other emotional experiences [1]. In other words, decreased visual complexity (VC) can allow the user to save time and effort required for the initial grasp of a UI or a web page, and at the same time can promote aesthetic impression. Correspondingly, UI designers often want to optimize VC, but this is not an easy undertaking without appropriate theoretical grounds and practical tools for assessing the VC in particular software products' UIs.

R. Yavorskiy et al. (Eds.): TMPA 2021, CCIS 1559, pp. 3–14, 2024.
https://doi.org/10.1007/978-3-031-50423-5_1

Indeed, the relation of VC with aesthetics is not straightforward though and is being actively studied lately in various contexts [2]. Most theoretical frameworks and practical tools dealing with VC of graphical UIs (e.g. [3]) agree that it incorporates the following groups of factors:

- **Scale:** size of UI, total number of UI elements, amount of content, etc.
- **Diversity:** number of different UI elements, different colors, etc.
- **Organization:** number of visually identifiable groups, relative positioning of UI elements, etc.

The latter group of factors incorporates alignment of UI elements, i.e. layout that fits them to a simple grid, and visual hierarchy, which is basically the order in which the user processes the elements and the content in UI. Effective hierarchy achieved in interface design clearly shows the relationship between the visual elements and structures the information so that the user can quickly understand the interface and distinguish between the main elements and the ones of secondary importance. This makes it easier to understand the information being communicated and provides the user with a sense of accomplishment [4].

Just like any other design, the "good" layout and visual hierarchy have to be immediately apparent and functional at first sight. This causes understandable difficulties for UI designers, as they are unable to assess their UIs' complexity from the user's perspective without a bias, being too familiar with their own designs [5]. At the same time, we still lack universally accepted quantitative measures of VC, as well as the agreement on the algorithms for automatically assessing it in a UI, although their development is largely seen as desirable [6]. There is a consensus though that the traditional code-based analysis of UIs that deals with HTML/CSS code is a poor fit for VC assessment, and most up-to-date approaches work with a graphical UI images (screenshots) [7].

For images in general (landscapes, drawings, photos etc.), the widely used measure of visual complexity is the file size in JPEG format, in accordance with the Algorithmic Information Theory [8]. However, there are research findings that suggest that graphical UIs constitute a particular class of visual stimuli with respect to VC perception. Previously, we found that the compression-based metrics obtained from UI grid mapping were better at predicting VC perception compared to the "raw" JPEG metric [9]. In that work we relied on 8 dedicated human labelers to identify the grids in 19 web UIs screenshots and code empty or meaningful cells in them, while in the current paper we present the algorithm for automation of the process. Having no humans in the loop would allow much faster analysis/testing of UIs and the accumulation of sizable datasets for modeling and predicting VC and possibly other visual perception dimensions in potential users.

The rest of our paper is structured as follows. In Sect. 2 we provide an overview of the existing techniques and tools for visual analysis of UIs and the VC assessment. We also briefly describe the informal "Squint Test" known in interface design, which served as an inspiration for our approach. In Sect. 3 we detail the proposed computer vision-based algorithm, demonstrate how changes in its parameters affect the end result, and validate it with 70 human subjects. In the final section, we summarize and discuss our results, note limitations of our current study and outline further research directions.

2 Methods and Related Work

The importance of simpler interfaces is already well established in Software Engineering, where they highlight that a user must not waste time interacting with a program, otherwise the overall performance is reduced. Recent studies in HCI suggest a clear link between subjective impressions in users, such as visual complexity and aesthetics, and the overall user experience and even productivity. For instance, various types of tasks were used, presented either on an aesthetic or an unaesthetic website according to a subjective assessment, with various instructions for their implementation, including target orientation. Although the results did not show significant influence of aesthetics and goal orientation in terms of quality and response time for each of the three tasks, it was nevertheless concluded that aesthetics should still be considered because of its positive impact on subjective user perception [10].

There are already several existing software tools implementing algorithms for automated identification of visual component of graphical interfaces, without involving human annotators. Among such user-independent tools developed over the past 10 years, we can mention XAOS [3], whose authors were among the first to propose formulas for assessing the complexity of graphical UIs. In the GUIEvaluator software [11], the emphasis was placed on assessing the complexity of the arrangement of elements in a UI. The authors highlighted factors such as alignment, grouping, size, density, and balance. The VC metrics proposed in [12] included visual clutter, color variability, symmetry, grid alignment, grouping, color density, contrast with the background, etc. Six of the metrics that allowed automatic calculation were included in the subsequently developed software tool Aalto Interface Metrics – AIM [13]. Of particular interest is the *Grid Quality* metric output by the tool, which corresponds to the number of grid alignment lines found for UI elements.

To the best of our knowledge, however, there are no solutions that overlay a grid to an existing UI in a manner that a design mockup does (which would mean performing a sort of reverse engineering). We first proposed such a visual analysis method in [9], being inspired in particular by the informal "Squint Test" known in usability engineering and UI design. This simple method, performing in essence a coarsening of the visual perception, implies that a designer half-closes his or her eyes while observing a UI prototype and tries to infer visual hierarchy in it. A software implementation of the "Squint Test" was described in [14], but their focus was on predicting visual attention, not on obtaining grid-based data for subsequent analysis.

In our previous related study [9], the grids (vertical and horizontal alignment lines for UI elements, corresponding to rows and columns) for 19 web page screenshots were overlaid by 8 human labelers. It should be noted that each labeler would process all 19 screenshots, and then the outcomes were averaged for each screenshot. The results varied quite notably per different labelers – for instance, for the total number of identified grid cells the relative standard deviation was 27.8%, so the "ground truth" in the grid overlaying task is obviously hard to pinpoint. Correspondingly, the automating algorithm needs adjustable parameters, tuning which for better fit to human perception is a distinct issue.

3 Results

3.1 The Algorithm

All in all, we have devised and implemented the algorithm to automatically produce the location grids (layouts) of visual elements in UIs. The essence of this algorithm is as follows: the input is a UI screenshot (mobile, web, or desktop platforms are all supported), while the output contains a superimposed layout grid of interface elements (buttons, input fields, text, etc.). The algorithm also determines which cells of the grid are filled with elements, and in which there is mostly an empty background (whitespace). The developed algorithm consists of several stages.

In the first stage, the input image of the interface (Fig. 1) is converted into the image containing edges (Fig. 2) using the Canny edge detector function from the popular OpenCV computer vision library.

Fig. 1. The original image (screenshot) of a web user interface.

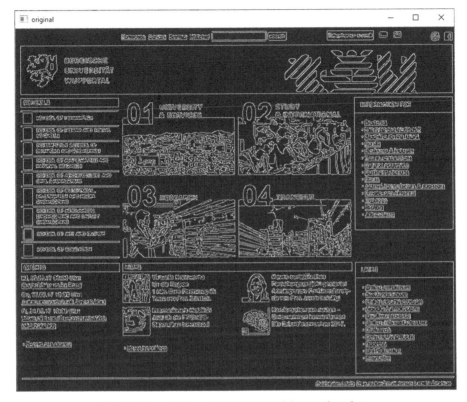

Fig. 2. Stage 1: Transformed image of the user interface.

Particularly, the following main steps are performed:

- removing noise and clutter from the image;
- calculating the image gradient;
- edge thinning;
- edge linking.

The following code is called for this (`aperture_size` is the parameter for Sobel's operator):

```
CVAPI(void) cvCanny( const CvArr* image, CvArr* edges, double
threshold1, double threshold2, int aperture_size CV_DEFAULT(3) );
```

In the second stage, the image with identified edges is compressed to obtain a "pixel" image (Fig. 3). The pixel image is necessary to make the boundaries between the elements better traceable for the algorithm to work. For this, the following is performed:

- the image size is reduced by the factor of 3;
- then the image is recovered to the original size.

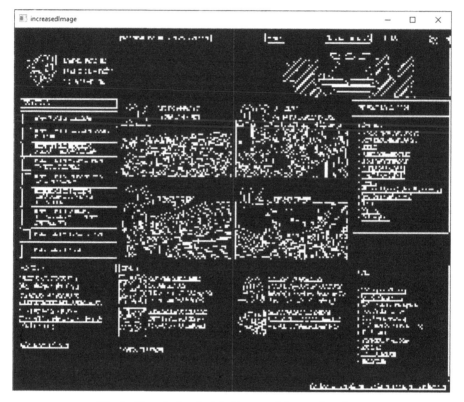

Fig. 3. Stage 2: the pixelated image of the user interface.

We used `cvResize()` function from the OpenCV library (`interpolation` is by default bilinear interpolation method default, which requires the minimal time for processing):

```
CVAPI(void) cvResize( const CvArr* src, CvArr* dst, int
interpolation CV_DEFAULT( CV_INTER_LINEAR ) );
```

In the third stage, the resulting image is analyzed and the grid is overlaid (Fig. 4 shows the outcome). The analysis starts by columns (vertical lines) in includes the following steps:

- looking for continuous segments of black and white pixels;
- depending on the `grid accuracy` parameter (allowed ratio of the segment's length to the column length) and the allowed noise – `error` (allowed percentage of irregular white or black pixels in the segment), decide on making a column;
- the next column is checked only after the `minimum grid step` (as the percentage of the whole image dimension).

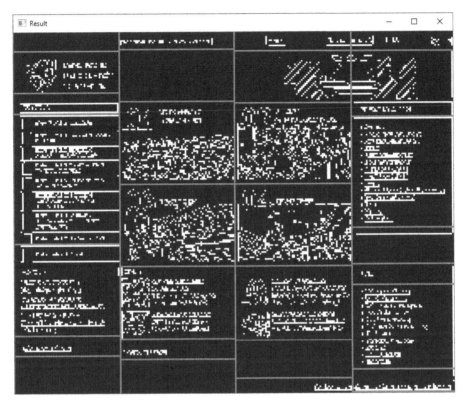

Fig. 4. Stage 3: the image of the user interface with the overlaid grid.

The analysis continues by rows (horizontal lines) following the same steps, but for each identified column. The `grid accuracy`, the `error` and the `minimum grid step` parameters are independently specified for the horizontal dimension.

In the fourth stage, each cell of the grid is assigned with 0 or 1 value, depending on the ratio of white pixels in the cell. We need to note that this is a fuzzy part of the algorithm, as selection of the threshold is justified by the particulars of human perception. The work on calibrating the threshold parameter to better match the perception of different categories of users is still ongoing in our project. Currently we settled on the default threshold value of 3%, which by and large produces the commonly expected 0/1 values.

Ultimately, the original UI image is recovered, with the grid superimposed on it and the cells coded with the values (Fig. 5).

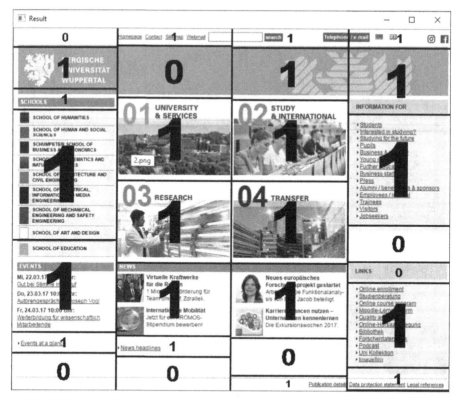

Fig. 5. Outcome: the user interface screenshot with the grid overlaid and the cells coded.

3.2 The Parameters Tuning

The algorithm is able to quickly process UI images and produce fairly accurate results depending on the configurable grid parameters. A drawback is that there are no universal settings for the configurable parameters for all UIs, since there are many interfaces that differ significantly from each other, particularly due to implementation in different platforms (e.g. desktop vs. web). Therefore, it is necessary to experiment with the parameters until the grid and the cell values meet the required accuracy requirements and appear adequate to the representative users.

Let us consider an example of the effect of the parameters' settings in the algorithm. Figure 6 demonstrates how the grid was overlaid with the default parameters. One can see that the small interface elements in the left side of the UI form separate grid cells containing 1–2 elements each. However, based on the semantics, these elements should have been joined in a group as menu items and identified as a single cell. To achieve this, we can increase the `Minimum border width` parameter from 2 to 3.

In Fig. 7 the improved result is presented, with the menu items now organized according to the semantics of UI elements and with the vertical spaces in the menus accounted for. Correspondingly, such outcome of the algorithm appears more accurate to a UI user and better matches the grid overlaying that a human labeler would perform.

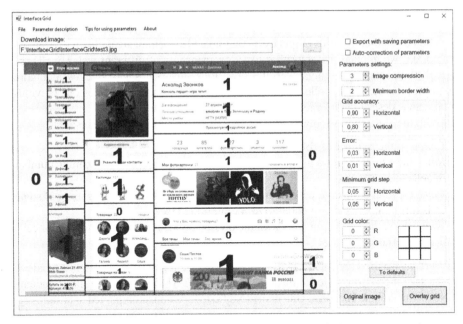

Fig. 6. A user interface processed by the algorithm with the default parameters settings.

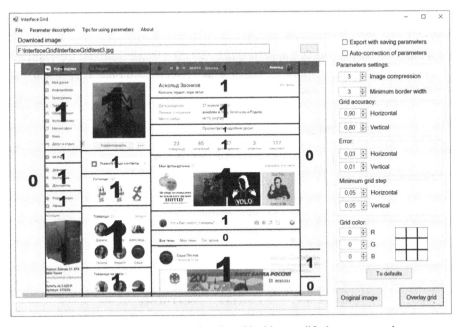

Fig. 7. An example of overlaying the grid with a modified parameter value.

3.3 The Validation

To validate whether the grids output by our automated algorithm are indicative of human perception, we applied the algorithm to 497 screenshots of different web UIs. These were the homepages for official websites of various universities and colleges, and more detail on their selection, collection and approval can be found in one of our previous publications describing a larger experimental study [15].

With the algorithm, we obtained the following metrics for each screenshot:

- *Columns*: the number of columns in the overlaid grid,
- *Rows*: the number of rows in the overlaid grid (corresponding to the maximum number of cells in a column),
- *Cells*: the total number of cells in the overlaid grid (note that due to spanning of some cells this number is less or equal to *Rows* multiplied by *Columns*),
- *Whitespace*: the number of cells with the 0 value divided by the total number of cells in the overlaid grid.

Further, we used the data from a survey with 70 participants (43 females, 27 males), whose age ranged from 18 to 29 (mean 20.86, SD = 1.75) [15]. They were either students of Novosibirsk State Technical University (NSTU) or specialists employed in IT industry. We asked them to provide their subjective assessments of the website screenshots per the three Likert scales (1 – lowest, 7 – highest):

- *Complexity*: how visually complex the UI appears in the screenshot,
- *Aesthetics*: how aesthetically pleasant is the UI,
- *Orderliness*: how orderly is the UI.

In total, we obtained 4235 full evaluations, per the 3 scales each (each screenshot was evaluated by 8–10 participants). The descriptive statistics for the independent and dependent variables in the study is presented in Table 1.

Table 1. The descriptive statistics for the variables in the study.

Variable	Range	Mean (SD)
Columns	1–5	3.03 (1.22)
Rows	2–13	8.34 (1.90)
Cells	3–25	15.17 (5.49)
Whitespace	0.00–0.92	0.41 (0.16)
Complexity	1.75–5.78	3.58 (0.65)
Aesthetics	1.71–6.25	4.12 (0.86)
Orderliness	2.11–6.13	4.44 (0.64)

Further, we constructed linear regression equations with the Backwards variable selection method for all three scales, using the four metrics obtained with the algorithm as the initial factors. All the regressions were highly significant, although the R^2s were rather moderate, particularly for the *Complexity* variable (see in Table 2). In accordance with UI design guidelines, the *Whitespace* factor was significant in all the models.

Table 2. Summary of the regression models with the factors based on the algorithm's output.

Dependent variable	Significant factors	Model
Complexity	*Whitespace* (Beta = -0.153, p = 0.001)	$R^2 = 0.024$, $R^2_{adj} = 0.022$, $F_{1,495} = 11.9$, p = 0.001
Aesthetics	*Columns* (Beta = -0.653, p < 0.001) *Cells* (Beta = 0.350, p < 0.001) *Whitespace* (Beta = 0.224, p < 0.001)	$R^2 = 0.246$, $R^2_{adj} = 0.242$, $F_{3,493} = 53.7$, p < 0.001
Orderliness	*Columns* (Beta = -0.471, p < 0.001) *Cells* (Beta = 0.260, p < 0.001) *Whitespace* (Beta = 0.186, p < 0.001)	$R^2 = 0.134$, $R^2_{adj} = 0.129$, $F_{3,493} = 25.4$, p < 0.001

4 Discussion and Conclusion

Automated testing of user interfaces is gaining in popularity, and particular focus is on evaluation of subjective perception aspects, such as visual complexity that affects many parameters in human-computer interaction. Code-based analysis of UIs is already well established as a fast and accurate method, but it is largely unable to predict visual perception aspects, while image-based analysis based on computer vision can "see" what the user sees in a graphical UI for any device, browser or platform.

Previously we proposed an analogue of the "Squint Test" method based on reduction of visual fidelity and demonstrated that the grids produced by human labelers for web UIs in its "manual" implementation were indeed good predictors of VC [9]. In our current paper, we describe the algorithm that automatically overlays the layout grid and codes the grid cells with the values of 0 (the cell is mostly blank) or 1 (the cell has UI elements or content). The several steps of the algorithm that we describe in detail are basically edge detection, image pixelization, grid overlaying, and cell coding. The technical implementation is supported by the respective functions available in OpenCV library, and we demonstrate how tweaking the configuration parameters affect the end result. The outcome of the algorithm is a coded representation of a graphical UI as 2D matrix, which is a convenient medium for further processing, e.g. application of compression algorithms that are known to be indicative of objects' visual complexity perception in humans [8]. Our algorithm can work in "batch" mode, taking the list of the UI screenshots filenames and outputting the grids and the coding data, thus allowing to obtain large datasets needed for up-to-date studies of VC.

The validation with 70 human subjects and 497 websites suggests that the factors resulting from the algorithm's output do have statistically significant relation with the perception of VC and some other subjective impressions. The regression model for *Complexity*, although highly significant, had R^2_{adj} considerably lower than the $R^2_{adj} =$

0.263 that we obtained for the manual grid overlaying in [9]. However, in that setup we only had 19 websites, i.e. 26 times less than the automated implementation of the algorithm has easily covered. Also, the R^2s that we now got for *Aesthetics* ($R^2_{adj} = 0.242$) and *Orderliness* ($R^2_{adj} = 0.129$) are already comparable to the R^2_{adj} [9], although in the latter work we did not consider any other perception dimensions besides VC.

A limitation of our current work is that so far we do not propose a formalized way to choose the values for the prominent configuration parameters of the algorithm depending of the particulars of UIs, platforms or users. We are working on auto-tuning of the algorithm parameters so that the output better matches human perception of VC. Still, we believe our results might be already of interest to HCI researchers and developers of software tools for UI testing.

References

1. Machado, P., et al.: Computerized measures of visual complexity. Acta Physiol (Oxf.) **160**, 43–57 (2015)
2. Miniukovich, A., Marchese, M.: Relationship between visual complexity and aesthetics of webpages. In Proceedings of the 2020 CHI Conference on Human Factors in Computer System, pp. 1–13 (2020)
3. Stickel, C., Ebner, M., Holzinger, A.: The XAOS metric–understanding visual complexity as measure of usability. In: Symposium of the Austrian HCI and Usability Engineering Group, pp. 278–290 (2010)
4. King, A.J., Lazard, A.J., White, S.R.: The influence of visual complexity on initial user impressions: testing the persuasive model of web design. Behav. Inf. Technol. **39**(5), 497–510 (2020)
5. Bakaev, M., Avdeenko, T.: A quantitative measure for information transfer in human-machine control systems. In: Proceedings of the IEEE International Siberian Conference on Control and Communications (SIBCON), pp. 1–4 (2015)
6. Wu, O., Hu, W., Shi, L.: Measuring the visual complexities of web pages. ACM Trans. Web (TWEB) **7**(1), 1 (2013)
7. Michailidou, E., et al.: Automated prediction of visual complexity of web pages: tools and evaluations. Int. J. Hum. Comput. Stud. **145**, 102523 (2021)
8. Donderi, D.C.: Visual complexity: a review. Psychol. Bull. **132**(1), 73 (2006)
9. Bakaev, M. et al.: Data compression algorithms in analysis of UI layouts visual complexity. In: Proceedings of the International Andrei Ershov Memorial Conference on Perspectives of System Informatics, pp. 167–184 (2019)
10. Thielsch, M.T., Haines, R., Flacke, L.: Experimental investigation on the effects of website aesthetics on user performance in different virtual tasks. PeerJ **7**, e6516 (2019)
11. Alemerien, K., Magel, K. GUIEvaluator: A metric-tool for evaluating the complexity of graphical user interfaces. In: SEKE, pp. 13–18 (2014)
12. Miniukovich, A., de Angeli, A.: Quantification of interface visual complexity. In: Proceedings of the International Working Conference on Advanced Visual Interfaces, pp. 153–160 (2014)
13. Oulasvirta, A. et al.: Aalto interface metrics (AIM) a service and codebase for computational GUI evaluation. In: Adjunct Proceedings 31st Annual ACM Symposium on User Interface Software and Technology, pp. 16–19 (2018)
14. Kim, N.W., et al.: BubbleView: an interface for crowdsourcing image importance maps and tracking visual attention. ACM Trans. Comput.-Hum. Interact. (TOCHI), **24**(5), 36 (2017)
15. Boychuk, E., Bakaev, M.: Entropy and compression based analysis of web user interfaces. In: Proceedings of International Conference on Web Engineering (ICWE), pp. 253–261 (2019)

Process Mining Algorithm for Online Intrusion Detection System

Yinzheng Zhong$^{(\boxtimes)}$, John Y. Goulermas , and Alexei Lisitsa

Department of Computer Science, University of Liverpool, Liverpool, UK
yinzheng.zhong@outlook.com, {goulerma,a.lisitsa}@liverpool.ac.uk

Abstract. In this paper, we consider the applications of process mining in intrusion detection. We propose a novel process mining inspired algorithm to be used to preprocess data in intrusion detection systems (IDS). The algorithm is designed to process the network packet data and it works well in online mode for online intrusion detection. To test our algorithm, we used the CSE-CIC-IDS2018 dataset which contains several common attacks. The packet data was preprocessed with this algorithm and then fed into the detectors. We report on the experiments using the algorithm with different machine learning (ML) models as classifiers to verify that our algorithm works as expected; we tested the performance on anomaly detection methods as well and reported on the existing preprocessing tool CICFlowMeter for the comparison of performance.

Keywords: Intrusion detection · Process mining · Deep learning · Anomaly detection · Cybersecurity

1 Introduction

With the growth of applications that relies on internet communication, cybercrime became a serious issue that affects many areas. By estimation, about 33 billion records of personal information including addresses, credit card information, or social security numbers etc., will be stolen in 2033 [9]. The intrusion detection systems (IDS) protect computer systems by monitoring the network or system activities. One of the main challenges in the design of IDS is to have fast and robust methods for network traffic assessment to be used for the detection of attacks and malicious behaviour. The *process mining* has risen recently as a promising research direction aiming at systematic developments of the methods for building behavioural or workflow models from event logs [2,11]. The process mining is essentially approaches that takes information (e.g. cases, timestamps and events) from the event logs for building the workflow models (process models) which can then be used for analytical tasks. The process model describes the transitions of events within traces.

While the applications of process mining in the security have been considered, e.g. in [1], its applications in IDS remain largely unexplored. In this paper, we propose process mining inspired technique to be used at the preprocessing stage to

© Springer Nature Switzerland AG 2024
R. Yavorskiy et al. (Eds.): TMPA 2021, CCIS 1559, pp. 15–25, 2024.
https://doi.org/10.1007/978-3-031-50423-5_2

generate a behaviour model, which subsequently be classified as attack/no attack or normal/malicious behaviour by trained machine learning models. There are similar approaches for IDS, for example, based on *data mining* [8] and *machine learning* [3,6]. In most of the cases, however, these approaches can only detect the threats after features been generated based on flows. In our approach, the process mining is used as the preprocessing step, while machine learning is used as the classifier. Our proposed algorithm for process mining of network data can be seen as a modification of the initial model mentioned in the fuzzy mining algorithm [5]. The latter was modified for better online processing, and techniques such as aggregation and abstraction in fuzzy mining could also be applied. The rest of the paper is organized as follows. In the next section, we give a short outline of the related work. After that, in Sect. 4 we present the proposed process mining inspired algorithm. The setup for machine learning is discussed in Sect. 5. Section 6 reports on experiments and Sect. 7 presents the discussion and outlines the future work.

2   Related Work

The fuzzy mining algorithm was introduced in [5]. The process model is built on the initial model with various filterings and abstractions. The initial model is the high-level description of processes that preserves all relations. We tried to use fuzzy and inductive mining traditionally for intrusion detection by performing conformance checking, but the result is far worse than expected [1]. We get the inspiration from fuzzy mining and modified the algorithm to perform online mining, which can then be used as a preprocessing step for online intrusion detection. The algorithm will be described in Sect. 4.

CICFlowMeter is a preprocessing tool that generates features, such as bytes per second, inter arrival time, packets per second etc., based on the network flows. The TCP flow terminates at FIN packet, where for UDP connections a timeout value needs to be set. The CICFlowMeter has been introduced in [7]. We compare the performance of CICFlowMeter with our preprocessing algorithm in Sect. 6.

We use multi-layer perceptron (MLP), long short-term memory (LSTM), convolutional neural network (CNN), and k-nearest neighbours (KNN) in our binary classification and multi-class classification setups. The reason we choose these classifiers is:

- MLP is a simple feedforward model.
- LSTM is a recurrent model that can be applied on time series data.
- CNN works directly on 2D inputs and it has been widely used in image classification problems.
- KNN is an example of traditional distance based classifier.

For the anomaly detection setup, we used the following outlier detectors.

- Multivariate normal distribution (MND).
- Copula-Based Outlier Detection (COPOD).

- AutoEncoder.
- Angle-Based Outlier Detection (ABOD).
- Clustering-Based Local Outlier Factor (CBLOF).
- Histogram-based Outlier Score (HBOS).
- Isolation Forest (IForest).
- K-nearest Neighbors (KNN).
- Local Outlier Factor (LOF).
- Principal Component Analysis (PCA).

Note that the reason we choose these models as our classifiers is because they have different properties and characteristics, and the purpose of comparing them is just to verify that the preprocessing algorithms works as expected so it can be applied onto different classifiers.

3   Dataset

The dataset we used in this experiment is the CSE-CIC-IDS2018 dataset [10]. The dataset contains common attacks such as Bruteforce, DoS, and Botnet etc. The dataset comes with two formats, the extracted features in CSV spreadsheets and the PCAP binary packet data. We used Tshark to extract necessary attributes (IPs, ports, and flags) of TCP packets from the PCAP data for our algorithm. We also generated dataset with CICFlowMeter using the same PCAP data that were used as the training set for our preprocessing algorithm.

4   Process Mining and Measuring Frequency of Transitions

The packets observed on the wire is the sequence $P = \langle p_i \rangle_{i=1}^n$, where p_i is each individual packet. The observed packets can also form a set of TCP flows $T = \{t_i\}_{i=1}^m$, where each flow t_i can be constructed according to the IP addresses and ports of two hosts (T can also be considered as the event log from a perspective of process mining). Please note that in process mining, a flow would correspond to a *trace*, and both of these terms may be used in this paper interchangeably. We define that a new TCP flow is started when a packet that has flag SYN set but without ACK set (first packet of three-way handshake) is received, also, this initial packet determines the IP addresses and ports of two hosts. For example, the packet has *Source IP : Port* $= IP_1 : PORT_1$ and *Target IP : Port* $= IP_2 : PORT_2$. The bidirectional flows can be reconstructed based on forward direction ($IP_1 : PORT_1 \rightarrow IP_2 : PORT_2$) and backward direction ($IP_2 : PORT_2 \rightarrow IP_1 : PORT_1$). We define the TCP flow as completed when the packet that has the FIN flag or RST flag set is received.

As mentioned above, instead of analysing the flows, we analyse the relations between packets in flows, which is the basic idea of process mining [11]. Before we discuss the algorithm we need to define the concepts of *transitions* and *event classes*.

Given a sequence of packets P, we define a *transition* in P as a pair of consecutive packets (p_i, p_j) within a flow in P.

Here is an example, giving two traces t_1 and t_2, where $t_1 = \langle p_1, p_3, p_5 \rangle$ and flow $t_2 = \langle p_2, p_6 \rangle$, we will get two transitions for t_1: (p_1, p_3) and (p_3, p_5); one transition for t_2: (p_2, p_6). Packets p_1 and p_2 come from two consecutive packets, however, these packets will not be considered as a transition as they belong to different flows.

An *event class* $ec(p)$ of a packet p is the concatenation of enabled flags of a packet followed by an indicator. e.g. 000.SYN.|C, where the last character is an indicator that indicates either the packet is sent from the client or the server. In this case, C indicates the packet is sent from the client.

A *type* of the transition (p_i, p_j) is a pair of corresponding event classes $(ec(p_i), ec(p_j))$. We will also refer to types of transitions as *relations*. e.g. (000-.SYN.|C, 000.ACK.SYN.|S) is a *relation* and which indicates that a packet has SYN flag enabled is followed by a consecutive packet that has ACK and SYN enabled.

We have 23 possible event classes that were observed from the IDS2018 dataset of normal traffic data. We assume these 23 event classes cover the majority of possible flag combinations. All other packets that have flag combinations that were not observed in the dataset can be simply classified as OTHERS as a default rear case handling, or the event classes can be adjusted according to a particular situation.

There are 26 event classes in total, including 23 event classes from the flag data and 3 default classes (START, END and OTHERS). Therefore, there will be $26^2 = 676$ possible *relations* if we assume every classes can be paired with other classes. These 26 event classes are available in Table 1.

Our proposed online algorithm operates as follows. Given a sequence of packets P (even log), the algorithm outputs the sequence (stream) of frequencies of relations observed in the last l packets (for some l), organized in a form of adjacency matrix (26×26). Here, the frequencies of relations observed in the last l packets are process models.

We want to measure the frequency by counting the incoming relations into an adjacency matrix A, however, we will only calculate the frequency based on the last l packets, and the frequency of the transitions needs to be updated per each new packet.

If the initial packet p_1 in trace t_1 carries 000.SYN.|C, then the weight of $A(START, 000.SYN.|C)$ will be increased by one; and if the next packet p_3 in the same trace carries 000.ACK.SYN.|S, then the weight in $A(000.SYN.|C, 000.ACK.SYN.|S)$ will be increased by one.

In our experiments, we have limited the number of packets l that used to calculate the frequency of transitions to 500 by using the sliding window. The limitation here is just our choice based on various experiment and any number is possible to be used here. The sliding window starts from p_1 and covers $\langle p_i \rangle_{i=1}^{l}$, and the frequency of transitions A' is calculated as A/l, then the window will be shifted one step further which covers $\langle p_i \rangle_{i=2}^{l+1}$. This process results in a sequence $\langle A'_i \rangle_{i=1}^{n-l+1}$ and each A'_i is a snapshot of a process model with l events. In process

Table 1. Possible event classes used.

000.SYN.|C	000.ACK.SYN.|S	000.ACK.|C	000.ACK.PSH.|C
000.ACK.PSH.|S	000.ACK.FIN.|C	000.ACK.|S	000.ACK.FIN.|S
000.ACK.RST.|C	000.ACK.RST.|S	000.RST.|S	000.ACK.PSH.FIN.|S
000.RST.|C	000.CWR.ECE.SYN.|C	000.ECE.ACK.SYN.|S	000.NS.ACK.FIN.|S
000.ACK.PSH.FIN.|C	000.CWR.ACK.PSH.|C	000.CWR.ACK.|C	000.CWR.ACK.|S
000.CWR.ACK.PSH.|S	000.CWR.ACK.RST.|S	000.CWR.ACK.RST.|C	START
END	OTHERS		

mining, the events are instances of event classes. The process of producing A is similar to mining the fuzzy model where t_i is traces and P is the event log. However, the modification here is that the last state that is outside the window of each flow t_i was kept in the state table so the START and END tokens will only occur at the beginning and end of a particular TCP flow, not where it begins and end in each sliding window. As the last state is known, the relation can be mined even if the window has already passed the previous event. In other words, the original process mining takes the entire event log P into account, and in that case P generates a single huge adjacency matrix A. However, this is not suitable for online processing, therefore, we keep the states of traces through the entire event log P but limit the process model generation based on l packets only. This keeps all the transition information and makes it suitable for online systems.

For the purpose of performance and ease of use, we used the l-sized buffer to keep the transitions that are inside the sliding window instead of count every transition again in each loop, and we ignored the transition to END, therefore, we only need to update two elements in A for each packet (decrease the frequency for the packet that goes off the buffer and increase the frequency for the packet that goes on the buffer). When computing the frequencies of transitions, we also produced the output for machine learning based on the labelled data provided from the dataset. The dataset provides the source of a certain attack, therefore, if the most recent packet in A_i was sent from or to the IP that was labelled as a certain attack (13 types of attacks in total), A_i will be marked as a model that contains attack. For better demonstration, Fig. 1 of Botnet attacks is provided, where attacks are marked in red colour. The red bar at the bottom of the chart in Fig. 2 indicates the locations of attacks. In summary, we have two outputs from this process, the frequencies of the transitions A_i' and the location of attacks. The pseudocode (Algorithm 1) is given in Appendix A below and Fig. 2 shows the example of the output of 20 relations.

5 Experiments

5.1 Knowledge-Based Detection

The proposed workflow applicable in knowledge-based (signature-based) IDS is as follows. The IP and flag information of network packets are captured,

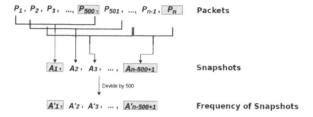

Fig. 1. Diagram of Algorithm 1. Packets P_{500} and P_n belong to traces that are marked as attacks, therefore, A_1 and $A_{n-500+1}$ are also labelled as attacks for training classifiers.

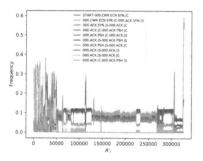 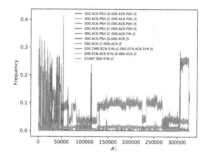

Fig. 2. The chart show frequency fluctuation under Botnet attacks. 20 out of 676 possible relations are given as the example. 10 relations in the first chart and 10 relations in the second chart. In the first chart, the attack happens between $50,000^{th}$ to $310,000^{th}$ packets (ground truth), and it's clear that the frequency starts to stabilise.

and the flows are reconstructed according to the IPs. The flows go through our preprocessor, then a series of snapshots A'_i matrices are generated. These snapshots will be reshaped if needed and then get fed into the ML classifiers trained to recognize *known* attacks. Finally, the classifier will raise the alarm whenever we got an attack.

Except for the input of CNN, A'_i (26 by 26 matrices) was flattened into 676-dimensional vectors (the elements of the vector are the frequencies of transitions), and which was used as the input for MLP, LSTM, and KNN. For binary classifications, the output data are 2-D vectors where $[1\ 0]^{\mathsf{T}}$ stands for normal traffic and $[0\ 1]^{\mathsf{T}}$ stands for intrusions; for multi-class classifications, the output was 14-dimensional one-hot vectors that encode the output to be normal or one of 13 types of attacks. As all of the locations of attacks were marked, the output data can be generated from the algorithm above (Sect. 4). We have not reduced the dimension as we want the classifiers to handle the input data.

The multi-layer perceptron was constructed with 4 dense layers (676, 128, 128 and 2 units for each layer) followed by a softmax layer; the LSTM was built with 2 layers of LSTM (128 units each), one dense layer with 2 units and one softmax layer lastly; the CNN model is similar to the model used in [6], however, we increased the input shape to 26-by-26 and added one dense layer (32 units) before the output layer. For multi-class classification, the number of units for the last dense layer had been increased from 2 to 14 for all neural networks. All instances had been tested through 5-fold cross-validation. We have three setups for the LSTM with 50, 100 and 250 timesteps.

The dataset has imbalanced normal and anomalous entries. Therefore, normal data has been added into samples or been removed to match the number of the attack data for binary classifications. This helps to train the neural networks but does not affect the F-score. Also, attack types SQL-Injection and Infiltration have been discarded in binary classifications due to an insufficient amount of data.

5.2   Anomaly-Based Detection

The proposed workflow for anomaly-based IDS is as follows. The necessary information of network packets are captured, and flows are reconstructed, then the flows go through the preprocessor, which generates snapshots. These steps are identical to the signature-based IDS. The snapshots are reshaped into vectors and fed into outlier detectors, then the outlier detectors provide the outlier scores, where a higher outlier score indicates the data has a higher probability of being an anomaly intrusion.

We use the PyOD python library for anomaly-based detection, and hyperparameters of all outlier detectors remain default. The data format is the same as the one used in the binary classification, where all data have been reshaped to 676-dimensional vectors. For data generated with CICFlowMeter, we did the column-wise normalisation before feeding them into the detectors. We only use the normal data that do not contain any attack to train the detectors, then used mixed data, which contain both normal data and attack data for testing.

6   Results

We compared the results of binary classification in Table 2, and the results of binary classification have also been compared with the results from [6] (Table 4). The LSTM gives worse result compared to other models, especially in multi-class classification (Table 3). Some F1 scores produced by LSTM multi-class classification display NaN (not a number) or 0, meaning these classes have 0 in both precision and recall (i.e. 0 on the diagonal line in the confusion matrix), or 0 in either precision or recall. However, this may indicates that with the preprocessing step, the classifiers do not require the historical data to perform the classification, as the historical data have already been encoded during the process showing in Fig. 1.

We focus on the preprocessing step, so we compare our results with CICFlowMeter in Table 4. Both column uses CNN as the classifier, and the result of our approach is promising.

Table 2. The F1 scores for binary classification.

Attack	MLP	LSTM-50	LSTM-100	LSTM-250	KNN	CNN
FTP-BruteForce	0.9990	0.9976	0.9984	0.9982	**0.9991**	0.9990
SSH-Bruteforce	0.9763	0.9764	0.9763	0.8907	0.9732	**0.9764**
DoS-GoldenEye	0.9212	0.9680	0.7457	0.9498	**0.9821**	0.9434
DoS-Slowloris	0.9945	0.8490	0.8513	0.7770	0.9947	**0.9948**
DoS-SlowHTTP	0.9983	0.9798	0.9937	0.9803	**0.9985**	0.9984
DoS-Hulk	0.7309	0.6732	**0.7731**	0.7313	0.7381	0.7314
DDoS-LOIC-HTTP	**0.9968**	0.7606	0.7129	0.7443	0.8353	0.8406
DDOS-HOIC	**0.9687**	0.7072	0.7922	0.6935	0.7879	0.7559
BruteForce-Web	**0.9962**	0.9588	0.9621	0.9631	0.9789	0.9741
BruteForce-XSS	**0.9985**	0.9676	0.9674	0.9788	0.9868	0.9827
Botnet	0.8168	**0.9644**	0.9137	0.8308	0.8754	0.8623

Table 3. The F1 scores for multi-class classifications.

Attack Type	MLP	LSTM-50	LSTM-100	LSTM-250	KNN	CNN
Normal	0.5533	0.4117	0.5401	0.3115	**0.8306**	0.6457
FTP-BruteForce	0.9734	NaN	NaN	NaN	**0.9991**	0.9743
SSH-Bruteforce	0.9772	0.9254	0.9206	0.9215	0.9753	**0.9774**
DoS-GoldenEye	0.9287	0.9219	0.9209	0.9215	**0.9618**	0.9277
DoS-Slowloris	0.9830	0.2433	0.9573	0.8323	**0.9935**	0.9837
DoS-SlowHTTP	0.9070	0.5056	0.5042	0.5546	**0.9981**	0.8844
DoS-Hulk	0.8241	0.8245	0.8212	0.7611	0.7688	**0.8244**
DDoS-LOIC-HTTP	**0.8755**	0.8754	0.524	0.8668	0.8480	**0.8755**
DDOS-HOIC	0.8188	0.8232	0.2553	0.8078	**0.8253**	0.8203
BruteForce-Web	0.9659	0.0334	NaN	0	0.9679	**0.9687**
BruteForce-XSS	0.9634	NaN	NaN	0	**0.9847**	0.9756
SQL-Injection	0.1765	NaN	NaN	NaN	**0.4941**	0.2908
Infiltration	0.0898	0.0417	0.142	0.0179	**0.4334**	0.0149
Botnet	0.6473	0.6465	0.6295	0.4089	0.6277	**0.6540**

We compared the receiver operating characteristic (ROC) for the anomaly-based intrusion detection setup in Fig. 3. The type of attacks was not separated, so what we have here is the overall performance. It's clear that our algorithm works better in anomaly-based intrusion detection.

We have published the preprocessed data and some of the experiment results online.[1]

---

[1] https://zenodo.org/record/5616678.

Table 4. Comparison between preprocessors.

Attack Type	Our Preprocessor	CICFlowMeter
FTP-BruteForce	**0.9990**	0.98
SSH-Bruteforce	**0.9764**	0.96
DoS-GoldenEye	**0.9434**	0.47
DoS-Slowloris	**0.9948**	0.66
DoS-SlowHTTP	0.9984	1
DoS-Hulk	0.7314	1
DDoS-LOIC-HTTP	0.8406	1
DDOS-HOIC	0.7559	1
BruteForce-Web	**0.9741**	0.3
BruteForce-XSS	**0.9827**	0.65
Botnet	0.8623	1

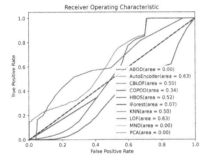 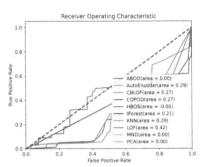

Fig. 3. The receiver operating characteristic (ROC) for anomaly-based intrusion detection setup. The first chart shows the performance of our preprocessor, where the second chart shows the performance of CICFlowMeter.

7 Conclusion and Discussion

We proposed the online process mining algorithm that preprocesses packet data for intrusion detection. The initial process mining algorithm was modified to adapt online process mining, which produces a series of process model snapshots with fixed window sizes. The snapshots were normalized and being used as the input data for machine learning. For signature-based intrusion detection, we used several machine learning models for binary and multi-class classification and yielded high accuracy. Though our preprocessing algorithm does not produce better results for every aspect, the performance was consistently high. On the anomaly-based intrusion detection side, the result is not impressive; however, considering the nature of anomaly-based intrusion detection and the performance of CICFlowMeter, we are satisfied with our preprocessing algorithm. We take it as a starting point to further extend the research on process mining applications in intrusion detection.

Currently, we use snapshots similar to the initial model of the fuzzy miner, and it is possible to apply abstraction on the snapshots easily; therefore, our model can be easily extended with process mining techniques.

As mentioned in Sect. 6, the classification step does not require any historical snapshots as the historical information has already been packed into the latest snapshot. This might be more efficient than using a recurrent neural network (RNN) to directly classify the latest n packet data without separate the flows; and it might be more accurate as our approach keeps the state of the flow until connection closed, not just getting information from the last n packets. It needs to be clarified here that this is just a hypothesis.

Because this algorithm is used for preprocessing, other methods for classification can be easily applied. The output of our preprocessor is normalised and can be directly fed into many classifiers or outlier detectors without much modification. Furthermore, the only attribute we used to generate event classes is the flag, so there is still a large set of unconsidered attributes we could use. These could be verified in our future research. Another problem for machine learning on IDS is that when training the neural networks with one dataset but test the accuracy with a different dataset, the accuracy drops massively [4]. We are planning to verify if process-mining based preprocessing can help to resolve such an issue.

A   Pseudocode

Algorithm 1: pseudocode of packet preprocessing.

```
 1  in P = [n];                                    /* load n packets */
 2  in l = 500;                                    /* define the window size */
 3  A = [26 by 26];                                /* a 26 * 26 adjacency matrix */
 4  list_A' = [ ];                                 /* initialise list of A'_i */
 5  list_attacks = [ ];                            /* initialise list of attacks */
    /* a dictionary where the key is the concatenation of IPs and Ports
       ("IP_1 : PORT_1|IP_1 : PORT''_1) of hosts, and the value is the flags of the previous
       packet                                                                    */
 6  dict_state_table = {};
 7  buffer = [l];         /* an FIFO buffer that keeps the last l transitions (events) */
    /* initialise with first l packets                                          */
 8  for i = 1 to l do
       /* check if the packet belong to any existing flow                       */
 9     if "IP_1 : PORT_1|IP_2 : PORT''_2" in dict_state_table.key() or
          "IP_2 : PORT_2|IP_1 : PORT''_1" in dict_state_table.key() then
             /* count the transition into A                                     */
10           A[dict_state_table["IP_1 : PORT_1|IP_2 : PORT''_2"], current_flags] += 1;
             /* update the state of the flow to the current flags into the dict */
11           dict_state_table["IP_1 : PORT_1|IP_2 : PORT''_2"] = current_flags;
12           push current_flags into buffer;
             /* check whether TCP flow terminates                               */
13           if "FIN" in current_flags or "RST" in current_flags then
14              |  remove key "IP_1 : PORT_1|IP_2 : PORT''_2" from dict_state_table;
15           end
       /* check if new TCP flow starts                                          */
16     else if "SYN" in current_flags and "ACK" not in current_flags then
17        |  A[dict_state_table["START"], current_flags] += 1;
18        |  push current_flags into buffer; /* push the transition (event) into buffer */
19     end
20  end
```

```
21  append A/l to list_A';           /* append the frequency of transitions into the list */
22  for i = l + 1 to n do
23  |   if "IP₁ : PORT₁|IP₂ : PORT₂''" in dict_state_table.key() or
    |      "IP₂ : PORT₂|IP₁ : PORT₁''" in dict_state_table.key() then
24  |   |   A[pop buffer] −= 1;   /* sub 1 for transition that went outside the window */
25  |   |   A[dict_state_table["IP₁ : PORT₁|IP₂ : PORT₂''], current_flags] += 1;
26  |   |   dict_state_table["IP₁ : PORT₁|IP₂ : PORT₂''] = current_flags;
27  |   |   push current_flags into buffer;
    |   |   /* check whether TCP flow terminates                                            */
28  |   |   if "FIN" in current_flags or "RST" in current_flags then
29  |   |   |   remove key "IP₁ : PORT₁|IP₂ : PORT₂''" from dict_state_table;
30  |   |   end
    |   /* check if new TCP flow starts                                                    */
31  |   else if "SYN" in current_flags and "ACK" not in current_flags then
32  |   |   A[pop buffer] −= 1;
33  |   |   A[dict_state_table["START"], current_flags] += 1;
34  |   |   push current_flags into buffer;
35  |   end
36  |   append A/l to list_A';
    |   /* Attack IP is from the labelled data                                             */
37  |   if Attack IP in current_flags then
38  |   |   append i to list_attacks
39  |   end
40  end
    Output: list_A';
    Output: list_attacks;
```

References

1. Van der Aalst, W.M., de Medeiros, A.K.A.: Process mining and security: detecting anomalous process executions and checking process conformance. Electron. Notes Theor. Comput. Sci. **121**, 3–21 (2005)
2. Van der Aalst, W.M., Weijters, A.J.: Process mining: a research agenda. Comput. Ind. **53**(3), 231–244 (2004)
3. Agarap, A.F.M.: A neural network architecture combining gated recurrent unit (GRU) and support vector machine (SVM) for intrusion detection in network traffic data. In: Proceedings of the 2018 10th International Conference on Machine Learning and Computing, pp. 26–30. ACM (2018)
4. Al-Riyami, S., Coenen, F., Lisitsa, A.: A re-evaluation of intrusion detection accuracy: alternative evaluation strategy. In: Proceedings of the 2018 ACM SIGSAC Conference on Computer and Communications Security, pp. 2195–2197 (2018)
5. Günther, C.W., van der Aalst, W.M.P.: Fuzzy mining – adaptive process simplification based on multi-perspective metrics. In: Alonso, G., Dadam, P., Rosemann, M. (eds.) BPM 2007. LNCS, vol. 4714, pp. 328–343. Springer, Heidelberg (2007). https://doi.org/10.1007/978-3-540-75183-0_24
6. Kim, J., Shin, Y., Choi, E., et al.: An intrusion detection model based on a convolutional neural network. J. Multimedia Inf. Syst. **6**(4), 165–172 (2019)
7. Lashkari, A.H., Draper-Gil, G., Mamun, M.S.I., Ghorbani, A.A.: Characterization of tor traffic using time based features. In: ICISSp, pp. 253–262 (2017)
8. Lee, W., Stolfo, S.: Data mining approaches for intrusion detection (1998)
9. Norton: 10 cyber security facts and statistics for 2018. https://us.norton.com/
10. UNB: Ids 2017 dataset. https://www.unb.ca/cic/datasets/ids-2017.html
11. Van Der Aalst, W.: Process Mining: Discovery, Conformance and Enhancement of Business Processes, vol. 2. Springer, Cham (2011)

Bayesian Optimization with Time-Decaying Jitter for Hyperparameter Tuning of Neural Networks

Konstantin A. Maslov[✉]

Division for Information Technology, Tomsk Polytechnic University, Tomsk, Russia
kam20@tpu.ru

Abstract. This paper introduces a modification of the ordinary Bayesian optimization algorithm for hyperparameter tuning of neural networks. The proposed algorithm utilizes the time-decaying parameter ξ (jitter) to dynamically balance between exploration and exploitation. This algorithm is compared with the ordinary Bayesian optimization algorithm with various constant values of ξ; for that, diverse artificial landscapes were used. In this comparison, the proposed algorithm shows a better performance for some artificial landscapes and numbers of dimensions of the search domain. For some others, the ordinary algorithm outperforms the proposed one, but in most cases, there is no statistically significant difference between the two algorithms. Both algorithms then are used to tune hyperparameters of a neural network for semantic image segmentation. The corresponding analysis has shown that both algorithms give a comparable performance.

Keywords: Hyperparameter tuning · Bayesian optimization · time-decaying jitter · semantic image segmentation

1 Introduction

The performance of deep learning algorithms can significantly depend on the values of the hyperparameters used to define the topology of neural networks, to tune the optimization algorithms for finding the best weight coefficients, to preprocess and augment the datasets, etc. [1]. Therefore, in order to achieve the best possible performance of the neural networks, it is necessary to carry out the procedure for hyperparameters tuning. In the literature, this problem is addressed using brute force (exhaustive search) algorithms [2], random search algorithms [3], and various metaheuristics such as genetic algorithms [4] and swarm intelligence algorithms [5]. In the number of recent studies, Bayesian optimization methods have gained particular popularity for the hyperparameter tuning [1, 6], since, unlike the others, they can significantly reduce the number of calls to the objective function, which becomes especially important against the background of constantly increasing datasets, the depth of neural networks and, consequently, the training time for one model.

© Springer Nature Switzerland AG 2024
R. Yavorskiy et al. (Eds.): TMPA 2021, CCIS 1559, pp. 26–40, 2024.
https://doi.org/10.1007/978-3-031-50423-5_3

It is important that an optimization algorithm makes it possible to balance between exploration (sampling from unconsidered areas of the search domain) and exploitation (using knowledge about the possibility to find a more optimal value in the local area). Some algorithms, such as brute force or random search algorithms in their original formulation, do not allow this. In metaheuristics, such balancing is usually incorporated in the algorithm's design and is accompanied by a very large number of calls to the objective function. Bayesian optimization algorithms use posterior distributions obtained as the output of a Gaussian process to assess the degree of exploration of a certain region of the search domain and make a decision about which new point from the search domain to investigate. However, in Bayesian optimization algorithms, typically, it is possible to distinguish an explicit random search phase (exploration) and a phase of the further search for optimal values (combining both exploration and exploitation). It forces the researcher to determine an additional parameter of the optimization algorithm—the number of iterations for the random search—and may also lead to suboptimal results if, in the further search phase, the optimization algorithm paid too much attention to either exploration or exploitation.

This paper proposes a modification of the ordinary Bayesian optimization algorithm that utilizes the time-decaying parameter ξ (jitter) for dynamic balancing between exploration and exploitation and compares it with the ordinary one on a number of artificial landscapes and when solving a practical problem of semantic image segmentation.

The rest of this paper is organized as follows: Sect. 2 describes the ordinary and the proposed Bayesian optimization algorithms; Sect. 3 presents several artificial landscapes, which are test functions for optimization algorithms, and gives a comparison of both algorithms on these landscapes; in Sect. 4, the practical problem of the semantic image segmentation is described and the considered algorithms are evaluated on this problem; and, finally, Sect. 5 concludes the main points of the paper and gives some ideas about the direction of further research in the field of the modifications of Bayesian optimization algorithms.

2 Implemented Optimization Algorithms

The idea behind Bayesian optimization is to replace the objective with a surrogate model, Gaussian process, and solve the optimization problem for this surrogate model. Optimization for the surrogate model is reduced to the optimization of so-called acquisition functions, one of the most popular acquisition functions is Expected Improvement (EI) given by [7]:

$$\text{EI}_\xi(\boldsymbol{\theta}) = \begin{cases} \left(\mu(\boldsymbol{\theta}) - g\left(\boldsymbol{\theta}^*\right) - \xi\right)\Phi(Z) + \sigma(\boldsymbol{\theta})\phi(Z) & \text{if } \sigma(\boldsymbol{\theta}) > 0 \\ 0 & \text{if } \sigma(\boldsymbol{\theta}) = 0 \end{cases}, \tag{1}$$

$$Z = \begin{cases} \frac{\mu(\boldsymbol{\theta}) - g\left(\boldsymbol{\theta}^*\right) - \xi}{\sigma(\boldsymbol{\theta})} & \text{if } \sigma(\boldsymbol{\theta}) > 0 \\ 0 & \text{if } \sigma(\boldsymbol{\theta}) = 0 \end{cases}, \tag{2}$$

where $g(\boldsymbol{\theta})$ is the surrogate model, $\boldsymbol{\theta}^*$ is the best set of the parameters sampled, $\mu(\boldsymbol{\theta})$ is the mean, $\sigma(\boldsymbol{\theta})$ is the standard deviation of the surrogate model posterior predictive at $\boldsymbol{\theta}$, Φ is the cumulative distribution function and ϕ is the probability density function of $N(0, 1)$. The parameter ξ governs the degree of exploration and exploitation, higher values of ξ lead to more frequent sampling from the regions of high uncertainty. Each optimization of the acquisition function allows obtaining a new vector of parameters potentially closer to the global minimum or maximum (depending on the task). All the parameter vectors and the corresponding values of the objective are saved and utilized to build the successive surrogate models.

In this paper, two Bayesian optimization algorithms are considered. The first one—Algorithm 1—is ordinary with the explicit random search phase and the constant parameter ξ. The pseudocode of Algorithm 1 is presented below.

Algorithm 1. Ordinary Bayesian optimization algorithm with constant jitter

Input: f: the objective, D: the search domain, ξ: the jitter parameter, N: the number of iterations at the first (random search) phase, M: the number of iterations at the second phase.

Output: θ^*: the best hyperparameters found.

1: $best\_value = -\infty$
2: repeat N times
3:          $\theta = \mathrm{random}(D)$ // sample uniformly from the search domain
4:          $value = f(\theta)$
5:          if $value > best\_value$ then
6:                  $best\_value = value$
7:                  $\theta^* = \theta$
8:          end if
9: end repeat
10: repeat M times
11:         fit a Gaussian process $g(\theta)$ approximating $f(\theta)$
12:         $\theta^+ = \mathrm{argmax}\ \mathrm{EI}_\xi(\theta)$ // utilizing $g(\theta)$, maximize the EI function parameterized with ξ
13:         $value = f(\theta^+)$
14:         if $value > best\_value$ then
15:                 $best\_value = value$
16:                 $\theta^* = \theta$
17:         end if
18: end repeat

This study proposes another algorithm—Algorithm 2—without the explicit random search phase and with the time-decaying parameter ξ. Pseudocode of Algorithm 2 can be found below.

Algorithm 2. Bayesian optimization algorithm with time-decaying jitter

Input: f: the objective, D: the search domain, ζ': the initial jitter parameter, N: the number of iterations.

Output: θ^*: the best hyperparameters found.

1: $\theta^* = random(D)$ // sample uniformly from the search domain
2: *best_value* $= f(\theta^*)$
3: for $i = 2, \ldots, N$ do
4:          $\zeta = \zeta' / i$
5:          fit a Gaussian process $g(\theta)$ approximating $f(\theta)$
6:          $\theta^+ = \text{argmax } EI_\zeta(\theta)$ // utilizing $g(\theta)$, maximize the EI function parameterized with ζ
7:          *value* $= f(\theta^+)$
8:          if *value* > *best_value* then
9:                  *best_value* = *value*
10:                 $\theta^* = \theta$
11:         end if
12: end for

It should be clarified that the pseudocodes of the algorithms are given for the problem of finding the global maximum. To find the global minimum, it is necessary to multiply the objective function by -1.

3   Evaluation on Artificial Landscapes

To evaluate and compare the implemented optimization algorithms, eight artificial landscapes were used, the description of which is given below, d denotes the number of dimensions:

1. Sphere—a convex function [8]:

$$f(\mathbf{x}) = \sum_{i=1}^{d} x_i^2, \tag{3}$$

2. Zakharov—a convex function with a large valley-like area [9]:

$$f(\mathbf{x}) = \sum_{i=1}^{d} x_i^2 + \left(\sum_{i=1}^{d} \frac{i}{2} x_i\right)^2 + \left(\sum_{i=1}^{d} \frac{i}{2} x_i\right)^4, \tag{4}$$

3. Rosenbrock—a non-convex function with a large valley-like area [8]:

$$f(\mathbf{x}) = \sum_{i=1}^{d-1} \left(100\left(x_{i+1} - x_i^2\right)^2 + (1 - x_i)^2\right), \tag{5}$$

4. Styblinski-Tang—a non-convex function with several basins [9]:

$$f(\mathbf{x}) = \frac{1}{2} \sum_{i=1}^{d} \left(x_i^4 - 16x_i^2 + 5x_i\right), \tag{6}$$

5. Schwefel—a non-convex multimodal function [8]:

$$f(\mathbf{x}) = \sum_{i=1}^{d} \left(-x_i \sin\left(\sqrt{|x_i|}\right) \right),$$ (7)

6. Rastrigin—a non-convex multimodal function [8]:

$$f(\mathbf{x}) = 10d + \sum_{i=1}^{d} \left(x_i^2 - 10\cos(2\pi x_i) \right),$$ (8)

7. Griewank—a non-convex multimodal function, at large scales it resembles a bowl-shaped function [8]:

$$f(\mathbf{x}) = \frac{1}{4000} \sum_{i=1}^{d} x_i^2 - \prod_{i=1}^{d} \cos\left(\frac{x_i}{\sqrt{i}}\right) + 1,$$ (9)

8. Ackley—a non-convex multimodal function with large gradients near the global minimum; $a = 20$, $b = 0.2$ and $c = 2\pi$ [8]:

$$f(\mathbf{x}) = -a\exp\left(-b\sqrt{\frac{1}{d}\sum_{i=1}^{d} x_i^2} \right) - \exp\left(\frac{1}{d}\sum_{i=1}^{d} \cos(cx_i) \right) + a + e.$$ (10)

For the above artificial landscapes, the minimization problem was being solved. Table 1 summarizes the data on global minima and search domains for the landscapes.

Table 1. Artificial landscapes for evaluation of the implemented optimization algorithms, d denotes the number of dimensions.

Function	Global minimum, $i = 1,\ldots, d$	Search domain, $i = 1,\ldots, d$
Sphere [8]	$f(\mathbf{x}) = 0$, $x_i = 0$	$-2 \le x_i \le 2$
Zakharov [9]	$f(\mathbf{x}) = 0$, $x_i = 0$	$-5 \le x_i \le 10$
Rosenbrock [8]	$f(\mathbf{x}) = 0$, $x_i = 1$	$-2.048 \le x_i \le 2.048$
Styblinski-Tang [9]	$f(\mathbf{x}) = -39.16599d$, $x_i = -2.903534$	$-5 \le x_i \le 5$
Schwefel [8]	$f(\mathbf{x}) = -418.9829d$, $x_i = 420.9687$	$-500 \le x_i \le 500$

(*continued*)

Table 1. (*continued*)

Function	Global minimum, $i = 1,...,d$	Search domain, $i = 1,...,d$
Rastrigin [8]	$f(\mathbf{x}) = 0,$ $x_i = 0$	$-5.12 \leq x_i \leq 5.12$
Griewank [8]	$f(\mathbf{x}) = 0,$ $x_i = 0$	$-600 \leq x_i \leq 600$
Ackley [8]	$f(\mathbf{x}) = 0,$ $x_i = 0$	$-32.768 \leq x_i \leq 32.768$

Figure 1 shows the surface plots of these artificial landscapes for the case $d = 2$ which allow to assess their diversity and identify potential challenges for the optimization algorithms—vast flat areas, many local minima, and maxima or a non-convex landscape.

For each artificial landscape, cases $d = 5, 10, 50$ were considered as representing situations of small, medium, and large numbers of parameters. For each artificial landscape and each value of d, different configurations of Algorithm 1 ($N = M = 50$; $\xi = 0.001, 0.01, 0.1$) and Algorithm 2 ($N = 100$; $\xi' = 0.1, 0.5, 1$) were employed. Note that the number of calls to the objective functions is equal for every configuration, therefore, it is expected that computational costs are also equal. Thirty runs of the algorithms were performed for each configuration. In that way, for each configuration algorithms produced a series of near-optimal values for every artificial landscape. Table 2 and Table 3 list min, mean, and max absolute errors for every series.

For each function and each value of d, the best (by mean) result for Algorithm 1 and Algorithm 2 was selected, and pairwise Wilcoxon tests were carried out for the corresponding series of the found near-optimal values to determine if there is a statistically significant difference in the results obtained by both algorithms. The results of the pairwise Wilcoxon tests are demonstrated in Table 4.

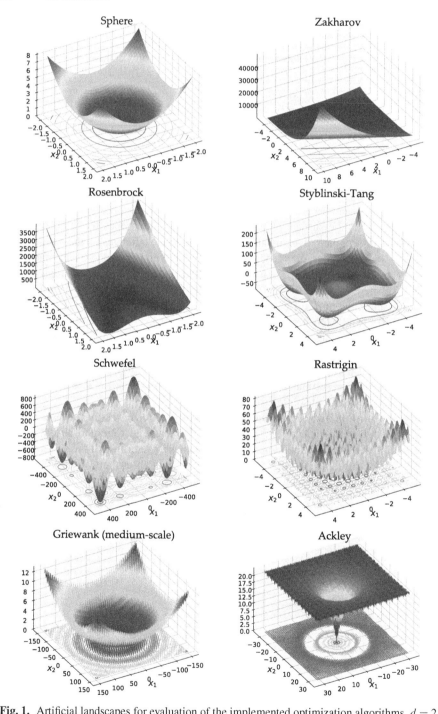

Fig. 1. Artificial landscapes for evaluation of the implemented optimization algorithms, $d = 2$

Table 2. Min, mean, and max absolute errors obtained with Algorithm 1 (with constant jitter)

Function	$d = 5$			$d = 10$			$d = 50$		
	ξ			ξ			ξ		
	0.001	0.01	0.1	0.001	0.01	0.1	0.001	0.01	0.1
Sphere	2.52e − 7	1.85e − 7	6.60e − 8	1.23e − 2	1.84e − 2	2.80e − 2	1.94	1.80	4.11
	6.71e − 5	6.21e − 4	**5.50e − 5**	**5.38e − 2**	6.73e − 2	1.46e − 1	2.16e + 1	2.11e + 1	**2.06e + 1**
	9.20e − 4	1.85e − 2	7.44e − 4	1.51e − 1	1.95e − 1	4.83e − 1	2.98e + 1	3.68e + 1	2.77e + 1
Zakharov	4.84	3.69	1.05e + 1	6.81e + 1	5.71e + 1	9.31e + 1	9.94e + 2	6.52e + 3	4.70e + 2
	5.18e + 1	**4.84e + 1**	5.89 + 1	**1.72e + 2**	1.82e + 2	1.80e + 2	9.74e + 10	8.98e + 10	**5.93 + 10**
	1.62e + 2	1.21e + 2	1.48e + 2	3.44e + 2	3.98e + 2	3.04e + 2	4.21e + 11	6.12e + 11	2.60e + 11
Rosenbrock	2.35	3.16	7.22	2.33e + 1	2.23e + 1	3.90e + 1	5.12e + 2	6.02e + 2	7.65e + 2
	6.68	9.08	2.10e + 1	5.62e + 1	**5.38e + 1**	9.03e + 1	1.89e + 3	1.96e + 3	**1.79 + 3**
	1.06e + 1	2.98e + 1	3.89e + 1	1.07e + 2	1.00e + 2	1.41e + 2	4.00e + 3	4.39e + 3	4.88e + 3
Styblinski-Tang	7.71e − 2	2.88	3.51	1.55e + 1	4.22	2.79e + 1	6.77e + 2	6.61e + 2	6.96e + 2
	1.90e + 1	1.70e + 1	**1.65e + 1**	6.45e + 1	**5.83e + 1**	7.40e + 1	**9.26e + 2**	9.42e + 2	9.45e + 2
	3.54e + 1	4.45e + 1	3.26e + 1	1.09e + 2	1.17e + 2	1.56e + 2	1.24e + 3	1.36e + 3	1.32e + 3
Schwefel	6.49e + 2	7.12e + 2	6.43e + 2	1.95e + 3	1.82e + 3	2.05e + 3	1.64e + 4	1.60e + 4	1.59e + 4
	1.03e + 3	1.08e + 3	**9.82e + 2**	2.62e + 3	**2.56e + 3**	2.71e + 3	1.76e + 4	1.75e + 4	**1.74e + 4**
	1.32e + 3	1.34e + 3	1.27e + 3	3.15e + 3	3.03e + 3	3.05e + 3	1.85e + 4	1.88e + 4	1.84e + 4
Rastrigin	6.03	3.29	4.28	2.48e + 1	2.75e + 1	3.15e + 1	5.36e + 2	5.77e + 2	5.34e + 2
	1.33e + 1	1.44e + 1	**1.26e + 1**	6.77e + 1	**6.52e + 1**	7.30e + 1	6.37e + 2	6.68e + 2	**6.28e + 2**
	2.49e + 1	2.49e + 1	2.22e + 1	1.20e + 2	1.02e + 2	1.14e + 2	7.59e + 2	7.60e + 2	7.07e + 2
Griewank	8.15	6.76	0.89	4.63e + 1	3.48e + 1	3.89e + 1	8.61e + 2	8.16e + 2	9.55e + 2
	2.70e + 1	2.68e + 1	**2.68e + 1**	1.12e + 2	**1.07e + 2**	1.12e + 2	1.03e + 3	**1.02e + 3**	1.07e + 3
	4.67e + 1	4.78e + 1	4.64e + 1	1.67e + 2	1.52e + 2	1.84e + 2	1.16e + 3	1.13e + 3	1.18e + 3
Ackley	1.50	2.83	2.67	1.09e + 1	1.18e + 1	1.15e + 1	2.04e + 1	2.03e + 1	2.06e + 1
	7.95	7.30	**5.48**	1.70e + 1	1.70e + 1	**1.66e + 1**	**2.08e + 1**	2.08e + 1	2.08e + 1
	1.91e + 1	1.90e + 1	1.51e + 1	2.05e + 1	2.03e + 1	2.00e + 1	2.10e + 1	2.10e + 1	2.09e + 1

Thus, it has been shown that for a part of the functions and the numbers of dimensions (Sphere, $d = 50$; Rosenbrock, $d = 5$) Algorithm 2 consistently shows the results better than Algorithm 1, for another part (Sphere, $d = 5$; Zakharov, $d = 10$; Styblinski-Tang, $d = 10$)—worse, and for most of the artificial landscapes, no statistically significant difference was found between Algorithm 1 and Algorithm 2. The results do not allow to make an unambiguous conclusion about the preference of one or another of the algorithms when optimizing the hyperparameters of deep learning algorithms, and therefore it is necessary to conduct additional research on practical problems.

Table 3. Min, mean, and max absolute errors obtained with Algorithm 2 (with time-decaying jitter)

Function	$d = 5$			$d = 10$			$d = 50$		
	ξ'			ξ'			ξ'		
	0.1	0.5	1.0	0.1	0.5	1.0	0.1	0.5	1.0
Sphere	3.58e − 4	1.00e − 2	9.03e − 8	1.31e − 2	1.29e − 2	6.65e − 2	4.38e − 1	5.86e − 1	7.36e − 1
	1.43e − 2	4.60e − 2	7.32e − 2	**4.77e − 2**	1.04e − 1	1.52e − 1	7.28	**3.62**	4.16
	5.12e − 2	8.86e − 2	1.47e − 1	9.46e − 2	2.15e − 1	2.21e − 1	4.94e + 1	3.42e + 1	4.18e + 1
Zakharov	1.23e + 1	1.15e + 1	4.30	1.03e + 2	7.78e + 1	1.08e + 2	1.10e + 6	7.69e + 3	5.13e + 6
	4.48e + 1	5.70e + 1	5.70e + 1	2.44e + 2	**2.35e + 2**	2.40e + 2	**8.36e + 10**	9.06e + 10	1.01e + 11
	8.56e + 1	1.33e + 2	1.28e + 2	3.83e + 2	4.14e + 2	4.28e + 2	3.26e + 11	6.79e + 11	4.14e + 11
Rosenbrock	5.83e − 1	1.81	2.00	1.99e + 1	2.50e + 1	2.82e + 1	6.83e + 2	6.41e + 2	4.99e + 2
	3.40	4.57	6.56	**4.65e + 1**	4.92e + 1	5.82e + 1	2.68e + 3	**1.91e + 3**	2.84e + 3
	5.33	8.92	1.23e + 1	8.43e + 1	9.72e + 1	1.08e + 2	1.41e + 4	1.38e + 4	1.34e + 4
Styblinski-Tang	1.84e − 1	6.29e − 1	1.68e − 1	4.18e + 1	4.08e + 1	5.79e + 1	6.88e + 2	7.28e + 2	7.10e + 2
	1.79e + 1	1.90e + 1	1.95e + 1	**8.26e + 1**	1.01e + 2	9.38e + 1	1.00e + 3	1.02e + 3	**9.68e + 2**
	4.75e + 1	4.28e + 1	3.75e + 1	1.38e + 2	1.58e + 2	1.34e + 2	1.28e + 3	1.33e + 3	1.26e + 3
Schwefel	5.86e + 2	7.10e + 2	7.19e + 2	2.19e + 3	1.73e + 3	2.23e + 3	1.60e + 4	1.54e + 4	1.59e + 4
	1.01e + 3	1.08e + 3	1.02e + 3	**2.63e + 3**	2.68e + 3	2.71e + 3	1.76e + 4	**1.74e + 4**	1.75e + 4
	1.27e + 3	1.39e + 3	1.30e + 3	3.05e + 3	3.17e + 3	3.12e + 3	1.88e + 4	1.85e + 4	1.86e + 4
Rastrigin	2.35	6.03	7.04	2.96e + 1	3.62e + 1	3.41e + 1	5.35e + 2	5.28e + 2	5.18e + 2
	1.54e + 1	1.69e + 1	1.61e + 1	**6.86e + 1**	8.04e + 1	7.85e + 1	**6.50e + 2**	6.60e + 2	6.50e + 2
	3.10e + 1	3.49e + 1	3.63e + 1	1.13e + 2	1.32e + 2	1.18e + 2	7.41e + 2	7.45e + 2	7.32e + 2
Griewank	6.21	5.89	8.34	4.91e + 1	6.80e + 1	3.20e + 1	8.56e + 2	9.32e + 2	9.05e + 2
	2.30e + 1	2.61e + 1	2.45e + 1	1.09e + 2	**1.09e + 2**	1.09e + 2	1.05e + 3	1.04e + 3	**1.03e + 3**
	5.01e + 1	4.36e + 1	4.66e + 1	1.66e + 2	1.55e + 2	1.51e + 2	1.17e + 3	1.17e + 3	1.16e + 3
Ackley	9.20e − 1	1.04	9.37e − 1	1.22e + 1	9.89	9.97	2.06e + 1	2.04e + 1	2.06e + 1
	9.53	9.29	**7.71**	**1.69e + 1**	1.71e + 1	1.70e + 1	2.08e + 1	2.08e + 1	**2.08e + 1**
	1.91e + 1	1.90e + 1	1.94e + 1	2.02e + 1	2.02e + 1	1.99e + 1	2.10e + 1	2.10e + 1	2.09e + 1

Table 4. Pairwise Wilcoxon signed-rank tests

Function	d	T	p-value	Statistically significant? ($\alpha = 0.05$)	Better algorithm
Sphere	5	0	1.7e − 6	Yes	Algorithm 1
	10	220	0.80	No	Equivalent
	50	8	3.9e − 6	Yes	Algorithm 2
Zakharov	5	232	0.99	No	Equivalent
	10	106	9.3e − 3	Yes	Algorithm 1
	50	166	0.17	No	Equivalent
Rosenbrock	5	27	2.4e − 5	Yes	Algorithm 2
	10	175	0.24	No	Equivalent
	50	148	8.2e − 2	No	Equivalent

(continued)

Table 4. (*continued*)

Function	d	T	p-value	Statistically significant? ($\alpha = 0.05$)	Better algorithm
Styblinski-Tang	5	229	0.94	No	Equivalent
	10	81	$1.8e-3$	Yes	Algorithm 1
	50	180	0.28	No	Equivalent
Schwefel	5	222	0.83	No	Equivalent
	10	187	0.35	No	Equivalent
	50	209	0.63	No	Equivalent
Rastrigin	5	152	$9.8e-2$	No	Equivalent
	10	206	0.59	No	Equivalent
	50	166	0.17	No	Equivalent
Griewank	5	171	0.21	No	Equivalent
	10	216	0.73	No	Equivalent
	50	213	0.69	No	Equivalent
Ackley	5	181	0.29	No	Equivalent
	10	212	0.67	No	Equivalent
	50	216	0.73	No	Equivalent

4 Evaluation on Semantic Image Segmentation Problem

To compare Algorithm 1 and Algorithm 2 in solving practical problems, the problem of semantic segmentation of *Abies sibirica* trees damaged by *Polygraphus proximus* in unmanned aerial vehicles imagery was addressed [10]. The imagery consists of five classes—four classes of the life condition of the trees (living, dying, recently dead and long dead) and the background class. It is also worth noting a serious imbalance and limitations of the training set [10], in connection with which the importance of choosing a good set of hyperparameters increases, since this can significantly increase the performance of deep learning models.

To deal with the problem, a fully convolutional network based on the original U-Net architecture [11] was utilized. Fully convolutional networks have a specific topology of the computational graph—it includes an encoder and a decoder. Usually, the encoder reduces the spatial dimensions of the input image and increases the number of feature maps. The decoder, on the other hand, restores the original image dimensions and reduces the number of feature maps, outputting the probabilities of each class for every pixel in a patch. The U-Net architecture differs from typical fully convolutional networks in the presence of skip-connections that copy feature maps from the encoder directly to the decoder, therefore, increasing the ability of the networks to recover fine-grained details of the input patch and partially solving the vanishing gradient problem [11]. Figure 2 demonstrates the architecture of the proposed neural network.

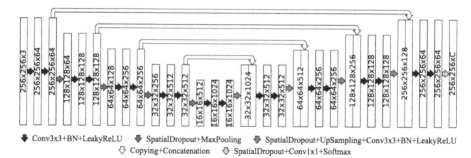

Fig. 2. U-Net architecture for *Abies Sibirica* trees segmentation

In the addressed problem, the objective is the mean Jaccard coefficient (J) which should be maximized:

$$J = \frac{1}{C} \sum_{c=1}^{C} J_c, \qquad J_c = \frac{\text{TP}_c}{\text{TP}_c + \text{FP}_c + \text{FN}_c}, \tag{11}$$

where TP_c, FP_c, FN_c are, respectively, the true positives, the false positives and the false negatives for the class c and C stands for the number of classes.

To train a segmentation model, the maximization of the following J approximation was employed:

$$\tilde{J}(\mathbf{T}, \mathbf{P}) = \frac{1}{C} \sum_{c=1}^{C} \left(\frac{\sum_{i=1}^{H} \sum_{j=1}^{W} \text{LS}(\mathbf{T})_{ijc} \cdot \mathbf{P}_{ijc} + \theta_{loss\_s}}{\sum_{i=1}^{H} \sum_{j=1}^{W} \left(\text{LS}(\mathbf{T})_{ijc} + \left(1 - \text{LS}(\mathbf{T})_{ijc}\right) \cdot \mathbf{P}_{ijc} \right) + \theta_{loss\_s}} \right), \tag{12}$$

$$\text{LS}(\mathbf{T}) = \left(1 - \theta_{label\_s}\right) \cdot \mathbf{T} + \frac{\theta_{label\_s}}{C}, \tag{13}$$

where $\mathbf{T}$ is the expected output, $\mathbf{P}$ is the predicted output, H and W are the height and the width of an image, $\theta_{loss\_s} > 0$ is the loss smoothing coefficient to eliminate the singularity and $0 \leq \theta_{label\_s} < 1$ is the label smoothing coefficient.

In total, 10 hyperparameters were identified. They are related to the optimization algorithm used for searching the best weight coefficients, to the regularization, to the approximation of J, and to the online augmentation techniques. Table 5 lists all the identified hyperparameters and the corresponding search domain.

Both algorithms described above were applied to search for the optimal values of the U-Net hyperparameters for the semantic segmentation problem. Figure 3 shows the corresponding convergence curves.

Table 5. List of hyperparameters

#	Hyperparameter	Description	Search domain
1	$\log_{10}\theta_{lr}$	The logarithm of the learning rate	$-8 \leq \log_{10}\theta_{lr} \leq -2$
2	θ_d	Spatial dropout rate	$0 \leq \theta_d \leq 0.5$
3	$\log_{10}\theta_{loss\_s}$	The logarithm of the loss smoothing coefficient	$-7 \leq \log_{10}\theta_{loss\_s} \leq -3$
4	θ_{label_s}	Label smoothing coefficient	$0 \leq \theta_{label\_s} \leq 0.8$
5	θ_z	Zoom rate for random clipping	$0.5 \leq \theta_z \leq 1$
6	θ_b	Brightness change rate	$0 \leq \theta_b \leq 0.6$
7	θ_c	Contrast change rate	$0 \leq \theta_c \leq 1$
8	θ_α	Elastic transformation coefficients [12]	$30 \leq \theta_\alpha \leq 300$
9	θ_σ		$3 \leq \theta_\sigma \leq 20$
10	θ_{lr_d}	Exponential learning rate decay rate	$0.7 \leq \theta_{lr\_d} \leq 1$

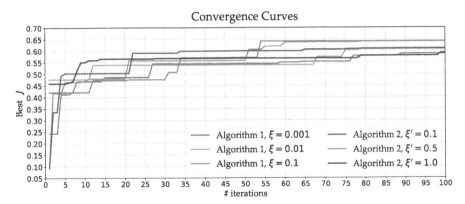

Fig. 3. Convergence curves for the semantic image segmentation case study

As can be seen from Fig. 3, both Algorithm 1 and Algorithm 2 are suitable for the addressed hyperparameter tuning problem. Although Algorithm 2, $\xi' = 0.5$ produced the best result ($J = 0.6412$), it is worth noting that the amount of the carried out computational experiments do not allow to make any conclusions about the statistical significance of the obtained results. In fact, only one near-optimal value of the objective was calculated with every configuration.

Figure 4 depicts the segmentation results of the test area with the use of the best U-Net model produced during the hyperparameter tuning. The corresponding values of the Jaccard coefficient for every class and the mean Jaccard coefficient are listed in Table 6.

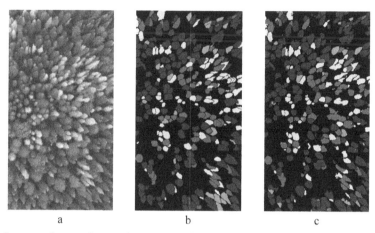

| a | b | c |

Fig. 4. Segmentation results: a—the test area, b—the ground truth, c—the output of the best model

Table 6. Jaccard coefficients obtained with the best model for the test area

J_c					J
Background	Living	Dying	Recently dead	Long dead	
0.8561	0.7509	0.4072	0.7808	0.6919	0.6974

The obtained model successfully classifies ($J_c > 0.5$ corresponds to the good quality of segmentation) four out of five target classes. The low segmentation quality for dying trees can be explained by their underrepresentation in the training set and visual similarity with living trees and *Picea* trees, which are a part of the background.

5   Conclusion and Future Work

This study proposed a Bayesian optimization algorithm with a time-decaying parameter ξ (jitter) for finding the optimal hyperparameters of neural networks (Algorithm 2). This algorithm was compared with the ordinary Bayesian optimization algorithm (Algorithm 1) on the artificial landscapes and when solving the problem of semantic image segmentation. The comparison on the artificial landscape has shown that for a part of the landscapes and the numbers of dimensions (Sphere, $d = 50$; Rosenbrock, $d = 5$) Algorithm 2 consistently shows the results better than Algorithm 1, for another part (Sphere, $d = 5$; Zakharov, $d = 10$; Styblinski-Tang, $d = 10$)—worse, and for most of the artificial landscapes, no statistically significant difference was found between Algorithm 1 and Algorithm 2. When tuning the hyperparameters of the neural network for the semantic image segmentation problem, the proposed algorithm produced the best result, but it cannot be argued that this fact is not random and the results obtained are significantly higher than those obtained using the ordinary algorithm. One of the unambiguous advantages of the proposed algorithm is the smaller number of parameters due to the absence of the explicit random search phase.

The fact that the proposed algorithm shows greater performance in some cases, or at least comparable to the performance of the ordinary one, allows asserting the potential usefulness of further research in this direction. For instance, it makes sense to consider various mechanisms of decreasing the parameter ξ in time and other value ranges of ξ, which differ from the one described in this paper. Also, an interesting direction of research could be the use of adaptive changes in the parameter ξ.

Acknowledgements. The research has been carried out with the financial support of the RFBR and the Tomsk region (Project 18–47-700010).

References

1. Snoek, J., Larochelle, H., Adams, R.P.: Practical Bayesian optimization of machine learning algorithms. In: Proceedings of the 25th International Conference on Neural Information Processing Systems, vol. 2, pp. 2951–2959. Curran Associates Inc., Red Hook, New York (2012)
2. Erten, G.E., Keser, S.B., Yavuz, M.: Grid search optimised artificial neural network for open stope stability prediction. Int. J. Min. Reclam. Environ. **35**(8), 600–617 (2021). https://doi.org/10.1080/17480930.2021.1899404
3. Bergstra, J., Bengio, Y.: Random search for hyper-parameter optimization. J. Mach. Learn. Res. **13**(10), 281–305 (2012)
4. Young, S.R., Rose, D.C., Karnowski, T.P., Lim, S.-H., Patton, R.M.: Optimizing deep learning hyper-parameters through an evolutionary algorithm. In: Proceedings of the Workshop on Machine Learning in High-Performance Computing Environments, p. 5. Association for Computing Machinery, New York (2015). https://doi.org/10.1145/2834892.2834896
5. Zhang, R., Qiu, Z.: Optimizing hyper-parameters of neural networks with swarm intelligence: a novel framework for credit scoring. PLoS ONE **15**(6), 35 (2020). https://doi.org/10.1371/journal.pone.0234254
6. Sameen, M.I., Pradhan, B., Lee, S.: Application of convolutional neural networks featuring Bayesian optimization for landslide susceptibility assessment. CATENA **186** (2020). https://doi.org/10.1016/j.catena.2019.104249
7. GPyOpt: A Bayesian Optimization Framework in Python (2016). http://github.com/SheffieldML/GPyOpt
8. Molga, M., Smutnicki, C.: Test Functions for Optimization Needs (2005). https://robertmarks.org/Classes/ENGR5358/Papers/functions.pdf
9. Virtual Library of Simulation Experiments: Test Function and Datasets. Optimization Test Problems. https://www.sfu.ca/~ssurjano/optimization.html
10. Kerchev, I.A., Maslov, K.A., Markov, N.G., Tokareva, O.S.: Semantic segmentation of damaged fir trees in unmanned aerial vehicle images. Curr. Probl. Remote Sens. Earth Space **18**(1), 116–126 (2021). https://doi.org/10.21046/2070-7401-2021-18-1-116-126

11. Ronneberger, O., Fischer, P., Brox, T.: U-Net: convolutional networks for biomedical image segmentation, p. 8 (2015). arXiv:1505.04597
12. Simard, P.Y., Steinkraus, D., Platt, J.C.: Best practices for convolutional neural networks applied to visual document analysis. In: Proceedings of the International Conference on Document Analysis and Recognition, pp. 958–963 (2003)

Investigation of the Capabilities of Artificial Neural Networks in the Problem of Classifying Objects with Dynamic Features

N. V. Laptev$^{(\boxtimes)}$ ⑩, V. V. Laptev ⑩, O. M. Gerget ⑩, D. Yu. Kolpashchikov ⑩, and A. A. Kravchenko ⑩

Tomsk Polytechnic University, Street Lenina 30, Tomsk 634050, Russia
nikitalaptev77@gmail.com

Abstract. Image classification is a classic machine learning (ML) problem. Neural networks are widely used in the problem of object classification. Despite the existence of a large number of image classification algorithms, very little attention is paid to the issue of video data classification. In the case of using convolutional neural networks to classify frames of a video sequence, it is necessary to combine image features to obtain a prediction. However, with this approach, the signs of object dynamics will be ignored, since the images are processed sequentially. Therefore, the issue of analyzing objects with dynamically changing characteristics remains relevant. To solve this issue, the authors propose to use a neural network with long-term short-term memory (LSTM). In contrast to classical convolutional neural networks (CNN), the proposed network uses information about the sequence of images, thereby providing a higher classification accuracy of detected objects with dynamic characteristics. In the study, the authors analyze the classification accuracy of smoke cloud detection in a forest using various machine learning methods. In the work, the authors present models for the classification of one frame and a sequence of frames of a video sequence. The results of the work of machine learning models are presented, as well as a comparative analysis of the classification of one frame and a sequence of frames. The accuracy of the video sequence classification by the model of a recurrent neural network with an LSTM layer was 85.7%.

Keywords: Neural networks · traditional machine learning · classification · image · detection of fire hazards

1 Introduction

The amount of data in the form of images and videos is growing every year. Complex algorithms and models of feature extraction are using to automate the description of such data. One of the most important directions of digital data analysis is classification. The classification methods could be divided into two groups: traditional ML algorithms and artificial neural networks (ANN).

Object classification on images by traditional ML is carried out in two stages:

© Springer Nature Switzerland AG 2024
R. Yavorskiy et al. (Eds.): TMPA 2021, CCIS 1559, pp. 41–51, 2024.
https://doi.org/10.1007/978-3-031-50423-5_4

1. Feature extraction. The most common feature extraction methods are function descriptors: HOG [1], LPB [2], SURF [3], etc. Based on extracted features, a feature vector is formed.
2. Classification. The obtained features are subdivided into classes by classification algorithms: k-nearest neighbors [4], SVM [5], RandomForest [6], etc.

It should be noted that the listed feature extraction methods have significant drawbacks. They are related to the manual selection of important features by experts. In this way, the result depends on the expert's qualifications. Nevertheless, traditional ML algorithms have a number of advantages: low requirements for computing resources and high processing speed.

ANN are devoid of these drawbacks, but they are not an ideal solution. To obtain an ANN model with the high generalizing ability and good accuracy, large volumes of "high-quality" data are required. It is also worth noting the high requirements for computing resources. Despite this, the popularity of using deep learning is fully justified. Neural networks automate the feature extraction stage: during the learning process, the ANN strives to improve the quality of the generated feature vector using the input data.

CNN is the most popular approach to image classification [7]. Despite a large number of image classification algorithms [8], very little attention is paid to video data classification. In the case of using CNN to classify frames of a video sequence, it is necessary to combine features of an image to obtain a prediction. However, with this approach, the dynamic features of the object will be ignored, since the frames are processed sequentially. Therefore, this algorithm is not always suitable for the classification of video sequences.

Recurrent neural networks (RNN) [9] have a more complex architecture and allow evaluating dynamic features since they are able to extract temporal characteristics. Long short-term memory (LSTM) is an artificial recurrent neural network (RNN) architecture [10] used in the field of deep learning. Unlike standard feedforward neural networks, LSTM has feedback connections. It can process not only single data points (such as images), but also entire sequences of data (such as speech or video). For example, LSTM is applicable to tasks such as unsegmented, connected handwriting recognition, speech recognition [11, 12] and anomaly detection in network traffic or IDSs (intrusion detection systems). A common LSTM unit is composed of a cell, an input gate, an output gate and a forget gate. The cell re-members values over arbitrary time intervals and the three gates regulate the flow of information into and out of the cell. Gated recurrent units (GRUs) are a gating mechanism in recurrent neural networks [13]. The GRU is like a long short-term memory (LSTM) with a forget gate [14], but has fewer parameters than LSTM, as it lacks an output gate [15].

In this article, we propose to use RNN with LSTM [16]. This type of neural network is well suited for sequence analysis. We propose a neural network architecture with an LSTM layer for classifying fire hazardous objects in a forest. The problem of classifying such objects is the absence of constant features of a smoke cloud, namely: inconstancy of the shape and smoke outflow rate, changes in the intensity of the color component. Video sequence analysis allows you to extract dynamic features specific to a smoke cloud. This allows classifying the objects in the frame with higher accuracy.

This study is a continuation of work [17]. The main task is to improve the detection quality of a smoke cloud in a forest by classifying the previously allocated area of interest. The article provides a comparative analysis of the applicability of various algorithms for extracting static features of a smoke cloud. Also, presents an analysis of comparison with algorithms for extracting dynamic features. Particular attention is paid to the development of a model of RNN for the extraction of dynamic features from a video sequence.

2 Research

2.1 Problem Statement

We considered two approaches for the classification of fire hazardous objects in the forest. The first approach is described in Sect. 2.2. This approach analyzes a single frame from a video sequence by ML. The second approach is described in Sect. 2.3. This approach splits the initial video into a frame sequence. From the resulting sequence, n frames are selected with equal time intervals, so that it is possible to analyze the entire video. The next step is the feature vector forming for each analyzed frame and its classification.

2.2 Single Frame Classification

Feature Vector Forming. To form a feature vector, the following feature extraction models are compared:

- MobileNetV2
- ResNet50
- InceptionV3
- EfficientNetB1

A dataset of 8135 images was collected to train models. The test sample consisted of 2440 images. 1220 images were labeled "fire hazardous object", the rest - "no fire". The size of the input tensor was $128 \times 128 \times 3$. The number of training iterations was 75 epochs. We consider binary classification accuracy as a qualitative indicator of forming a feature vector. Binary classification accuracy was obtained as a result of adding a fully connected layer of dimension 1 with a linear activation function ReLu (Rectified Linear Unit).

Based on the results shown in Table 1, we conclude that the most effective model for forming a feature vector for the problem of classifying fire hazardous objects is the InceptionV3 model with trainable parameters. However, the model accuracy at this stage was only 62%.

Classification Based on the Feature Vector. We search the classification model, both among traditional ML methods and by the construction of a new CNN architecture. We use AutoML service [18], to select a classification model among traditional machine learning algorithms. AutoML service offers the following classification models:

- XGBoost [19]
- LightGBM [20]

Table 1. Results of neural network models for forming a feature vector

Model name	Frozen weights	Accuracy, %	Processing time, s
MobileNetV2	True	53	0,053
	False	50	0,056
ResNet50	True	60	0,074
	False	46	0,54
InceptionV3	True	62	0,056
	False	46	0,05
EfficientNetB1	True	60	0,081
	False	56	0,054

- Random Forest [21]
- CatBoost [22]
- ElasticNet [23]
- ExtraTree [24]

Also we constructed a new CNN architecture (Fig. 1). The neural network model was built using the following deep machine learning libraries: Tensorflow [25], Keras [26].

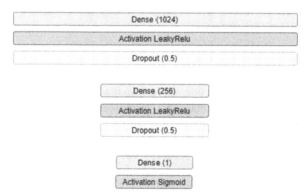

Fig. 1. The architecture of the neural network for the classification of fire hazardous objects.

According to the results shown in Table 2, the neural network architecture proposed by the authors is superior in accuracy compared to classical machine learning algorithms in the task of smoke cloud classification. The difference in processing speed is considered insignificant. It should be noted, despite the rather high accuracy rates, the presented classification algorithms make mistakes in the identification of fire hazardous objects. These errors may be associated with the absence of a smoke cloud in this frame at the current time and the absence of dynamic features in the analysis.

Table 2. Comparison of classification algorithms

	Traditional ML algorithms			CNN
Model name	XGBoost	LightGBM	Random Forest	Own CNN architecture
Accuracy, %	82	80	71	83,6
Processing time, s	0,032	0,048	0,057	0,062
Traditional ML algorithms				
Model name	CatBoost		ElasticNet	ExtraTree
Accuracy, %	50		84	64,1
Processing time, s	0,039		0,059	0,044

2.3 Frame Sequence Classification

Two approaches were considered to solve the issue of the absence of a smoke cloud in the frame at the current time, as well as to extract dynamic features from the studied objects:

- Classification of a frames sequence by the arithmetic weighted average result (Fig. 2.)
- Classification of a sequence of images using recurrent neural networks with a layer of LSTM and GRU (Fig. 3.)

We assess the effectiveness of the classification by accuracy and the frame processing time. The video sequence length is 10 s. - this is the average camera shooting time before

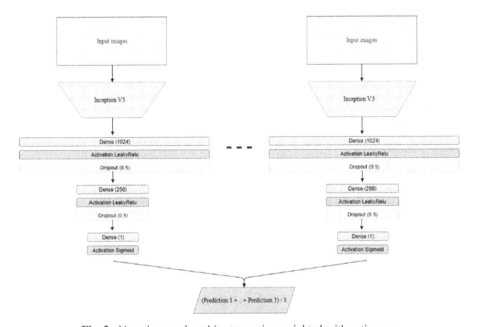

Fig. 2. Neural network architecture using weighted arithmetic mean

changing the angle of view. For training the models, we used a fixed size of the input tensor of 128 × 128 × 3 and a sequence of three frames.

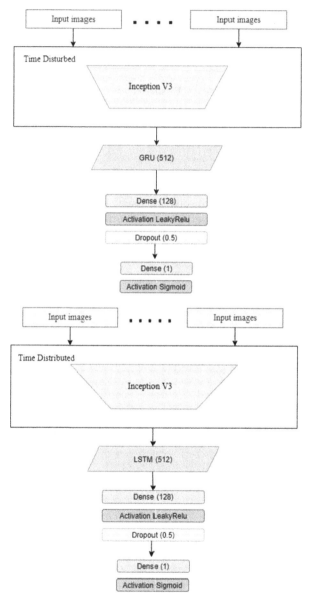

Fig. 3. Recurrent neural network architectures with a layer of LSTM and GRU

Table 3. Comparison of Frame Sequence Classification Models

	RNN		Fully connected neural networks
	GRU Network	LSTM Network	
Accuracy,%	74,8	77,3	69,3
Processing time, s	0,19	0,18	0,06

Table 3 shows that the most effective model is LSTM Network. It is also worth noting that the quality of the classification is not final, since more fine tuning of the input parameters of the neural network is required. When manually analyzing the data, it was revealed that there are sequences of three frames, where the smoke cloud is traced only in one of them, which in turn negatively affects the final result. It should also be noted that there is a decrease in errors in the identification of fire hazardous objects in the video in comparison with the approach that analyzes one frame.

Long Short-Term Memory Network. As noted earlier, the LSTM network requires optimization of the input tensor parameters and the number of simultaneously analyzed frames. The results of optimization of the input parameters presented in Table 4. The list of model training hyperparameters is given in Table 5.

Table 4. Fine tuning the input parameters of the LSTM network.

Number of processed frames	Frame size	Accuracy, %	Time, s
3	28 × 28	68,98	0,04
	32 × 32	72,12	0,07
	64 × 64	75,05	0,11
	128 × 128	77,33	0,21
5	28 × 28	79,97	0,06
	32 × 32	83,21	0,08
	64 × 64	85,4	0,12
	128 × 128	85,7	0,25
7	28 × 28	73,74	0,18
	32 × 32	75,32	0,30
	64 × 64	78,5	0,41
	128 × 128	77,79	0,75
11	28 × 28	65,74	0,27
	32 × 32	68,54	0,49
	64 × 64	70,66	0,98
	128 × 128	71,03	1,12

Table 5. Classification Model Learning Hyperparameters.

Input tensor	$5 \times 64 \times 64 \times 3$
Batch size	32
Loss function	Binary cross entropy
Optimizer	RectifiedAdam
Learning rate	0.0002
Epochs	125
Transfer learning model	Inception V3
Weight training TL model	False

Results show that model achieves the greatest efficiency with the input tensor size 5 $\times$ 128 $\times$ 128 $\times$ 3. The final classification accuracy of the video is 85.7%. Visualization of the classifier's work is shown in image 4. Detailed statistics are presented in Table 6.

Table 6. Model test results.

TP	FP	TN	FN	Precision	Recall	Accuracy
238	31	42	15	0,885	0,94	0,854

Where *TP* (*True Positive*) - real smoke is detected in the frame, *FP* (*False Positive*) - there is no smoke, but there is detection, *TN* (*True Negative*) - there is no smoke, and there is no detection, *FN* (*False Negative*) - real smoke, no detection (Fig. 4).

Fig. 4. Visualization of the work of the classifier: a) Visualization of object selection by the object detection model; b) Visualization of the work of the classifier

3 Conclusion

The paper study classification of frames of a video. The paper presents the results of comparing classification algorithms for single frame and frame sequence. The results of ML algorithms for the classification of smoke cloud features in single frame are presented. Despite the high accuracy rates of 83,6%, the presented classification algorithms make mistakes in the identification of fire hazardous objects. This error is critical, so this result cannot be considered satisfactory. The indicated error may be due to the absence of a smoke cloud in the frame at the current moment and the absence of dynamic features in the analysis. To solve this problem, an approach based on the analysis of frame sequences is considered. The results of comparison of various neural network models for frame sequence analysis are presented. As a result of the analysis, the LSTM network showed the highest efficiency with the accuracy 85.7%. The article also provides a description of the selection of RNN input parameters. Study proved hypothesis about the importance of analyzing dynamically signs of a smoke cloud. As a result, the error of incorrect classification of fire hazardous objects is minimized. It should be noted that the proposed neural network model is not ideal and allows errors associated with incorrect classification of rain clouds, which are identical in texture to smoke clouds. In general, the work of the system is assessed by experts as high.

Acknowledgements. The study has been funded with support from the Russian Foundation for Basic Research, projects No. 20-38-90143 and Russian Federation Governmental Program 'Nauka' No. FFSWW-2020-0014.

References

1. Zhu, Q., Avidan, S., Yeh, M.C., Cheng, K.T.: Fast human detection using a cascade of histograms of oriented gradients. In: Proceedings of IEEE Computer Society Conference on Computer Vision and Pattern Recognition, pp. 1491–1498 (2006)
2. Pietikäinen, M., Hadid, A., Zhao, G., Ahonen, T.: Computer Vision Using Local Binary Patterns. Springer, London (2011)
3. Bay, H., Tuytelaars, T., Van Gool, L.: SURF: Speeded up robust features.In: Leonardis, A., Bischof, H., Pinz, A. (eds) Computer Vision – ECCV 2006. ECCV 2006, vol. 3951, pp. 404–417. Lecture Notes in Computer Science. Springer, Heidelberg (2006) https://doi.org/10.1007/11744023_32
4. Laaksonen, J., Oja, E.: Classification with learning k-nearest neighbors. In: IEEE International Conference on Neural Networks - Conference Proceedings, pp. 1480–1483 IEEE (1996)
5. Zhao, J., Zhang, Z., Han, S., Qu, C., Yuan, Z., Zhang, D.: SVM based forest fire detection using static and dynamic features. Comput. Sci. Inf. Syst. **8**(3), 821–841 (2011)
6. Biau, G., Scornet, E.: A random forest guided tour. TEST **25**(2), 197–227 (2016)
7. O'Shea, K., Nash, R.: An introduction to convolutional neural networks (2015)
8. Rawat, W., Wang, Z.: Deep convolutional neural networks for image classification: a comprehensive review. Neural Comput. **29**(9), 2352–2449 (2017)
9. Medsker, L.R., Jain, L.C.: Recurrent neural networks. Des. Appl. **5**(64–67), 2 (2001)
10. Hochreiter, S., Schmidhuber, J.: Long short-term memory. Neural Comput. **9**(8), 1735–1780 (1997)
11. Graves, A., Liwicki, M., Fernández, S., Bertolami, R., Bunke, H., Schmidhuber, J.: A novel connectionist system for unconstrained handwriting recognition. IEEE Trans. Pattern Anal. Mach. Intell. **31**(5), 855–868 (2008)
12. Sak, H.H., Senior, A., Google, B.: Long short-term memory recurrent neural network architectures for large scale acoustic modeling (2014)
13. Cho, K., et al.: Learning phrase representations using RNN encoder-decoder for statistical machine translation. In: EMNLP 2014 - 2014 Conference on Empirical Methods Nat. Lang. Process. Proc. Conf, pp. 1724–1734 (2014)
14. Gers, F.A., Schmidhuber, J., Cummins, F.: Learning to forget: continual prediction with LSTM. Neural Comput. **12**(10), 2451–2471 (2000)

15. Britz, D.: Recurrent neural network tutorial, part 4 implementing a GRU/LSTM RNN with python and theano
16. Sundermeyer, M., Schlüter, R., Ney, H.: LSTM Neural Networks for Language Modeling (2012)
17. Laptev, N., Laptev, V., Gerget, O., Kravchenko, A., Kolpashchikov, D.: Visualization system for fire detection in the video sequences. Sci. Vis. **13**(2), 1–9 (2021)
18. Cloud AutoML Custom Machine Learning Models | Google Cloud. https://cloud.google.com/automl
19. Ramraj, S., Uzir, N., Sunil, R., Banerjee, S.: Experimenting XGBoost algorithm for prediction and classification of different datasets. Int. J. Control Theory Appl. **9**(40), 651–662 (2016)
20. Wang, D., Zhang, Y., Zhao, Y.: LightGBM: An Effective miRNA Classification Method in Breast Cancer Patients. In: Proceedings of 2017 International Conference on Computational Biology Bioinformatics - ICCBB 2017 (2017)
21. Liaw, A., Wiener, M.: Classification and regression by randomforest. R News **2**, 18–22 (2002)
22. Hancock, J.T., Khoshgoftaar, T.M.: CatBoost for big data: an interdisciplinary review. J. Big Data **7**(1), 1–45 (2020)
23. Shen, B., Liu, B.D., Wang, Q.: Elastic net regularized dictionary learning for image classification. Multimedia Tools Appl. **75**, 8861–8874 (2016)
24. Sharaff, A., Gupta, H.: Extra-tree classifier with metaheuristics approach for email classification. Adv. Intell. Syst. Comput. **924**, 189–197 (2019)
25. TensorFlow, https://www.tensorflow.org/
26. Keras: the Python deep learning API. https://keras.io/

Analysis of Hardware-Implemented U-Net–Like Convolutional Neural Networks

Zoev Ivan, Maslov Konstantin, Markov Nikolay⬮, and Mytsko Evgeniy(✉)⬮

School of Computer Science and Robotics, Tomsk Polytechnic University, 30, Lenin Avenue,
Tomsk 634050, Russia
{markovng,evgenvt}@tpu.ru

Abstract. Two convolutional neural networks (CNNs)—modification of classic U-Net and U-Net with the use of dilated convolutions—were implemented. In order to train and test the CNNs, we utilised unmanned aerial vehicle images containing *Abies sibirica* trees damaged by *Polygraphus proximus*. The images consist five classes: four classes of the trees depending on their condition and background. The weights of the CNNs, obtained as a result of the training, were then used to implement the CNNs in the field-programmable gate array–based system on a chip platform (Xilinx Zynq 7000). The paper also presents a comparison of the hardware-implemented CNNs in terms of segmentation quality and time efficiency.

Keywords: convolutional neural networks · field-programmable gate array · hardware implementation of convolutional neural networks · U-Net

1 Introduction

Nowadays the problems of recognizing different objects (human faces, cars, objects on the earth's surface, etc.) and their state monitoring are relevant. Various architectures of convolutional neural networks (CNNs) have been successfully used to address these problems [1, 2]. However, there is a need to use unmanned aerial vehicles (UAVs) with special equipment for solving some of these problems such as monitoring of hard-to-reach objects (hazardous technological objects in the fields, forests in mountainous areas, etc.). In such cases, it is required to equip each UAV with an intelligent computer vision system (CVS) which includes a video camera, a thermal imager and a computing unit (CU) with a hardware-implemented CNN. The CVS would allow to solve problems of recognition of various objects (cars, technological objects, people, etc.) Designing such mobile monitoring systems with intelligent CVS requires keeping a balance between the speed of the CU, the CNN performance for object recognition and the mass and power consumption of this device to increase the UAV flight time.

This paper is devoted to the study of the effectiveness of hardware-implemented U-Net–like CNN models with the use of field programmable gate array (FPGA) of modern systems on a chip (SoC). The dataset of images from UAVs of *Abies sibirica* trees damaged by *Polygraphus proximus* was used for training, validation and evaluation of

© Springer Nature Switzerland AG 2024
R. Yavorskiy et al. (Eds.): TMPA 2021, CCIS 1559, pp. 52–63, 2024.
https://doi.org/10.1007/978-3-031-50423-5_5

these CNN models. The images contain trees of four *Abies sibirica* classes depending on the degree of damage by the pests and the background class. We also provide a comparison of these hardware-implemented and software-implemented models in terms of the segmentation quality, time efficiency and power consumption.

2 Related Work

A number of recent studies have addressed the use of FPGA-implemented CNN models for semantic image segmentation. These CNN models usually include fully convolutional networks such as U-Net and SegNet or their modifications. Over the last years, this area has been developing very intensively and the largest numbers of studies have been carried out on the U-Net models implemented in FPGAs [3–5]. Important results for SegNet models are given in [6, 7] where the authors present large-scale studies of the performance and power consumption of accelerators which are implemented on an Intel Arria-10 GX1150 FPGA SoC. However, only in [7] the quality of image segmentation was evaluated using the optimized SegNet model implemented in an accelerator. Note that FPGAs of modern SoCs (e.g., Intel Arria-10 GX1150 in [6, 7] and Xilinx Zynq ZC706 in [8]) are mainly used to develop accelerators. However, in [3] an outdated Altera Cyclone V FPGA with low resources and minimal power consumption was used.

In most studies, it is proposed to reduce the complexity of the U-Net and SegNet models to improve the performance of accelerators in FPGAs. For example, a simple encoder-decoder is used with depthwise separable convolutions in [3, 4]. In [5], one vector multiplication module is used for the efficient implementation of convolution and deconvolution and different levels of parallel computations are applied. In addition, operations on 8-, 16-, and 32-bit fixed-point numbers are used [5, 7, 8] to increase the performance of FPGA accelerators. Analysis of the accelerator performance when using 32-bit floating-point numbers is given only in [4] but there are no studies for the case of using 16-bit floating-point numbers. Although studies of the accelerators performance using new architectures in the presented works have been carried out on a large-scale, studies of the segmentation quality loss for new architectures are not complete. Sometimes unsubstantiated theses are given that the quality for a particular new CNN model is somewhat reduced in comparison with the segmentation quality given by the original U-Net or SegNet models. All this indicates the relevance of large-scale studies on segmentation quality obtained with modifications of the original U-Net and SegNet models and the use of floating-point arithmetic.

Only accelerators which are considered in [3, 5] were developed taking into account the specifics of the segmentation problems of remote sensing images. Moreover, simple problems of binary image segmentation using CNN models in FPGAs are considered in [3] and problems of object recognition for many classes are not addressed in detail. This once again underlines the relevance of the studies on image segmentation performance and the corresponding computational costs while solving multiclass problems using FPGA-implemented U-Net–like models.

3   U-Net Models

The addressed problem was to perform semantic segmentation of UAV images of *Abies sibirica* trees damaged by *Polygraphus proximus*. The images consist five classes: four classes of the trees (living, dying, recently dead and long dead trees) depending on their degree of the damage by the forest pest and the background class. U-Net models proposed for solving this problem are developed on the basis of the original fully convolutional network U-Net [1]. A typical U-Net model consists of an encoder and a decoder. A distinctive feature of U-Net is the presence of concatenation operations connecting feature maps in the encoder with feature maps in the decoder in order to increase the detail of the resulting segmentation maps.

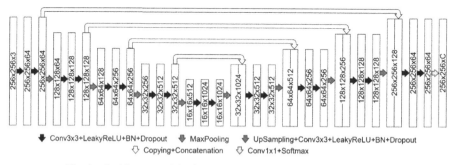

Fig. 1.   Architecture of the implemented CNN model based on U-Net

Minor modifications to the original U-Net have been made to deal with the multiclass problem. Figure 1 shows the architecture of the proposed model. Every rectangle depicts a tensor, or a multidimensional array representing a set of feature maps. The numbers correspond to the sizes of the tensors. The arrows depict the following operations: convolutions (Conv3×3, Conv1×1); LeakyReLU calculation (we also considered ReLU and ELU); batch normalization (BN); downsampling by choosing the maximum value in the 2 by 2 patches of the feature maps (MaxPooling); upsampling with the nearest neighbor interpolation (UpSampling); copying of the tensor and its concatenation with another one (Copying + Concatenation); dropping out values of the tensor by setting them to zero at random positions during the training (Dropout). The categorical distribution at the output of the decoder is modeled for each pixel by applying the multivariate logistic function, Softmax. In contrast to the original U-Net, the described model has the following minor modifications: the input image of the network is represented by a 256 × 256 × 3 tensor, which corresponds to an ordinary RGB image; convolutions do not reduce the size of the feature maps; cropping is not used; batch normalization is applied after every non-linearity; the output tensor is calculated using C convolutions with 1 × 1 kernels, thereby allowing to classify the pixels of C classes.

On the basis of this CNN model, we propose another CNN model with the use of dilated convolutions [9]. Dilated convolutions differ from ordinary convolutions by inflating the convolution kernel by inserting zero coefficients between its elements. Dilated convolutions are governed by dilation rate that shows the distance between neighboring nonzero coefficients of the kernel. In the new model, every two consequent convolutions with 3×3 kernels in the model shown in Fig. 1 are replaced by one dilated convolution with 3×3 kernels and the dilation rate of 2 (thus, giving 5×5 receptive field). This leads to a significant simplification of the CNN model and, therefore, should decrease the inference time.

In order to evaluate the quality of the CNN models, intersection over union (IoU) [10] was used. It is considered a widely recognized metric for the problems of semantic image segmentation. IoU values greater than 0.5 are considered to correspond to acceptably high segmentation quality. An aggregate indicator of the quality of the models is mean intersection over union ($mIoU$) which is average of IoU by class.

4 U-Net Models Training

To implement in software the CNN models, we utilized Python programming language and keras library [11]. To train the models, to validate and evaluate them, we used a dataset created from dataset consisting UAV images of *Abies sibirica* trees affected by *Poligraphus proximus* [12]. The subject to recognition in the images are four classes of *Abies sibirica* trees describing their condition and the background class. For the formation of training and validation sets, the images from the dataset were rotated several times and cut into patches of 256 by 256 pixels with the offset of 128 pixels. Data leakage from the validation set was eliminated by imposing Boolean masks on the original images and blocking the possibility of moving the corresponding pixels into the training set. Thus, it was ensured that the features of the validation samples are not repeated among the training samples. In total, 2004 training and 672 validation patches were obtained. Online augmentation technique was applied in order to improve the generalizing ability of the CNN models.

In order to find optimal weight coefficients, $mIoU$ was maximized and the gradient-based optimization algorithm Adam was utilized. The optimization of $mIoU$ allows to partially solve the issue of the imbalanced training set shown earlier. To find the best sets of the hyperparameters for the proposed CNN models, we employed Bayesian approach to optimization.

During the hardware implementation of the CNN models, their weight coefficients obtained in the described above way were transferred to the SoC.

5 Features of the Hardware Implementation of the Proposed CNN Models

A modern intelligent CVSs should have low power consumption, for example, no more than 10–12 Watts in the case of UAVs. Therefore, the CU of such CVS should be developed on the basis of modern SoCs with FPGAs which have low power consumption and high performance. We used SoC Zinq 7000 (Kintex FPGA) from Xilinx [13].

The architecture of most SoCs allows one to organize direct access of a hardware-implemented CNN to external memory. The implementation of this method of interaction of the FPGA with external memory allows performing some operations that differ from the convolution and subsample procedures of the CNN on the SoC processor. Also, in [14] an original method for performing computations in a hardware-implemented CNN on a FPGA was proposed. It differs from the known methods by using unified computational convolution and subsampling blocks. The unification of the convolution/subsample blocks is achieved by extracting parameters of this blocks usually specified at the stage of their synthesis and placing them in a separate variable FPGA memory area, called the configuration memory region ("CONFIG space"). Thereby, it allows to use the blocks of the suitable type in the layers of the CNN with different architectural parameters. Moreover, the universal unified blocks (the blocks of only one type) are used in the layers of convolution and subsampling of the hardware-implemented CNN. These blocks contain both convolution sub-blocks and subsampling sub-blocks [15]. This makes it possible to organize computations in the hardware-implemented CNN in a more flexible way. The implementation of the method assumes that the number of computing blocks involved in the hardware-implemented CNN can vary.

It is necessary to organize access of the SoC processor to this memory area and to develop the appropriate software when implementing the unification method, in addition to allocate the configuration memory area.

Taking into account the interaction of the FPGA with external memory, the unification of computing blocks of the CNN and the way proposed in [16] of organizing computations in SoC made it possible to implement a mobile CU of CVS based on the Avnet Mini-ITX developing board with the SoC Zynq 7000 (Kintex FPGA). The enlarged functional diagram of this CU is shown in Fig. 2.

The CU (Fig. 2) contains two main functional units. The SoC is the first one. It contains a processor system (PS) and FPGA. The PS in turn includes a DDR3 external memory controller and two ARM Cortex A9 800 MHz processor cores. We developed a controller of direct access to external memory (DMA controller) in FPGA, the block "Hardware implementation of CNN" and configuration memory "CONFIG space" which is included in this block (configuration memory in Fig. 2 is taken out of the block for the clarity of the CU scheme presentation). The block "Hardware implementation of CNN" consists of a neural computing unit (NCU). The NCU performs the computations of the convolution and subsampling procedures for the U-Net models. NCU contains 64 universal computing blocks that simultaneously work on each layer of the CNN. The second functional unit is external DDR3 memory with 800 MHz clock frequency.

An algorithm for the NCU operations is proposed and implemented for parallel computations which are carried out within each layer of the CNN model. The idea of the algorithm is that each universal computing block of the NCU performs a sequential calculation of the elements of the assigned output feature map in the current layer. It turns out that each output feature map is simultaneously formed by a separate block. If the output feature maps of the layer are greater than the number of computational blocks in the NCU then one block sequentially produces several output feature maps of the layer.

A multifunctional software driver for the Linux kernel OS was developed to ensure the interaction between the FPGA, PS and external memory. This driver was written in C programming language. We have developed a library for the interaction of users with the CU settings using C++ language.

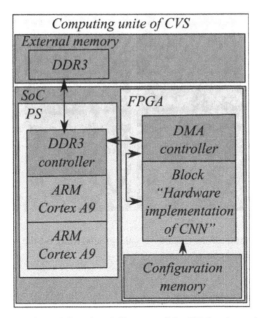

Fig. 2. The enlarged functional diagram of the CU for the mobile CVS

A software tool was developed using Python with Cython procedures (inserts) to quickly reconfigure NCU on FPGAs and to simplify the hardware implementation of various CNN models. This tool also makes it possible to choose the option for implementing the CNN model on a microprocessor system ($\times86$ or ARM) or on an FPGA.

6 The Results and Discussion of the CNN Models Analysis

6.1 Evaluation of the Software-Implemented CNN Models

The trained models were applied to the semantic segmentation of the test area image of an *Abies sibirica* forest. A visual analysis of the test area image (Fig. 3a), the ground truth map (Fig. 3b) and the outputs of the CNN models (Fig. 3c and Fig. 3d) has shown that both models are capable of delineating the boundaries between the trees and classifying successfully a considerable part of the *Abies sibirica* crowns. At the same time the biggest challenge for the both CNN models is to classify correctly dying trees.

Table 1 lists *IoU* values for the both CNN models (using LeakyReLU activation function) and for every class. It also shows *mIoU* values to evaluate the overall performance of the models while classifying the test area image. The both CNN models successfully classify all classes but dying trees. The low segmentation quality for dying trees can be explained by their underrepresentation in the training set and visual similarity with living trees and *Picea* trees, which are a part of the background.

We also conducted a comparison of the time efficiency of the implemented in software CNN models. For that, inference times needed to process a $256 \times 256 \times 3$ patch were recorded for the both models. The corresponding results are summarized in Table 2,

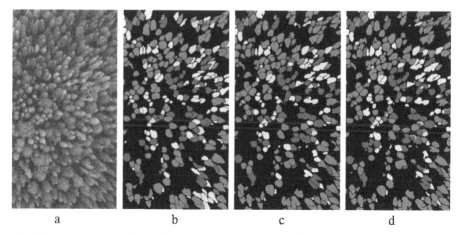

a   b   c   d

Fig. 3. Segmentation result: a—the test area, b—the ground truth, c—the output of U-Net, d—the output of U-Net with dilated convolutions.

Table 1. Quality of segmentation for U-Net and U-Net with dilated convolutions (U-Net*)

Model	*IoU*					*mIoU*
	Background	Living	Dying	Recently dead	Long dead	
U-Net	0.87	0.77	0.39	0.75	0.62	0.68
U-Net*	0.86	0.76	0.37	0.75	0.62	0.67

the use of the median and MAD is reasoned by the skewness of the inference time distributions. The comparison has been carried out on a PC with an Intel Core i7-8700 CPU, 31 GB RAM and an NVIDIA GeForce GTX 1080 Ti GPU (3584 CUDA cores with the 1582 MHz boost clock, 11 GB GDDR5X memory with the 1372 MHz frequency and 352-bit interface width). The graphics card power is 250 Watts.

Table 2. Inference time for U-Net and U-Net with dilated convolutions (U-Net*)

Model	*One patch inference time, ms*	
	Median	MAD
U-Net	30.78	0.16
U-Net*	27.67	0.16

As can be seen from Table 2, U-Net with dilated convolutions gives an advantage in inference time of a patch of about 3 ms on a PC, while providing a comparable segmentation quality (see Table 1).

6.2 Evaluation of the Hardware-Implemented CNN Models

Computational experiments on the semantic segmentation of the image patches from UAVs of the test area were carried out to study the effectiveness of the hardware-implemented CNN models. Image patches with a size of $256 \times 256 \times 3$ were fed to the input of the U-Net and U-Net with dilated convolutions hardware-implemented models.

Experiments with the U-Net model were carried out using both 16-bit (float16) and 32-bit (float32) floating point numbers and with different activation functions: ELU, ReLU and LeakyReLU. The results for this model are shown in Table 3.

Table 3. Quality of segmentation for U-Net with different activation functions and floating-point formats

Activation function	*IoU*					*mIoU*
	Background	Living	Dying	Recently dead	Long dead	
float16						
ELU	0.84	0.72	0.39	0.74	0.63	0.66
ReLU	0.82	0.68	0.28	0.76	0.66	0.64
LeakyReLU	0.84	0.72	0.36	0.77	0.65	0.67
float32						
ELU	0.84	0.72	0.39	0.74	0.63	0.66
ReLU	0.83	0.68	0.29	0.76	0.66	0.64
LeakyReLU	0.84	0.72	0.36	0.77	0.65	0.67

We see that the best results in terms of the image patch segmentation quality were obtained using the U-Net model with the LeakyReLU activation function. Coefficients of software-implemented CNN models only with this (LeakyReLU) activation function were used for further studies of the effectiveness of hardware-implemented CNN models.

Table 4 shows the values of the semantic segmentation quality obtained using the U-Net model with dilated convolutions and the LeakyReLU activation function. Tables 3 and 4 show that the results of the segmentation quality of patches for each CNN model with this activation function and with 16-bit floating point values do not differ from the results with 32-bit floating point values for some tree classes.

The use of dilated convolutions leads to a slight loss of segmentation quality (by about 0.02 for the *mIoU* metric) relative to the U-Net model. However, in comparison with the software-implemented models of the CNN the results for which are presented in Table 1 there is a decrease in quality by 0.02–0.04 according to the *mIoU* metric depending on the activation function used in the model. Note that the drop in segmentation quality is even higher for some classes of *Abies sibirica* trees. So, for example, for dying trees the difference is 0.03–0.06 according to the *IoU* metric.

Computing speed evaluation of the hardware-implemented CNN models was conducted by semantic segmentation of one $256 \times 256 \times 3$ patch. The SoC used made it

Table 4. Quality of segmentation for U-Net with dilated convolutions and different floating-point formats

IoU					
Background	Living	Dying	Recently dead	Long dead	*mIoU*
float16					
0.83	0.69	0.33	0.78	0.62	0.65
float32					
0.83	0.69	0.33	0.78	0.62	0.65

possible to operate the FPGA with a clock frequency of 100 MHz and to organize the use of 64 universal computing blocks in the NCU. The inference time medians and MADs for the both float32 and float16 are summarized in Table 5 (note the use of seconds, not milliseconds, as oppose to Table 2). It follows that U-Net model with dilated convolutions makes it possible to analyze an image patch on the FPGA more than 25% faster than the U-Net model with float32 and float16. Using float16 («IEEE float16») numbers leads to a drop in performance due to the fact that upsample and the last CNN layer are processed on an PS which does not support half-precision floating point numbers. Converting numbers from float32 to float16 format requires additional costs which is the bottleneck of the system.

The speed computation of patch semantic segmentation with software-implemented CNN models (Table 2) on a personal computer with an Intel Core i7–8700 CPU, 31 GB of RAM and an NVIDIA GeForce GTX 1080 Ti GPU is almost a thousand times higher than the computation speed of these CNN models on FPGAs. This is due to the significantly higher CPU clock frequency (3200 MHz) of the computer used than the FPGA clock frequency (100 MHz) and to the presence of the computer with more advanced RAM and GPU.

Table 5. Inference time for hardware-implemented U-Net and U-Net with dilated convolutions (U Net*)

Model	One patch inference time, s			
	float32		float16	
	Median	MAD	Median	MAD
U-Net	31.12	0.07	38.03	0.12
U-Net*	23.47	0.03	27.58	0.05

Table 6 shows the results of measuring the power consumption of the SoC and the FPGA resources in the form of the various types number of cells for each U-Net models with float32 and float16 formats. From these results, we can say that the use of float16 allows to reduce the power consumption of the SoC and the required FPGA resources for storing the input data and weight coefficients of the CNN model in comparison with float32 values. The power consumption of SoCs with FPGAs is slightly more than 5 Watts which is 50 times less than NVIDIA GeForce GTX 1080 Ti GPU with power consumption of 250 Watts.

Table 6. SoC power consumption and FPGA resources

Power consumption and FPGA resources				
Type	Power, Watts	LUT, count	LUTRAM, count	BRAM, count
float16	4.32	138917	2074	225,5
float32	5.33	165278	871	328,5

All these results once again indicate that the main advantage of devices based on modern SoCs with FPGAs is low power consumption. Moreover, modern SoCs have a very low mass in comparison with the same graphics accelerators.

Note that all the obtained results of the study of the U-Net models which were hardware-implemented on FPGAs are very important for the developers of intelligent CVSs as part of mobile monitoring systems based on UAVs. Developers of such CVSs must maintain a balance between the speed of the used CU, the quality of recognizing objects on the earth's surface using the CNN and the mass and power consumption of this device in order to increase the flight time of the UAV. It is important for developers to analyze the given research results and make appropriate design decisions when searching for a balance. For example, if a CVS is created with a relatively low segmentation quality of monitored object images then you can use the U-Net model with dilated convolutions and perform calculations of this model on FPGAs with 16-bit floating point numbers. All this will significantly reduce CU power consumption and resource requirements for the selected FPGA.

7   Conclusion

The tasks of creating intelligent CVSs as a part of mobile systems for monitoring objects of the earth surface based on UAVs are relevant today. Is this study, modifications of the U-Net model are proposed, software-implemented and trained for the subsequent development of such a CVS. Then these CNN models are hardware-implemented on the FPGA of the modern SoC Zynq 7000 (Kintex FPGA). For training, validation and research of these CNN models a dataset which was created from UAV images of *Abies sibirica* trees damaged by *Polygraphus proximus* was used.

Comprehensive studies of these software-implemented CNN models and the CU which is based on this SoC have been carried out. There is a decrease in the quality of image segmentation by 0.02–0.04 according to the *mIoU* metric in comparison with the software-implemented CNN models for the hardware-implemented CNN models in FPGA. The drop in segmentation quality is even higher for some classes of *Abies sibirica* trees, e.g., for dying trees the difference is 0.03–0.06 according to the *IoU* metric. The use of dilated convolutions in the CNN model leads to an insignificant loss of segmentation quality (by about 0.02 for the *mIoU* metric). The results on segmentation quality with 16-bit floating point numbers in FPGA calculations do not differ from the results with 32-bit floating point numbers.

In the study of the CU performance it was revealed that the U-Net model with dilated convolutions allows to analyze a $256 \times 256 \times 3$ image patch in the FPGA more than 25% faster than the original U-Net model. However, the speed of computing these CNN models in CU is almost a thousand times slower compared to the speed of the software-implemented CNN models on a personal computer with an Intel Core i7–8700 processor, 31 GB of RAM and an NVIDIA GeForce GTX 1080 Ti GPU.

The obtained results of measuring the SoC power consumption and the required FPGA resources in the hardware implementation of the U-Net models indicate that the use of 16-bit floating point numbers when performing the calculations of the CNN models can reduce the power consumption of the SoC and the required FPGA resources in comparison with the case using 32-bit floating points. The power consumption of SoCs with FPGAs is a little more than 5 Watts and it is 50 times less than that of the same NVIDIA GeForce GTX 1080 Ti graphics accelerator.

We can assume that the results of complex studies of software-implemented and FPGA-implemented CNN models are of great scientific and practical importance for developers of intelligent CVSs as a part of mobile systems for monitoring objects of the earth surface based on UAVs. The use of these results will allow them to make informed design decisions when creating intelligent CVSs for solving various applied problems.

Acknowledgments. The research was funded by RFBR and Tomsk region, project number 18–47-700010.

References

1. Ronneberger, O., Fischer, P., Brox, T.: U-Net: Convolutional Networks for Biomedical Image Segmentation. arXiv preprint arXiv: 1505.04597v1 (2015)
2. Bochkovskiy, A., Wang, C.Y., Mark Liao, H-Y.: YOLOv4: optimal speed and accuracy of object detection. arXiv preprint arXiv:2004.10934v1 (2020)
3. Bahl, G., Daniel, L., Moretti M., Lafarge, F.: Low-power neural networks for semantic segmentation of satellite images. In: IEEE/CVF International Conference on Computer Vision Workshop (ICCVW), pp. 2469–2476. IEEE, Seoul, South Korea (2019)
4. Liu, B., Zou, D., Feng, L., Feng, S., Fu, P., Li, J.: An FPGA-based CNN accelerator integrating depthwise separable convolution. Electronics **8**(3), 1–18 (2019)
5. Liu, S., Luk, W.: Towards an efficient accelerator for DNN-based remote sensing image segmentation on FPGAs. In: Proceedings of 29th International Conference on Field Programmable Logic and Applications (FPL), pp. 187–193. IEEE, Barcelona, Spain (2019)
6. Huang, H., et al.: EDSSA: an encoder-decoder semantic segmentation networks accelerator on OpenCL-based FPGA platform. Sensors. **20**(14), 1–18 (2020)
7. Yu, M., et al.: Optimizing FPGA-based convolutional encoder-decoder architecture for semantic segmentation. In: Proceedings of 9th IEEE International Conference on CYBER Technology in Automation, Control, and Intelligent Systems, pp. 1436–1440. IEEE, Suzhou, China (2019)

8. Liu, S., Fan, H., Niu, X., Ng, H.-C., Chu, Y., Luk, W.: Optimizing CNN-based sementation with deeply customized convolutional and deconvolutional architectures on FPGA. ACM Trans. Reconfigurable Technol. Syst. **11**(3), 1–22 (2018)

9. Fisher, Y.: Multi scale context aggregation by dilated convolutions. arXiv preprint arXiv: 1511.07122v3 (2016)

10. Taha, A., Hanbury, A.: Metrics for evaluating 3D medical image segmentation: analysis, selection, and tool. BMC Med. Imaging **15**(29), 1–28 (2015)

11. Keras. https://keras.io/. Accessed 05 Oct 2021

12. Kerchev, I.A., Maslov, KA., Markov, N.G., Tokareva, O.S.: Semantic segmentation of damaged fir trees in unmanned aerial vehicle images. Sovremennye problemy distantsionnogo zondirovaniya Zemli iz kosmosa. **18**, 116–126 (2021)

13. Xilinx. https://xilinx.com/products/silicon-devices/soc/zynq-7000.html. Accessed 05 Oct 2021

14. Zoev, I.V., Markov, N.G., Beresnev, A.P., Yagunov, T.A.: FPGA-based hardware implementation of convolutional neural networks for images recognition. In: GraphiCon 2018 – 28th International Conference on Computer Graphics and Vision, vol. 2, pp. 200–203. Tomsk, Russian Federation (2018)

15. Zoev, I.V., Markov, N.G., Ryzhova, S.E.: Intelligent computer vision system for unmanned aerial vehicles for monitoring technological objects of oil and gas industry. Bull. Tomsk Polytech. Univ. Geo Assets Eng. **330**(11), 34– 49 (2019)

16. Zoev, I.V., Markov, N.G., Ryzhova, S.E.: The monitoring system of hazardous technological objects based unmanned aerial vehicles. In: E3S Web of Conferences, vol. 223 03005, pp. 1–6 (2020)

Early Detection of Tasks
with Uncommonly Long Run Duration
in Post-trade Systems

Maxim Nikiforov[1]([✉]), Danila Gorkavchenko[2], Murad Mamedov[3],
Andrey Novikov[4], and Nikita Pushchin[4]

[1] Exactpro Systems Limited, London, UK
maxim.nikiforov@exactpro.com
[2] Exactpro Systems LLC, Saratov, Russia
danila.gorkavchenko@exactpro.com
[3] Exactpro Systems LLC, Tbilisi, Georgia
murad.mamedov@exactpro.com
[4] Syndata.io, Moscow, Russia
andrey.novikov@exactpro.com
http://exactpro.com

Abstract. The paper describes the authors' experience of implementing machine learning techniques to predict deviations in the service workflows duration, long before the post-trade system reports them as not completed on time. The prediction is based on analyzing a large set of performance metrics collected every second from modules of the system, and using regression models to detect running workflows that are likely to be hung. This article covers raw data pre-processing, data set dimensionality reduction, the applied regression models and their performance. Problems to be resolved and the project roadmap are also described.

Keywords: Model-based testing · Software testing · Post-Trade · Performance testing · Monitoring

1 Introduction

1.1 Goal of the Research

The idea of our research is to predict delays in scheduled activities based on the telemetry logs produced by the system components.

The system is a distributed high-loaded post-trade platform performing clearing, settlement and risk management. Being designed as a real-time platform to process up to 20 millions trades daily with minimal latency, it also contains a scheduler that launches various data processing jobs in a time-based manner. It is very important that these events are successfully executed without any delays because a delay or failure of just one activity can create a delay of the entire daily life cycle of the system.

© Springer Nature Switzerland AG 2024
R. Yavorskiy et al. (Eds.): TMPA 2021, CCIS 1559, pp. 64–74, 2024.
https://doi.org/10.1007/978-3-031-50423-5_6

Such situations should be detected during the non-functional testing phase when the performance, capacity, and resiliency testing are run against the target system. And for any of the scheduled jobs, it is required to get an understanding of the system's bottlenecks, limitations and possible delays that can happen due to various reasons. The duration of most of the activities can vary at the time of the test, even if conditions are the same. We also could see test runs when duration of the workflows was significantly longer than usual. Often it can be a defect that required an immediate attention of the development team as it blocks testing process in particular environment. So for the sake of time efficiency it would be useful to monitor the duration of the jobs and notify the QA team if there is a significant deviation from the normal duration.

The target system, that contains more than 200 running components during a regular business day, produces telemetry logs with the information about all of the components. These logs store values of about 7500 parameters updated each second. Only less than 1% of them are considered by the development team as critical parameters that need to be monitored in production, so they are collected by external monitoring systems to get a high-level understanding of whether the system supports the current load or not. A major part of telemetry values is not documented, and, hence, not used during the production run. But these values represent the internal state of the components, and they can also be indicators of something going wrong. In some cases, they are also used to troubleshoot issues.

Due to the number of values and the size of the logs, it is not possible to explore these values manually in a reasonable time, so, in our research, we would like to develop an automated approach for this. And we would like to use this data to predict deviations from the normal scheduled jobs duration before they become obvious.

At the time its writing, this is ongoing work, so we share the current results and summarize the next steps.

1.2   Source Data Description

Batch Jobs Data. There are more than 100 batch activities, and they can be divided into different groups, depending on the frequency and regularity of the launches:

- **Activities which are executed several times a day.** Most of them are important, but they do not create significant delays for the system's life cycle.
- **Daily activities.** They are executed once per day and, usually, their completion is crucial for the business process.
- **Ad-hoc activities.** Instead of running in line with an internal system schedule, they are launched by a particular event in the system or by the business users' necessities, so their number can be different. For instance, one ad-hoc activity can run several times a day, while others have never been used in a regular business day.
- **Weekly and monthly events** are also mandatory, but they are also quite rare, and they don't usually have any critical dependencies.

In our research, the following attributes are used to describe any of the scheduled jobs:

- Unique identifier;
- Type of activity;
- Start time;
- End time;
- Completion status.

In Fig. 1, it is also possible to see that the duration for different activity types varies widely.

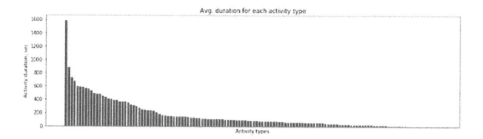

Fig. 1. Average duration for each activity type

Telemetry Logs Components. This is the information collected from all running components in the system, it is stored in text files. The format of the logs varies depending on the component, but they have a common high-level structure:

- Timestamp;
- Component ID;
- Group ID of the parameters;
- List of the parameters in a custom format.

Such a raw data format is not efficient and doesn't allow to get unified access to the values. During just one day, the system generates 30 GB of logs. In order to change this, the text files were converted to table format and processed data stores in CSV-format. Each row is a timestamp, and each column represents the history of updates of a particular component's parameter. This change allowed us to reduce the size of the logs by 93%.

Most of the values are numerical values: numerical IDs of the transaction, counters, buffer sizes, flags with Boolean values. A small part of them contains categorical values like the unique text ID of the current task.

2   Literature Review

The task of monitoring technical systems appears in different industries, including software [1,2], hardware [3], industrial machines, vehicles and others [4–6]. The purposes of monitoring include timely parts replacement, signalling on abnormal behavior, and even finding root causes of irregular systems operations. Machine learning on systems-assembled data is a common approach to address prediction tasks, with supervised algorithms prevailing in practical use.

In relation to our work, publications with practices we found useful or worth considering for our research, fall on the following two domains:

- **Equipment outage prediction and preventive maintenance** deals with analyzing a flow of telemetry data to predict the lifetime of hardware systems components and ensure raising timely alerts when their components are about to stop working.
- **Detection of anomalies in software processes** is a relatively newer field, where Machine learning techniques are applied to detecting anomalies, it is primarily based on the data produced by software components as part of their normal functioning.

2.1   Equipment Outage Predictions

Outage prediction and preventive maintenance for complex equipment based on data accumulated within the equipment components during their normal operation is a well-researched field, with applications widely used in the industry. The applications include computer hardware, automotive, banking ATMs and many more industries.

As the corresponding research is more business-oriented, and in many cases the prediction algorithm implemented in the hardware cannot be updated immediately, should and error be discovered, a "good enough" approach is mostly used, and many authors come to the use of tree-based algorithms.

In [7], authors use Random Forest classifier to predict an impending outage of computer hard disks (target variable) based on an array of 90 parameters produced by SMART (Self-monitoring and Reporting Technology) for a given hard disk. The research is based on a business data set of 50,000+ records, and the accuracy achieved is around 0,87.

In [8], a number of tree-based models is applied to predict an outage of agricultural equipment for the purposes of predictive maintenance.

The general direction of these papers is in line with our research, as both are focused on predicting some sort of a "lifespan" of the equipment in one case and unfinished processes in the other. However, the difference is that our business context requires identifying a process as frozen at an early stage, based on as small a set of initial data as possible, that forcing us to work on data augmentation, which is not the case for hardware where "everything is ok so far" is a desired and acceptable answer.

2.2 Software Systems Failure Prediction

The field of predicting crashes of software systems, while setting the same goal of early prediction of undesired states, is much different from the hardware outage prediction in the following ways:

- Many features are typically available (thousands to tens of thousands),
- Observation is performed in real time, producing a high frequency of recorded observations.

This makes dimensionality reduction and aggregation a core part of the developed algorithms.

The work [9] is centered around classifying software systems states into three levels: Red zone (5 min or less before crash), Orange zone (5 min before Red zone), and Green zone (everything that precedes the Orange zone).

Working with a dataset of around 40 features, authors tried a range of classification algorithms, including Decision tree, Naive Bayes, Support Vector Machines, K nearest neighbors, Random Forest and LDA/QDA, with the best results produced by Random Forest. A part of the work is dedicated to feature set reduction via the Lasso algorithm, resulting in reducing the number of features by 60%.

In our research, we both apply Machine Learning methods and construct an approach to a massive feature set reduction. Another way we use to reduce computational complexity is using the same set of aggregates for predicting the state of each of the many processes, this leading to another layer of data preprocessing that did not arise in the above-mentioned research.

3 Data Handling

3.1 Types of Data Sets

Based on the current problem, it was decided to split the research into 2 phases. Each phase has different goals, and a different data format is required:

1. **Activity-based data set.** Each row in the data set contains data for a run of one activity. It can be easily prepared based on the historical data. It is used for development purposes only.
2. **Time-based data set.** Each row of the data set contains data for a specific period of time for several activities, as they can be executed simultaneously in the system. The data set can be created in real time and is supposed to be used in a ready-to-use solution.

All the results demonstrated further in this work are presented for the first type of the data set. Time-based data set will be used in the future as a part of a PoC solution.

3.2   Activity-Based Data Set Preparation

The following approach is used to create an activity-based data set:

1. Categorical data processing: removing unique IDs from the source data, for non-unique values, the one-hot encoding technique is applied;
2. Once there are no text data in the data set, the telemetry data for each workflow is aggregated using a set of functions (min, mean, max);
3. Remove columns with constant values
4. Remove correlated columns

At first, we eliminated the columns with constant values and converted the columns with textual information to the number format using the one-hot encoding technique. During this operation, the quantity of columns increased (from 7.5K to 8.3K columns), however, the goal of data unification was achieved.

A major problem that is eliminated here is the length of the original data. If the duration of some activities is up to 1 h, it means that the telemetry data set also has to contain data for a corresponding number of seconds. To decrease the number of rows, we aggregated all parameters using functions - maximum, minimum and mean. As a result, each row in the dataframe represented one workflow run with aggregated values in the columns. The quantity of rows decreased from the total number of seconds to the total number of workflow runs, but the number of columns increased to the number of aggregates used (more than 25000, in our case).

At the last stage, we drop columns with constant data and remove the correlated columns (where correlation coefficient was more than 0.99). It allows us to reduce the number of columns approximately 10 times, to 2300. The resulting data set can be used for further research.

3.3   Data Modeling

Training a Model for 1 Activity Type. At the very beginning it was decided to evaluate a duration of just one activity type without any prediction (telemetry data for training was taken from the first to the last second of the jobs). Using a decision tree regressor model, we got the following results: RMSE = 202 sec, STD = 45 sec. Figure 2 represents the performance of such a model, which can hardly be considered acceptable. In most cases, especially for short activities, the regressor overestimated their durations, that would create too many false positive triggers in real life.

Training a Single Model for All Activities. In Fig. 2, it is possible to see that there is a correlation between real and predicted values, and longer activities also have bigger predicted values, that is a positive result. Also, as the goal is to develop a solution that can work for a varied number of activities, the way to create a single model for each activity type doesn't seem feasible.

So, it was decided to use a single model to predict the duration of all types of workflows, which required to get a resolution to several problems:

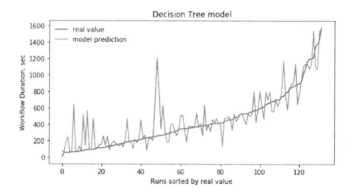

Fig. 2. Performance of the Decision Tree Regression model trained against a particular activity

- stratification of the data;
- adaption of the performance metrics;
- cleaning of the data.

During the experiments, we could see that longer activities produce a greater RMSE, if we measure it in seconds, even if the model has good performance for short activities. So, for business needs, it is required to resolve such problem to make sure that all activities contribute to RMSE equally. To resolve this, we suggest to calculate RMSE in relation to the target values using Formulae 1.

$$RMSE = \sqrt{\sum_{1}^{N} (\frac{y_{predicted}}{y_{test}} - \frac{y_{test}}{y_{test}})^2 \div N} \qquad (1)$$

The significant divergence of the target value also affects the performance of the model. Figure 3 shows that normalisation of the target value using a logarithm instead of the absolute value can increase the performance.

Also, in the Fig. 3, it is possible to see that some of the activities predicted with very low proximity. They are ad-hoc daily and weekly jobs executed rarely. So, we decided to exclude them, as their data wasn't enough for training.

After the above-mentioned changes, we compared the performance of the Decision Tree and the Random Forest Regression Models. For most cases, the performance of the Random Forest Models was significantly better (Fig. 4).

Prediction of Activities Duration. Up until now, we predicted the duration using the data from the beginning till the very end of the activities. The actual business scenario is to predict the duration based on analysing the telemetry on the initial period of expected run duration.

So, the hypothesis we checked is whether it is possible to predict the duration of the workflow based on the telemetry data from the components collected before the activity completes. We created 3 data sets based on the following criteria:

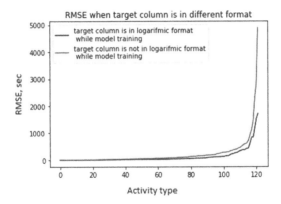

Fig. 3. Improvement of model quality after target value normalisation using logarithm function

- find D_{avg} average duration for each activity type
- create activity-based data set with telemetry data at 25%, 50% and 75% of D_{avg}

Models trained on each of the data sets do not show a quality improvement if the data was collected closer to the end point. The performance was on the same level as for the models trained at 100% point.

After that, these 3 data sets were joined into one with an additional column indicating at what point the data was collected. The model was trained with the same approach and its performance was significantly better (Fig. 5).

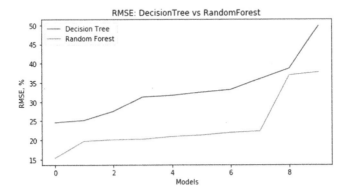

Fig. 4. Comparison of Decision Tree and Random Forest Regression models performance

As seen from Fig. 5, the overall medium result of prediction for different workflows, is, in the worst case, around 20% different from the actual value.

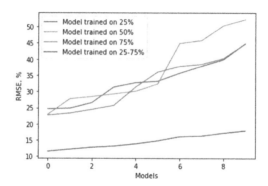

Fig. 5. Comparison of Decision Tree models predicted duration of activity based on telemetry data collected before activity completed

Random Forest Regressor Model trained on full list of activities using this approach shown RMSE = 25.6% with STD = 0.58%. This being the main result of this work.

Other effects from using additional data with aggregates at 25%, 50% and 75% expected workflow run duration, are the following:

- The overall prediction quality for the activities with a sufficient number of runs increases;
- Jobs with a low number of runs, like ad-hoc, weekly and monthly runs, can now also be addressed;
- For regular jobs, with data augmentation of this kind, we can accumulate sufficient data to train the model faster.

4   Conclusion

During the research using a distributed post-trade platform as a source of information, we found a way to pre-process the telemetry data and significantly reduce its size. A large amount of features is normal for systems like this, so we managed to significantly reduce their number from 8500 to 2300, considering generated aggregates. The reduction was done in the most general way, that would make it easy to adapt the approach to other data systems.

The experiments shown that Random Forest Regressor model predicts workflow duration with RMSE = 25.6% with STD = 0.58%. Such modeling results are acceptable and could only be achieved by enriching the source data set by additional intermediate records.

5   Future Work

As we get some results for the activity-based data set, we would like to prove that the same performance can be reached for a time-based data set and complete a PoC of the product, including the confirmation that the same level of performance can be reached for the time-based data set.

Aggregated functions (min, mean, max) used in the work are quite basic. It is required to research what aggregates can be used to collect more precise information about the original value to get better model performance.

As quite a big part of the most critical activities run just once a day, it is also required to focus on how much data we need to collect before getting an acceptable result. The ways of further data augmentation are also required to develop an approach to enlarge the data set.

After we get acceptable results in the prediction of workflow duration and deviation from the expected duration, we would like to focus on explaining the reason of the failure based on telemetry data.

References

1. Gámiz, M.L., Navas-Gómez, F.J., Raya-Miranda, R.: A machine learning algorithm for reliability analysis. IEEE (2020)
2. Behera, R.K., Shukla, S., Rath, S.K., Misra, S.: Software reliability assessment using machine learning technique. In: Gervasi, O., et al. (eds.) ICCSA 2018. LNCS, vol. 10964, pp. 403–411. Springer, Cham (2018). https://doi.org/10.1007/978-3-319-95174-4_32
3. Mahdisoltani, F., Stefanovici, I., Schroeder, B.: Proactive error prediction to improve storage system reliability. USENIX ATC (2017)
4. Xu, Z., Saleh, J.H.: Machine learning for reliability engineering and safety applications: review of current status and future opportunities. Reliab. Eng. Syst. Saf. **211**, 107530 (2021)
5. Li, G., Huang, Y., Bie, Z., Bing, T.: Machine-learning-based reliability evalution framework for power distribution networks. Instit. Eng. Technol. J. (2020)
6. Duchesne, L., Karangelos, E., Wehenkel, L.: Machine learning of real-time power systems reliability management response. In: IEEE Manchester Power Tech (2017)
7. Su, C.J., Yon, J.A.Q.: Big data preventive maintenance for hard disk failure detection. Int. J. Inf. Educ. Technol. **8**(7) (2018)
8. Kaparthi, S., Bumblauskas, D.: Designing predictive maintenance systems using decision tree-based machine learning techniques. Int. J. Qual. Reliab. Manage. **37**(4), 659–686 (2020)
9. Alonso, J., Belanche, L., Avresky, D.R.: Predicting software anomalies using machine learning techniques. In: 2011 IEEE 10th International Symposium on Network Computing and Applications, pp. 163–170 (2011) https://doi.org/10.1109/NCA.2011.29
10. Dias Neto, A.C., Subramanyan, R., Vieira, M., Travassos, G.H.: A survey on model-based testing approaches: a systematic review. In: WEASELTech '07: Proceedings of the 1st ACM International Workshop on Empirical Assessment of Software Engineering Languages and Technologies: Held in Conjunction with the 22nd IEEE/ACM International Conference on Automated Software Engineering (ASE) 2007, pp. 31–36 (2007)
11. Utting, M., Pretschner, A., Legeard, B.: A taxonomy of model-based testing. Technical report 04/2006. Department of Computer Science, University of Waikato (2006)

12. Villalobos-Arias L., Quesada-Lopez C., Martınez A., Jenkins M. :Model-based testing areas, tools and challenges: a tertiary study. CLEI Electr. J. **22**(1) (2019). Paper 3
13. Stachowiak, H.: Allgemeine Modelltheorie. Springer-Verlag, Wien and New York (1973)

Unpaired Image-To-Image Translation Using Transformer-Based CycleGAN

Chongyu Gu$^{(\boxtimes)}$ ⓘ and Maxim Gromov ⓘ

Tomsk State University, Tomsk, Russia
chongyugu@gmail.com

Abstract. The use of transformer-based architectures by computer vision researchers is on the rise. Recently, the implementations of GANs that use transformer-based architectures, such as TransGAN and ViTGAN, have demonstrated profitability for visual generative modeling. We introduced TransCycle-GAN, a novel, efficient GAN model, and explored its application to image-to-image translation. In distinction to the architectures above, our generator utilizes source images as input, not simply noise. We developed it and carried out preliminary experiments on the horse2zebra resized to 64 × 64. The experimental outcomes show the potential of our new architecture. An implementation of the model is available under the MIT license at GitHub.

Keywords: Image-to-Image Translation · Vision Transformer · Generative Adversarial Network

1 Introduction

Convolutional neural networks (CNNs) are the mainstay of computer vision today, thanks to their two core ideas: local connectivity and parameter sharing. Transformer architectures [11] are now displacing CNNs in image classification [13], semantic segmentation [23], object detection [24], and GAN tasks [12, 18]. Transformer architectures possess strong representation capabilities and are free from human-defined biases. CNNs, in comparison, have a strong bias toward feature locality and spatial invariance as a result of sharing filter weights between all locations.

TransGAN [12] and ViTGAN [18], which are GANs completely free of convolutions, have demonstrated profitability for the undertaking of visual generative modeling. These transformer-based generation models demonstrate the ability to generate better quality images compared to CNNs. We are inspired to investigate whether pure transformer-based architectures without using convolutions are capable of performing image-to-image translation. Moreover, we expect our transformer-based model to produce better quality results than CNNs.

TransCycleGAN is a new model that uses only transformers. It has customized memory-friendly generators and multi-scale discriminators. We apply adversarial losses, cycle consistency losses, and identity losses [7] to train the model. We run experiments on

© Springer Nature Switzerland AG 2024
R. Yavorskiy et al. (Eds.): TMPA 2021, CCIS 1559, pp. 75–82, 2024.
https://doi.org/10.1007/978-3-031-50423-5_7

the horse2zebra resized to 64×64. The results show that our model performs well. However, there are problems with low-resolution patches and artifacts. Section 4.2 demonstrates some good results. To the best of our knowledge, the proposed TransCycleGAN model is among the first approaches that leverage Vision Transformers [13] in GANs for the task of image-to-image translation.

The rest of the paper proceeds as follows. In Sect. 2, we discuss research related to unpaired image-to-image translation and GANs using Vision Transformers. Section 3 introduces the generator and discriminator design of our new architecture. Section 4 describes details of the experiment and the main result of our work. Section 5 briefly summarizes all the work.

2   Related Work

Generative Adversarial Networks (GANs) [1], a framework built using two neural networks to play a minimax game, made it possible to train generative models for unsupervised image synthesis. A generator network learns to produce realistic images, and a discriminator network is trained to distinguish between real and generated images. GANs are widely adopted in image synthesis [2–4], image super-resolution [5], image editing [6], image-to-image translation [7, 8], and text-to-image translation [9, 10].

Unpaired image-to-image translation refers to the process, which transforms an image from domain A into one in domain B. The training set consists of images from domains A and B, without pairs of corresponding images. A classical approach consists of training two generators ($A \rightarrow B$ and $B \rightarrow A$) and two corresponding discriminators. It may be advantageous to use a variational autoencoder like CoGAN [14], CycleGAN [7], and DualGAN [15]. These variants combine an adversarial loss induced by the discriminators with a cycle consistency constraint to retain semantic information throughout domain changes. As well as having an encoder, decoder, and residual block architecture roughly similar to CycleGAN, they incorporate elements from other networks, such as StyleGAN [3]. In our work, we use transformer-based generators and discriminators to replace the CNN-based ones in CycleGAN.

GANs Using Vision Transformers. As mentioned previously, the use of Vision Transformers for visual tasks is increasing. TransGAN is one of the first approaches to build a strong GAN completely free of convolutions. This transformer-based model introduces a novel generator using transformer encoder blocks. It uses upsampling modules composed of a reshaping and bicubic/pixelshuffle layer [16] to scale to higher-resolution images. Using a multi-scale structure, the discriminator takes patches of different sizes as inputs, thus balancing global and local contexts and increasing memory efficiency. TransGAN requires data augmentation as transformers are data-hungry architectures. The authors of [17] simplify training by combining a transformer-based generator with a convolutional discriminator. ViTGAN [18] is an under review paper. The ViT [13] architecture was integrated into GANs without using convolution or pooling. They introduced enforcing lipschitzness of transformer discriminator, improved spectral normalization, and overlapping image patches. These methods are not the same as ours, as our model provides the approach for image-to-image translation rather than image generation.

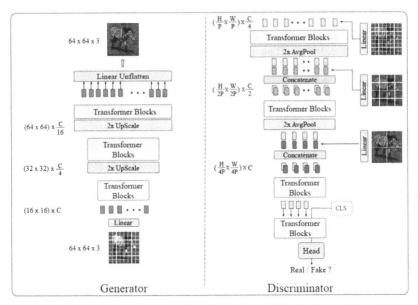

Fig. 1. The pipeline of the pure transform-based generator and discriminator of TransCycleGAN.

3   The Generator and Discriminator Networks

Our proposed model is a type of CycleGAN completely free of convolutions, using only pure transformer encoders [11]. An encoder consists of two blocks. A multi-head self-attention module constructs the first block, while a feed-forward multi-layer perceptron (MLP) with Gaussian Error Linear Unit (GELU) nonlinearity constructs the second. Both blocks make use of residual connections and have a normalization layer applied before them.

3.1   Generator Design

Inspired by TransGAN, we designed a generator structure to upscale the resolution repeatedly at several stages [2]. We may reduce the explosive cost of self-attention (quadratic w.r.t. the sequence length) by progressively expanding the input sequence and decreasing the embedding dimension.

Figure 1 (left) shows a memory-friendly transformer-based generator with several stages. Each stage contains several transformer blocks. We gradually increase the resolution of the feature map until it reaches the target resolution $H \times W$. Specifically, in contrast to TransGAN, the generator takes the source images as its input instead of the random noise. We reshape the image $x \in \mathbb{R}^{H \times W \times 3}$ into a sequence of flattened 2D patches $x_p \in \mathbb{R}^{N \times (P^2 \cdot 3)}$ and map to C dimensions, where (H, W) is the resolution of the source image, (P, P) is the resolution of each image patch, and $N = HW/P^2$ is the ensuring number of patches, which additionally serves as the effective input sequence length for the transformer encoder. Then we combine the resulting patch embeddings with the learnable position embedding to retain positional information. The resulting sequence of embedding vectors serves as input to the basic block.

After each stage, we insert an upsampling module that consists of a reshaping and resolution-upscaling layer to scale up to higher-resolution images. The upsampling module firstly reshapes the 1D sequence of token embedding back to a 2D feature map $X_i \in \mathbb{R}^{H_i \times W_i \times D}$. It then uses the pixelshuffle module to upsample its resolution. This method upsamples the resolution of the feature map by a factor of two while simultaneously reducing the embedding dimension to one-quarter of the input. This pyramid structure with modified upscaling stages mitigates the memory and computation explosion. The process will continue until the generator reaches the target resolution (H, W). Projecting the embedding dimension to 3 yields the RGB image.

3.2 Discriminator Design

In Fig. 1 (right), we use multi-scale discriminators to identify real and fake images. First, we used varied patch sizes $(P, 2P, 4P)$ to divide the input images $Y \in \mathbb{R}^{H \times W \times 3}$ into three different sequences. The longest sequence $\left(\frac{H}{P} \times \frac{W}{P}\right) \times 3$ is linearly converted to $\left(\frac{H}{P} \times \frac{W}{P}\right) \times \frac{C}{4}$ and then concatenated with the learnable position encoding to serve as the input of the first stage, where $\frac{C}{4}$ is the embedded dimension size.

The second and third sequences are also linearly converted to $\left(\frac{H}{2P} \times \frac{W}{2P}\right) \times \frac{C}{4}$ and $\left(\frac{H}{4P} \times \frac{W}{4P}\right) \times \frac{C}{2}$. They are then individually concatenated into the second and third stages. As a result, these three distinct sequences can extract both the semantic structure and the textual information. Between each stage, we adopt a 2DAverage Pooling layer to downsample the feature map resolution. Before the last block of the discriminator, a [class] token is attached at the beginning of the 1D sequence and then taken by the classification head to output the real/fake prediction.

3.3 Detailed Architecture Configurations

We present the architecture configurations of TransCycleGAN, shown in Figs. 2 and 3. Patch splitting and linear transformation are called "Layer Flatten" for generator designs, and "Block" represents the basic Transformer Block, which includes self-attention, normalization, and feed-forward MLP. The "input_shape" and "output_shape" correspondingly stand for the shape of the input and output feature map. According to Sect. 3.2, the output feature map of stages is concatenated with another sequence in the discriminator architecture. The last stage adds another [class] token and uses a transformer block to correspond the [class] token to the extracted representation. In the end, the Classification Head uses just the [class] token to determine if the image is real or false. The total number of parameters is 15.2 M (Table 1).

An implementation of the model is available at [22] (see Table 2).

Table 1. Architecture configuration of generator.

Generator			
Stage	Layer	Input Shape	Output Shape
–	Linear Flatten	$64 \times 64 \times 3$	$16 \times 16 \times 1024$
1	Block	$16 \times 16 \times 1024$	$16 \times 16 \times 1024$
	Block	$16 \times 16 \times 1024$	$16 \times 16 \times 1024$
	Block	$16 \times 16 \times 1024$	$16 \times 16 \times 1024$
	Block	$16 \times 16 \times 1024$	$16 \times 16 \times 1024$
	Block	$16 \times 16 \times 1024$	$16 \times 16 \times 1024$
2	PixelShuffle	$16 \times 16 \times 1024$	$32 \times 32 \times 256$
	Block	$32 \times 32 \times 256$	$32 \times 32 \times 256$
	Block	$32 \times 32 \times 256$	$32 \times 32 \times 256$
	Block	$32 \times 32 \times 256$	$32 \times 32 \times 256$
	Block	$32 \times 32 \times 256$	$32 \times 32 \times 256$
3	PixelShuffle	$32 \times 32 \times 256$	$64 \times 64 \times 64$
	Block	$64 \times 64 \times 64$	$64 \times 64 \times 64$
	Block	$64 \times 64 \times 64$	$64 \times 64 \times 64$
–	Linear Layer	$64 \times 64 \times 64$	$64 \times 64 \times 3$

4 Experiments

4.1 Experiment Setup

Datasets. We evaluate our methods on a standard dataset for image-to-image translations: horse2zebra resized to 64×64. The training set size of each class:1187(horse),1474 (zebra).

Implementation. We follow the setting of TransGAN and use the losses introduced in CycleGAN. We adopt a learning rate of $1e - 4$ for the generators and discriminators. Step decay schedule drops the learning rate by 0.98 every ten epochs. Adam optimizers with $\beta_1 = 0$ and $\beta_2 = 0.99$, exponential moving average weights for generator, and a batch size of 1 for generator and discriminator, for all experiments. The transformer-based architectures are highly data-hungry, so we utilized identity losses for generators for the first 750 epochs out of 1300, which are traditionally not employed for the horse to zebra translation. We apply {Translation, Color, Cutout} data augmentations [19] during the training process with probability {1.0, 0.3, 1.0}. We do not employ gradient penalty, typically used for training GANs, because it leads to serious discoloration problems. We use common evaluation metrics Frechet Inception Distance (FID) [20], with the code [21]. All experiments are set with 1 RTX 3090 GPU, using PyTorch 1.9.1.

Table 2. Architecture configuration of discriminator.

Discriminator			
Stage	Layer	Input Shape	Output Shape
–	Linear Flatten	$64 \times 64 \times 3$	$32 \times 32 \times 96$
1	Block	$32 \times 32 \times 96$	$32 \times 32 \times 96$
	Block	$32 \times 32 \times 96$	$32 \times 32 \times 96$
	Block	$32 \times 32 \times 96$	$32 \times 32 \times 96$
	AvgPooling	$32 \times 32 \times 96$	$16 \times 16 \times 96$
	Concatenate	$16 \times 16 \times 96$	$16 \times 16 \times 192$
2	Block	$16 \times 16 \times 192$	$16 \times 16 \times 192$
	Block	$16 \times 16 \times 192$	$16 \times 16 \times 192$
	Block	$16 \times 16 \times 192$	$16 \times 16 \times 192$
	AvgPooling	$16 \times 16 \times 192$	$8 \times 8 \times 192$
	Concatenate	$8 \times 8 \times 192$	$8 \times 8 \times 384$
3	Block	$8 \times 8 \times 384$	$8 \times 8 \times 384$
	Block	$8 \times 8 \times 384$	$8 \times 8 \times 384$
	Block	$8 \times 8 \times 384$	$8 \times 8 \times 384$
–	Add [class] token	$8 \times 8 \times 384$	$8 \times 8 + 1 \times 384$
	Block	$8 \times 8 + 1 \times 384$	$8 \times 8 + 1 \times 384$
	[Class] head	1×384	1

4.2 Main Results

Fig. 2. Good samples of the horse2zebra 64×64. **Odd columns**: source images. **Even columns**: images generated by TransCycleGAN.

Fig. 3. Good samples of the zebra2horse 64 × 64. **Odd columns**: source images. **Even columns**: images generated by TransCycleGAN.

Our model reaches FID of 80.54 on horse2zebra 64 × 64 and 93.05 FID on zebra2horse 64 × 64. Of course, it is better to compare these results with those obtained in other architectures. Since the benchmark resolution is 256 × 256 and the result we got, for now, is 64 × 64, it cannot be compared directly. Direct comparison will provide in our future work.

5 Conclusion and Limitation

We have introduced TransCycleGAN, the first pure transformer-based GAN for the task of image-to-image translation. Our experiments on the horse2zebra 64 × 64 benchmark demonstrate that the great potential of our new architecture.

TransCycleGAN still has much room for exploration, such as going towards high-resolution translation tasks (e.g., 256 × 256) and experimenting on more datasets like Apple ↔ Orange, Summer ↔ Winter Yosemite, and Photo ↔ Art for style transfer, which is our future directions.

Acknowledgments. This work was supported by China Scholarship Council (CSC) Grant #201908090255.

References

1. Goodfellow, I., et al.: Generative adversarial nets. In: Advances in Neural Information Processing Systems, vol. 27 (2014)
2. Karras, T., Aila, T., Laine, S., Lehtinen, J.: Progressive growing of gans for improved quality, stability, and variation. arXiv preprint: arXiv:1710.10196 (2017)
3. Karras, T., Laine, S., Aila, T.: A style-based generator architecture for generative adversarial networks. In: Proceedings of the IEEE/CVF Conference on Computer Vision and Pattern Recognition, pp. 4401–4410 (2019)

4. Karras, T., Laine, S., Aittala, M., Hellsten, J., Lehtinen, J., Aila, T.: Analyzing and improving the image quality of stylegan. In: Proceedings of the IEEE/CVF Conference on Computer Vision and Pattern Recognition, pp. 8110–8119 (2020)
5. Ledig, C., et al.: Photo-realistic single image super-resolution using a generative adversarial network. In: Proceedings of the IEEE Conference on Computer Vision and Pattern Recognition, pp. 4681–4690 (2017)
6. Lee, C.-H., Liu, Z., Wu, L., Luo, P.: MaskGan: Towards diverse and interactive facial image manipulation. In: Proceedings of the IEEE/CVF Conference on Computer Vision and Pattern Recognition, pp. 5549–5558 (2020)
7. Zhu, J.-Y., Park, T., Isola, P., Efros, A.A.: Unpaired image-to-image translation using cycle-consistent adversarial networks. In: Proceedings of the IEEE International Conference on Computer Vision, pp. 2223–2232 (2017)
8. Kim, J., Kim, M., Kang, H., Lee, K.: U-GAT-IT: unsupervised generative attentional networks with adaptive layer-instance normalization for image-to-image translation. arXiv preprint: arXiv:1907.10830 (2019)
9. Reed, S., Akata, Z., Yan, X., Logeswaran, L., Schiele, B., Lee, H.: Generative adversarial text to image synthesis. In: International Conference on Machine Learning, pp. 1060–1069. PMLR (2016)
10. Frolov, S., Hinz, T., Raue, F., Hees, J., Dengel, A.: Adversarial text-to-image synthesis: a review. arXiv preprint: arXiv:2101.09983 (2021)
11. Vaswani, A., et al.: Attention is all you need. In: Advances in Neural Information Processing Systems, pp. 5998–6008 (2017)
12. Jiang, Y., Chang, S., Wang, Z.: TransGAN: two pure transformers can make one strong GAN, and that can scale up. arXiv:2102.07074 [cs]. (2021)
13. Dosovitskiy, A., et al.: An image is worth 16x16 words: transformers for image recognition at scale. arXiv preprint: arXiv:2010.11929 (2020)
14. Liu, M.-Y., Tuzel, O.: Coupled generative adversarial networks. arXiv:1606.07536 [cs]. (2016)
15. Yi, Z., Zhang, H., Tan, P., Gong, M.: DualGAN: unsupervised dual learning for image-to-image translation. arXiv:1704.02510 [cs]. (2018)
16. Shi, W., et al.: Real-time single image and video super-resolution using an efficient sub-pixel convolutional neural network. arXiv:1609.05158 [cs, stat]. (2016)
17. Durall, R., et al.: Combining transformer generators with convolutional discriminators. arXiv: 2105.10189 [cs]. (2021)
18. Lee, K., Chang, H., Jiang, L., Zhang, H., Tu, Z., Liu, C.: ViTGAN: training GANs with vision transformers. arXiv:2107.04589 [cs, eess]. (2021)
19. Zhao, S., Liu, Z., Lin, J., Zhu, J.-Y., Han, S.: Differentiable augmentation for data-efficient GAN training. arXiv:2006.10738 [cs]. (2020)
20. Heusel, M., Ramsauer, H., Unterthiner, T., Nessler, B., Hochreiter, S.: GANs trained by a two time-scale update rule converge to a local nash equilibrium. arXiv:1706.08500 [cs, stat]. (2018)
21. pytorch-fid: FID Score for PyTorch. https://github.com/mseitzer/pytorch-fid. Accessed 04 Oct 2021
22. TransCycleGAN. https://github.com/ch0n9waiu/TransCycleGAN. Accessed 05 Oct 2021
23. Bao, H., Dong, L., Wei, F.: BEiT: BERT pre-training of image transformers. arXiv:2106. 08254 [cs]. (2021)
24. Caron, M., et al.: Emerging properties in self-supervised vision transformers. arXiv:2104. 14294 [cs]. (2021)

Model-Based Testing Approach for Financial Technology Platforms: An Industrial Implementation

Liubov Konnova[1,2(✉)], Ivan Scherbinin[1,2], Vyacheslav Okhlopkov[1,2], Levan Gharibashvili[1,2], Mariam Mtsariashvili[1,2], and Tiniko Babalashvili[1,2]

[1] Exactpro Systems Limited, London, UK
{luba.konnova,ivan.scherbinin,vyacheslav.okhlopkov,levan.gharibashvili, mariam.mtsariashvili,tiniko.babalashvili}@exactpro.com
[2] Exactpro Systems LLC Georgia, Tbilisi, Georgia
https://exactpro.com

Abstract. This paper looks at the industrial experience of using automated model-based approach for the black-box testing of trading systems. The approach, used by Exactpro, is described using two existing taxonomies. Then, the main future applications of the models in the test automation paradigm are outlined.

In our approach a model reflects a selection of the system under tests properties and serves to generate expected results from the input (built based on the specifications). Models are created in Python which provides flexibility for describing complex financial systems behaviors. Models are integrated into the Exactpro's th2 test automation framework, and expected results from the system under test and model are compared automatically.

Keywords: Model-based testing · Software testing · Test automation · Trading platforms · Exchanges · Black-box testing

1 Introduction

1.1 Model-Based Testing Definition

Testing is the process consisting of all life cycle activities, both static and dynamic, concerned with planning, preparation and evaluation of a component or system and related work products to determine that they satisfy specified requirements, to demonstrate that they are fit for purpose and to detect defects[1].

Model-based testing (MBT), as a promising solution, aims at formalizing and automating as many activities related to testing as possible and thereby to increase both the efficiency and effectiveness of testing [2].

MBT designates any kind of "testing based on or involving models" [10]. Models represent the system under test (SUT), its environment, or the test

---

[1] https://glossary.istqb.org/en/search/testing.

© Springer Nature Switzerland AG 2024
R. Yavorskiy et al. (Eds.): TMPA 2021, CCIS 1559, pp. 83–93, 2024.
https://doi.org/10.1007/978-3-031-50423-5_8

itself, which directly supports test analysis, planning, control, implementation, execution and reporting activities.

MBT is being increasingly adopted to automate testing and brings intelligence to quality assurance by combining model-based design and technologies [12].

1.2   Related Work

The ideas of MBT, then called dubbed specification-based testing, go back to the seventies [14]. MBT has received much attention since that time, both in academia and in industry. This interest has been stimulated by the success of the improved understanding of testing and formal verification in the last two decades. Indeed, when compared to conventional testing approaches, MBT has proven to increase both quality and efficiency of test campaigns [5]. However, the MBT approaches vary significantly, and there exists the myriads of technical proposals of MBT implementation.

The Google Scholar search with key-words "model-based testing" returns 18 300 results. The abundance of technical proposals lead to the appearance of multiple surveys in the area.

Surveys by Hierons et al. [6], by Dias-Neto et al. [1], for example, provide a comprehensive overview of the abundant technical literature in the MBT field. Dias-Neto et al. analysed 271 papers and counted more than 219 different MBT approaches that have been proposed, often with associated tools. With so many approaches in the field, it can be a daunting task for a practitioner or researcher to make sense of the myriads of technical proposals.

Utting et al. [15] summarize recent advances in model-based testing. They cover such questions as MBT process in general, current penetration of MBT in industry, languages for MBT modeling activities, technologies for model-based automated test generation, model-based security testing. As per [15], the past decade has seen continual improvements both in the MBT algorithms used to generate tests, and in the efficiency and flexibility of the underlying solver technologies used during test generation. These improvements have the incremental effect of allowing the tools to scale to larger problems, and producing better quality test suites. But with regards to industry adoption, the progress is slower. Shultze et al. [16] compare the efforts and benefits of the manual testing and MBT, coming to a conclusion that "MBT detected more issues with higher severity scores with less testing and analysis effort than manual testing. However, it required more initial effort, which eventually would pay off if several versions of the same system would be tested". Shultze et al. [16] point out that effort required for the MBT is one of the key issues regarding the penetration of MBT in industry.

Li W. et al. [11] surveyed and analysed a large number of open-source MBT tools from perspectives of model specification, test generation, test description and overall MBT support. The authors aimed at delivering a systematic analysis and comparison of MBT tools to facilitate the use of MBT and enlarge the MBT community. Plus, they claim having illustrated future directions following their survey to attract more research and development attention, to improve the MBT tools and to accelerate the development of MBT activities.

In September 2021 Mohd-Shafie M.L. et al. [8] performed a systematic literature review on MBT, model-based test case generation and model-based test case prioritization. The authors initially selected 7078 candidate studies then narrowed their search. From 295 distinct case studies identified, 93 were real-world case studies (i.e. originating in the industry) and 202 were toy case studies (i.e. not fulfilling real-world requirements). There were only 30 case studies that were real-world, open-source, and available. Real-world case studies are rarely used because most of them are proprietary as per [8].

Thus, the area of MBT seems to be heavily researched, with the body of knowledge containing MBT approaches and tools overview as well as multiple taxonomies proposed to describe the variety.

1.3   Objective

The objective of this paper is to describe an industrial experience of applying MBT to the black-box testing of complex distributed systems supporting business operations of global financial markets. In the paper, we show how models are integrated in the test automation framework for functional testing using both active and passive approaches. Though the core of the discussed test automation framework, th2[2], is open-source, the models mentioned in this research are not publicly shared since they contain customer proprietary logic. Thus, a description of the experience of using them can be viewed as a practical contribution for the industry.

The paper is organized as follows.

Section 2 outlines the characteristics of the MBT approach used at Exactpro[3] from the perspectives of the classification frameworks proposed in [1,2]. A descriptive approach based on a classification framework puts this paper into the knowledge domain context as well as aligns it with other existing research on the topic (e.g. see [3]). In Subsect. 2.1, our model approach is characterized according to six dimensions introduced by Utting et al., the description is accompanied by an updated schema reflecting the characteristics of the approach. Subsection 2.2 provides the approach description according to an alternative framework.

Section 3 provides further details of the approach as well as outlines the directions of future MBT developments.

Section 4 provides an assessment of the industrial experience with MBT outlined through analysis of survey responses. The survey was conducted among the Exactpro specialists involved in the project roll-out and was aimed to collect software tester's reflections on the main challenges of MBT approach.

Section 5 concludes the paper.

---

[2] https://github.com/th2-net.

[3] https://exactpro.com/.

2   Classification of the Approach

2.1   Taxonomy-Based Classification

Taxonomies in software engineering help clarify the key issues of a field and show the possible alternatives and directions. They can be used to classify tools and to help users to see which approaches and tools fit their specific needs more closely.

We use taxonomy of model-based testing approaches introduced by Utting et al. to classify our process in six dimensions (*scope, characteristics, paradigm, test selection criteria, technology, online/offline*) [2]. This taxonomy has been selected as having the highest citation rate on Google Scholar.

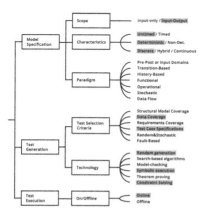

Fig. 1. Model Taxonomy.

Model Specification Scope: The *scope* of our models is *input-output*. Input-output models act as an oracle and can predict expected results for input scenarios. Input-output models are usually more useful than input-only models, which only generate a set of input parameters while testers should write expected results manually. Our exchange models are written in Python programming language and include precise implementations of various exchange validations and trading algorithms. Having an *input-output* model frees testers from having to manually specify expected results, allowing them to quickly generate large number of test cases. In our case these benefits outweigh costs of developing and validating the models, as manual test case creation involves assembling precise trading messages which is time-consuming for testers.

Test Execution: Our models directly interact with the SUT. This allows us to have online execution, meaning that after each user action, model automatically checks expected results against the SUT. Online execution saves time during test creation, as any abnormal behavior can be registered as soon as possible, without having to generate the whole test. It is also interactive, compared with offline execution, where testers would need to write the whole test case first and then execute it against system as a separate step.

Model Specification Characteristics: In terms of *characteristics*, our models can be considered as *untimed*, as they generate tests in synchronous manner. Model generates input messages that should be sent to the system (actions) and expected messages that should be checked against what is received from the system (expected results). Next message is normally sent as soon as a response for the previous one is received. This avoids any non-determinism that may appear if the messages are received by the system out of order. Although messages are usually sent immediately, sometimes it is necessary to wait before sending the next message (for example to wait for an auction to uncross). For expected messages from the system, model creates requests to the test environment to verify the structure of the message. These requests are created asynchronously and model immediately proceeds to the next action without checking status of verification. Testers can later check the results in a report.

The taxonomy differentiates between reactive and non-reactive models. Reactive models wait for the response from the SUT before the proceeding with the next action and can use the information in response for deciding how to proceed. This is useful for non-deterministic systems, where exact behavior of the system cannot accurately be predicted in advance. If the SUT is deterministic, then non-reactive models can be used, which can predict the whole scenario without relying on actual responses from the system. Our models wait for the response message before proceeding with the next action, so it can be classified as reactive. This is needed for certain identifiers generated by the system (e.g. Order ID, Trade ID). These fields cannot be predicted by the model and should be saved from the actual system response so that it can be reused for later messages. Reactive functionality is only used for this simple case, as rest of exchange functionality can be accurately predicted.

In terms of dynamics, our models are *discrete-event*. Discrete-event models only need to calculate expected results at particular time points, as opposed to continuous models where the state may be continuously changing, described by some equation (continuous models are usually used for simulating physical systems). The state of a stock exchange changes at particular time points where user interacts with it. In our case the discrete events are messages exchanged with the SUT.

Model Paradigm: The third dimension specifies what paradigm and notation are used to describe the model. There are many different modelling notations that have been used for modelling the behaviour of systems for test generation purposes [2].

We couldn't classify our model by the paradigms described in the paper from Utting et al. It comes closest to functional, however the exchange logic is not specified as an algebraic specification but rather as a Python code.

Test Selection Criteria defines strategies for managing the exploration of the model. We mainly use *data coverage* as the test selection criteria. Using pairwise combinatorial algorithm testers can check various order configurations using minimal number of test cases. Ad-hoc *test case specifications* are also utilized sometimes, using model only as a test oracle.

Technology: For test selection we use *constraint-solving* (n-wise combinatorial algorithm) combined with *random generation* for certain parameters. We created a Python library which is similar in functionality to Microsoft PICT[4]. In addition to above methods we have recently devised a method based on *symbolic execution* to generate test cases based on Python functions of model logic.

Figure 1 summarizes Exactpro MBT approach classification, applicable characteristics are marked in cyan.

2.2   Another Classification Approach

Arilo C. Dias Neto et al. [1] provide an overview of various model-based approaches and give an alternative classification of them. It might be useful to describe our MBT approach from a different angle.

Software Domain: Software domain defines the type of the system a MBT approach can be applied to. Currently, our approach is used for testing trading platforms which are large-scale time-critical complex distributed infrastructures (by distributed systems we mean the systems where computations are performed on multiple networked computers that communicate and coordinate their actions by passing messages [9]). In future, it might be applied to other systems of the global financial market.

Testing Level: Our MBT approach is applied to functional and regression system testing of the trading platforms. Some features like reference data upload, some downstream systems testing, non-functional testing are out of scope of our MBT approach.

Automation Level: The proportion of automated steps that compose an approach and the complexity level of its non-automated steps are relevant to automation level analysis as per [1].

We tend to have our models fully automated as our goal initially was to improve the speed of testing and increase accuracy of the test oracle. Some low-medium complexity steps, like providing reference data files for the model, are manual. The files themselves are generated automatically, though. Manual steps complexity depends on the tests done. If models do not have access to back-end or UI, analysts use 'Ask to continue' option to pause the model execution, do those required steps manually, and continue model execution.

Testers have to analyse the results of the testing. Comparison tables contain model-generated expected result versus results, returned from the SUT. Users review the comparison table. The failed steps are marked in red and all the required data for the investigation is provided for the user analysis.

---

[4] https://github.com/microsoft/pict.

Supporting Tools: Exactpro uses its bespoke test automation framework th2[5] for models execution. Models themselves are in Python. Incoming data, required for the model, are in .csv or in Python scripts. No other proprietary or freeware tools are used in our MBT approach.

Model Used for Test Case Generation: MBT approaches can be classified as per UML or non-UML models used. In our case, the aim of the model-based approach was to imitate the behavior of the matching engine of the trading platform. Matching engine is at the heart of every electronic exchange and it's extremely complex. Trading order book, orders are dynamic, frequently changeable entities. The above said were one of the reasons why the non-UML model was chosen. Another reason was existing expertise in a team. Due to the reasons above the Python programming language was chosen for the development of models. It's an area of future research to understand if existing UML modeling languages could be used to enhance our approach.

Qualitative Analysis: Testing Coverage Criteria: Since we are using models to generate expected results for the back-box testing, both data-flow and control-flow strategies haven't been implemented. These two strategies are applicable for the white box testing only [7]. It's still a question for us how we could measure test coverage on such a complex type of systems.

Qualitative Analysis: Behavior Model: Models should be correct to generate expected results accurately. Model is checked at the stage of the development that it corresponds to the specification, and later, when testers analyse the results of models run.

Cost and Complexity of Applying MBT Approach: The cost and complexity of applying our approach depends on the project and complexity of the system. The models for functional testing are more expensive in terms of resources and time used. But when functional model is debugged and moved to a regression tests pack, it brings benefits overtime. Regression tests pack has to be repeatedly run multiple times. The change of the features in the tested functionalities is also managed through models: when a particular model is changed, test cases are regenerated automatically.

3   Future Applications of the Model-Based Test Automation

This section describes main ideas that would be implemented in future in the model-based automation in Exactpro.

---

[5] https://github.com/th2-net; https://exactpro.com/test-tools/th2.

3.1   Passive Model

We refer to the model, described in the sections above as an "active" one since it can both send messages to the system, based on the tester input, and catch system replies and validate the expected result against the model output. Figure 2 shows how active model is integrated with the th2 services. Active model is the source of incoming test messages on the picture.

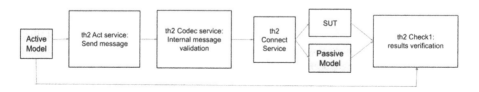

Fig. 2. Passive and Active Models Integration with th2.

Passive model is such kind of a model which will be directly connected to th2 and SUT. It will "catch" all incoming messages to the SUT and immediately validate responses from the SUT against the model result. Such model will always be a passive listener. Tester can't send messages via it. Incoming test messages are generated not by a model.

As part of the development of the passive model, we plan to migrate from using Python to Java or Kotlin. The reason for that is that our test automation framework th2 is created in Java, and it would be easier and faster to integrate a model in a similar language in th2.

3.2   External Exchange Stub

In order to test the "smart routing" functionality, it's required to simulate external exchange. Model could serve as a smart stub, automatically providing external exchange response based on the incoming message. Again, in this case, external exchange stub will be a replica of the real system, close in complexity to it.

The usage of such smart stub will allow deeper functional and regression testing in an automated way.

3.3   Interactive Model

This application is similar to the active model but testers will be able to connect to the UI and send the required messages to the SUT. This feature will be used for exploratory testing, smoke tests etc.

3.4 Generic Model

The aim of a generic model is to be able to reuse basic model for various exchanges and thus simplify the model adjustment for a new client. The plan is to reduce number of functions and mechanism, add logic to fill in default values for some fields. It will support some small number of functionalities but will be suitable for more exchanges. Generic model will be applicable to basic features, existing on all exchanges.

4 Models Related Challenges and Solutions

We have reflected on the challenges of using MBT enumerated by Paleska [5]:

1. If complex models have to be completed before testing can start, this induces an unacceptable delay for the proper test executions.
2. For complex SUT, like systems of systems, test models need to abstract from a large amount of detail, because otherwise the resulting test model would become unmanageable.
3. The required skills for test engineers writing test models are significantly higher than for test engineers writing sequential test procedures.

A survey has been conducted to discover whether these challenges are actual from the professionals perspective. The survey audience are software testers involved in the roll-out of the project. We have received 135 responses from specialists with QA experience from 1 to 20 years. Testers have been given the three challenges listed above. They could answer on a scale consisting of 10 points: 1 - strongly disagree, 10 - strongly agree. The survey results are given on Fig. 3.

The survey has shown that testers mostly agree with the relevance of these challenges to practical MBT implementations.

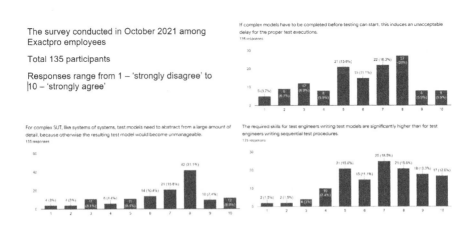

Fig. 3. Results of the survey on 3 challenges outlined by Peleska et al. (2013).

We are trying to address these challenges by incrementally developing the models and gradually covering additional functionality. At the start of the testing project, trading platforms functionalities, protocols, interfaces are analysed and accessed. At this stage, it's discovered what might be covered by models and what should be. This list is agreed on by the project participants. Models for some features, protocols etc. could be re-used from the previous projects. When the Generic Models, described in Subsect. 3.4, are implemented, the re-use of the existing models will be facilitated to the great extent.

The picture below Fig. 4 illustrates how model development fits into a short project. The upper line shows testing activities. Models-related actions are in green. For big projects the process of models introduction into testing is the same but it iterates over test cycles as well.

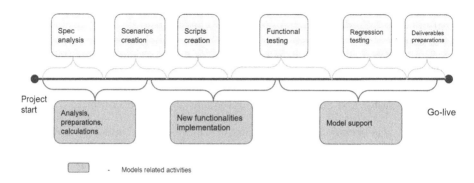

Fig. 4. Model Creation in Project Schedule.

The models, done for testing, are Python systems, quite complex. At the moment an additional dedicated models development team works on the models implementation. Testers can see the models code and try to understand their logic. If any issue is detected in the model, it is logged for the development team. Better and more efficient ways of this collaboration are a subject of our current and future research.

5   Summary

As a part of our work we've successfully applied MBT on an industrial scale to generate test cases, test oracles and execute black-box testing for a variety of exchange trading systems. We've confirmed the relevance of the existing MBT taxonomies to describing the practical implementation of the approach. We've also collated and contributed the outcome of the survey on the main challenges in applying MBT collected from a group of 135 specialists who represent a subset of a team involved in delivering the projects.

References

1. Dias Neto, A.C., Subramanyan, R., Vieira, M., Travassos, G.H.: A survey on model-based testing approaches: a systematic review. In: WEASELTech 2007: Proceedings of the 1st ACM International Workshop on Empirical Assessment of Software Engineering Languages and Technologies: Held in Conjunction with the 22nd IEEE/ACM International Conference on Automated Software Engineering (ASE) 2007, pp. 31–36 (2007)

2. Utting, M., Pretschner, A., Legeard, B.: A taxonomy of model-based testing. Special Issue: Model-based Testing Volume 1: Foundations and Applications of Model-Based Testing **22**(5) (2012)

3. Villalobos-Arias, L., Quesada, L.C., Martınez, A., Jenkins, M.: Model-based testing areas, tools and challenges: A tertiary study. CLEI Electron. J. **22**(1), 3-1 (2019)

4. Stachowiak, H.: Allgemeine Modelltheorie. Springer, Wien and New York (1973)

5. Peleska, J.: Industrial-strength model-based testing - state of the art and current challenges. Electronic Proceedings in Theoretical Computer Science (2013)

6. Hierons, R., et al.: Using formal specifications to support testing. ACM Comput. Surv. **41**(2), 9:1–9:76 (2009)

7. Santelices, R., Harrold, M.J.: Efficiently monitoring data-flow test coverage. Atlanta, Georgia, USA (2007)

8. Mohd-Shafie, M.L., Kadir, W.M.N.W., Lichter, H., Khatibsyarbini, M., Isa, M.A.: Model-based test case generation and prioritization: a systematic literature review. Softw. Syst. Model. **21**(2), 717–753 (2021)

9. Vain, J., Halling, E., Kanter, G., Anier, A., Pal, D.: Model-based testing of real-time distributed systems. In: Arnicans, G., Arnicane, V., Borzovs, J., Niedrite, L. (eds.) DB&IS 2016. CCIS, vol. 615, pp. 272–286. Springer, Cham (2016). https://doi.org/10.1007/978-3-319-40180-5_19

10. Kramer, A., Legeard, B.: Model-Based Testing Essentials: Guide to the ISTQB Certified Model-based Tester Foundation Level. Wiley, Hoboken (2016)

11. Li, W., Le Gall, F., Spaseski, N.: A survey on model-based testing tools for test case generation. In: Itsykson, V., Scedrov, A., Zakharov, V. (eds.) TMPA 2017. CCIS, vol. 779, pp. 77–89. Springer, Cham (2018). https://doi.org/10.1007/978-3-319-71734-0_7

12. Li, W., Le Gall, F., Vlacheas, P., Cheptsov, A.: Quality assurance for component-based systems in embedded environments (2018)

13. DTRON: a tool for distributed model-based testing of time critical applications (2017)

14. Chow, T.S.: Testing software design modeled by finite-state machines. IEEE Trans. Softw. Eng. **4**(3), 178–187 (1978)

15. Utting, M., Legeard, B., Bouquet, F., Fourneret, E., Peureux, F., Vernotte, A.: Chapter two - recent advances in model-based testing. Adv. Comput. **101**, 53–120 (2016)

16. Schulze C., Ganesan D., Lindvall M., Cleaveland R., Goldman D. Assessing model-based testing: an empirical study conducted in industry. In: Companion Proceedings of the 36th International Conference on Software Engineering, ICSE Companion 2014, Hyderabad, India, ACM, New York, NY, pp. 135–144 (2014)

Searching for Deviations in Trading Systems: Combining Control-Flow and Data Perspectives

Julio C. Carrasquel[(✉)] and Irina A. Lomazova

HSE University, Myasnitskaya ul. 20, 101000 Moscow, Russia
{jcarrasquel,ilomazova}@hse.ru

Abstract. Trading systems are software platforms that support the exchange of securities (e.g., company shares) between participants. In this paper, we present a method to search for deviations in trading systems by checking conformance between colored Petri nets and event logs. Colored Petri nets (CPNs) are an extension of Petri nets, a formalism for modeling of distributed systems. CPNs allow us to describe an expected causal ordering between system activities and how data attributes of domain-related objects (e.g., orders to trade) must be transformed. Event logs consist of traces corresponding to runs of a real system. By comparing CPNs and event logs, different types of deviations can be detected. Using this method, we report the validation of a real-life trading system.

Keywords: process mining · conformance checking · Petri nets · colored Petri nets · trading systems

1 Introduction

Trading systems are software platforms that support the exchange of securities (e.g., company shares) between participants [9]. In these systems, orders are submitted by users to indicate what securities they aim to buy or sell, how many stocks and their price. Investors buy securities with promising returns, whereas companies sell their shares to gain capital. These are some of the reasons why trading systems are a vital element in global finances, requiring software processes in these systems to guarantee their correctness. Among these processes, a crucial one is the management of orders in order books. Order books are two-sided priority lists where buy orders and sell orders that aim to trade the same security are matched for trading. A trading system must handle and match orders in these books according to its specification. Nonetheless, trading systems may be prone to deviate from their specification due to software errors or malicious users. This is why the validation of processes in trading systems, such as the management of orders, is a task of utmost importance. In this light, domain experts constantly seek for novel ways to detect system *deviations*, that is, to localize precise differences between a real system and its specification [10].

This work is supported by the Basic Research Program at the National Research University Higher School of Economics.

R. Yavorskiy et al. (Eds.): TMPA 2021, CCIS 1559, pp. 94–106, 2024.
https://doi.org/10.1007/978-3-031-50423-5_9

To detect deviations in trading systems, we consider *conformance checking* [1, 2]. Conformance checking is a process mining technique to search for differences between models describing *expected behavior* of processes and event logs that record *real behavior* of such processes [1]. Event logs consist of traces related to runs of processes; a trace is a sequence of events, where each event indicates an activity executed. To model expected behavior, we use *Petri nets*—a well-known formalism for modeling distributed systems [13]. Petri nets allow to describe the *control-flow* perspective of processes, that is, activities and their causal ordering, e.g., "a trade between two orders is preceded by the submission of both orders".

For trading systems, models should describe not only control-flow, but also how *data attributes* of objects such as orders change upon the execution of activities (e.g., "stocks of a sell order decrease by the number of stocks sold in a trade"). We resort to colored Petri nets (CPNs) to combine both control-flow and data perspectives [11]. CPNs are an extension of Petri nets where tokens progressing through the net carry data from some domains (referred to as "colors"). CPNs allow us to describe how trading systems handle objects (represented by tokens) and how their data attributes are transformed. This is an advantage over data-aware Petri net models used in other conformance methods, which do not directly relate data to tokens [12]. In [3–5] we presented how CPNs, as well as other Petri net extensions, allow to model different processes in trading systems.

We then developed conformance methods to replay traces of trading systems on CPNs. Replay comprises the execution of a model based on the information in events of a trace [14]. Deviations are found when a model cannot be executed as an event indicates. In [6] we consider deviations related only to control-flow, proposing a strategy to force the model execution when such deviations are found. In [7] we use replay to check if data attributes of objects are transformed by a real system in the same way that its model does. Yet, the method in [7] does not use any strategy to force the model execution if deviations are found, thereby halting the replay upon the first occurrence of a deviation in a trace.

This paper presents a comprehensive conformance method that integrates and extends the approaches presented in [6,7] in order to detect multiple kinds of deviations, including those related to control-flow and data attributes of objects. Notably, strategies are provided to force the execution of a CPN upon the occurrence of each kind of deviation. In particular, the following kinds of deviations can be detected when replaying a system's trace on a CPN that models the system specification: (*i*) *control-flow deviation:* the real system invoked an activity involving certain objects, but skipping some activities that should have been executed before to handle such objects; (*ii*) *priority rule violation:* an object was served before other objects with higher priority; (*iii*) *resource corruption:* object attributes were not transformed as the model specifies; (*iv*) *non-proper termination:* an object was not fully processed by the real system. The method returns a file with precise information about all deviations detected. We developed a prototypical implementation of the method, that we use to validate the management of orders in a real trading system. An experiment with artificial data is also reported.

The remainder of this paper is structured as follows. Sections 2 and 3 introduce the CPN models and event logs used in our method. Section 4 presents the conformance method. Section 5 reports the prototype and experiments conducted. Finally, Sect. 6 presents the conclusions.

2   Colored Petri Nets

Petri nets [13] are bipartite graphs consisting of two kinds of nodes: places and transitions. Places (drawn as circles) denote resource buffers, conditions, or virtual/physical locations. Transitions (drawn as boxes) account for system activities. Places store tokens, denoting control threads, resources, etc. Transitions consume tokens from input places and produce them in output places. We consider colored Petri nets (CPNs), where tokens carry data belonging to some data domains ("colors") [11]. Figure 1 depicts a CPN modeling a trading system handling buy/sell orders in one order book. Places p_1 and p_2 are sources for incoming buy and sell orders; p_3 and p_4 are buffers for submitted orders; p_5 and p_6 model the buy/sell side of the order book, whereas p_7 and p_8 are sinks for orders that traded or were canceled. Transitions t_1 and t_2 model submission of orders by users; t_3 and t_4 model insertion of orders in the order book. Transition t_5 (activity `trade1`) models a trade where two involved orders are filled (all their stocks were bought/sold); t_6, t_7 (activities `trade2` and `trade3`) model the cases where only one order is filled, whereas the second one is partially filled (returning to the order book). Transitions t_8 and t_9 model cancellation of orders.

Let $\mathfrak{D}$ be a finite set of *data domains*. A Cartesian product $D_1 \times ... \times D_n$, $n \geq 1$, between a combination of data domains $D_1, ..., D_n$ from $\mathfrak{D}$ is called a *color*. Σ is the set of all possible colors defined over $\mathfrak{D}$. A token is a tuple $(d_1, ..., d_n) \in \mathsf{C}$ s.t. C is a color in Σ, and we call the first component d_1 as the token's *identifier*. In Fig. 1, we have colors $\mathsf{OB} = O_\mathsf{B} \times \mathbb{N} \times \mathbb{R}^+ \times \mathbb{N}$ and $\mathsf{OS} = O_\mathsf{S} \times \mathbb{N} \times \mathbb{R}^+ \times \mathbb{N}$, where O_B and O_S are sets of identifiers for buy orders and sell orders, $\mathbb{N}$ is the set of natural numbers (including zero) and $\mathbb{R}^+$ is the set of positive real numbers; these colors denote orders with identifiers, arrival time, price and stock quantity, e.g., a token $(\mathsf{b1}, 1, 22.0, 5)$ denotes a buy order with identifier $\mathsf{b1}$, submitted in time 1, to buy 5 stocks at price 22.0 per stock. Thus, colors model classes of objects, whereas tokens are object instances. We fix a function `color` to indicate the color of tokens that each place stores (e.g., $\mathsf{color}(p_1) = \mathsf{OB}$). Arcs are labeled with expressions to specify how tokens are processed. We fix a language of expressions $\mathcal{L}$, where each expression is of the form $(e_1, ..., e_n)$ s.t., for each $i \in \{1, ..., n\}$, e_i is either a constant from a domain in $\mathfrak{D}$, a variable typed over an element in $\mathfrak{D}$, or a function whose domain and range are domains in $\mathfrak{D}$. For a variable v we denote its type by $\mathsf{type}(\mathsf{v})$, s.t. $\mathsf{type}(\mathsf{v}) \in \mathfrak{D}$. With slight abuse of notation, for an expression $(e_1, ..., e_n)$ we have that $\mathsf{color}((e_1, ..., e_n)) = D_1 \times ... \times D_n$ where, for each $i \in \{1, ..., n\}$, $D_i \in \mathfrak{D}$ and $D_i = \mathsf{type}(e_i)$ if e_i is a variable, $e_i \in D_i$ if e_i is a constant, or D_i is the range of e_i if e_i is a function.

Definition 1 (Colored Petri net). Let $\mathfrak{D}$ be a finite set of data domains, let Σ be a set of colors defined over $\mathfrak{D}$, let $\mathcal{L}$ be a language of expressions, and let $\mathcal{A}$ be a

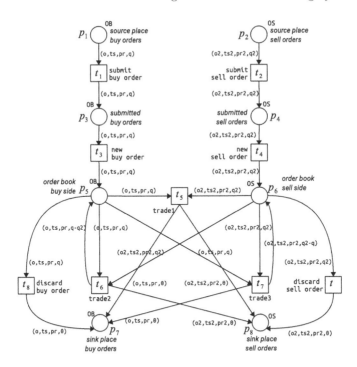

Fig. 1. CPN model of a trading system operating one order book.

set of activity labels. A colored Petri net is a 6-tuple $CP = (P, T, F, \text{color}, \mathcal{E}, \Lambda)$, where:

- P is a finite set of places, T is a finite set of transitions, s.t. $P \cap T = \emptyset$, and $F \subseteq (P \times T) \cup (T \times P)$ is a finite set of directed arcs;
- $\text{color} : P \to \Sigma$ is a place-coloring function, mapping each place to a color;
- $\mathcal{E} : F \to \mathcal{L}$ is an arc-labeling function, mapping each arc r to an expression in $\mathcal{L}$, such that $\text{color}(\mathcal{E}(r)) = \text{color}(p)$ where p is adjacent to r;
- $\Lambda : T \to \mathcal{A}$ is an activity-labeling function, mapping each transition to an element in $\mathcal{A}$, $\forall t, t' \in T : t \neq t' \iff \Lambda(t) \neq \Lambda(t')$.

In the following, for a transition $t \in T$ in a CPN, $^\bullet t = \{p \in P \mid (p, t) \in F\}$ denotes the set of *input places* of t, and $t^\bullet = \{p \in P \mid (t, p) \in F\}$ denotes the set of *output places* of t. Let $CP = (P, T, F, \text{color}, \mathcal{E}, \Lambda)$ be a CPN. A *marking* M is a function, mapping every place $p \in P$ to a (possibly empty) multiset of tokens $M(p)$ defined over $\text{color}(p)$. We denote by M_0 the *initial marking* of a CPN. A *binding* b of a transition $t \in T$ is a function, that assigns a value $b(\mathbf{v})$ to each variable $\mathbf{v}$ occurring in arc expressions adjacent to t, where $b(\mathbf{v}) \in \text{type}(\mathbf{v})$. Transition t is *enabled* in marking M w.r.t. a binding b iff $\forall p \in {^\bullet t} : b(\mathcal{E}(p, t)) \in M(p)$, that is, each input place of t has at least one token to be consumed. The *firing* of an enabled transition t in a marking M w.r.t. to a binding b yields a new marking M' such that $\forall p \in P : M'(p) = M(p) \setminus \{b(\mathcal{E}(p, t))\} \cup \{b(\mathcal{E}(t, p))\}$.

Finally, we define restrictions for CPNs in order to model processes in trading systems that handle different kinds of objects such as buy/sell orders [6,7]. We call *conservative-workflow* CPNs the models that comply with such restrictions.

Definition 2 (Conservative-Workflow Colored Petri Net). Let Σ be a finite set of colors, let $CP = (P, T, F, \texttt{color}, \mathcal{E}, \Lambda)$ be a CPN defined over Σ, and let M_0 be the initial marking of CP. We say that CP is a conservative-workflow CPN iff:

1. CP is a conservative colored Petri net, such that for every transition $t \in T$:
   - $\forall\, p \in {}^{\bullet}t\ \exists!\, p' \in t^{\bullet} : \mathcal{E}(p, t) = (\texttt{v}_1, ..., \texttt{v}_n) \wedge \mathcal{E}(t, p') = (\texttt{w}_1, ..., \texttt{w}_n) \wedge\ \texttt{v}_1 = \texttt{w}_1.$
   - $\forall\, p \in t^{\bullet}\ \exists!\, p' \in {}^{\bullet}t : \mathcal{E}(p', t) = (\texttt{v}_1, ..., \texttt{v}_n) \wedge \mathcal{E}(t, p) = (\texttt{w}_1, ..., \texttt{w}_n) \wedge\ \texttt{v}_1 = \texttt{w}_1.$

   The restriction above states that for each input arc (p, t) of a transition t with expression $(\texttt{v}_1, ..., \texttt{v}_n)$, there is exactly one output arc (t, p') of t with expression $(\texttt{w}_1, ..., \texttt{w}_n)$ s.t. $\texttt{w}_1 = \texttt{v}_1$; also, for each output arc of t with expression $(\texttt{w}_1, ..., \texttt{w}_n)$, there is exactly one input arc of t with expression $(\texttt{v}_1, ..., \texttt{v}_n)$ s.t. $\texttt{w}_1 = \texttt{v}_1$; when firing a transition t, this restriction guarantees the "transfer" of a token $(d_1, ..., d_n)$ from an input place p of t to an output place p' with the token's first component d_1 unchanged (its "identifier"); components $d_2, ..., d_n$ of the token may be modified by the expression of the output arc (t, p') abstractly meaning the transformation of the object represented by the token; thus, tokens with their identifiers cannot "disappear" or "duplicate".
2. There are no two tokens in the initial marking M_0 of CP with the same identifier, that is, all tokens have distinct identifiers. Note that if CP is conservative (as defined above), it follows that all tokens have distinct identifiers in every possible marking of CP reachable from the initial marking M_0.
3. For every color $\texttt{C} \in \Sigma$, there exists one distinguished pair of places in P, a source i and a sink o, where $\texttt{color}(i) = \texttt{color}(o) = \texttt{C}$, and there exists a path from i to o s.t. for each place p in the path $\texttt{color}(p) = \texttt{C}$. We respectively denote the sets of source and sink places in CP by P_0 and P_F.
4. $\forall t \in T : (\forall p, p' \in {}^{\bullet}t\ p \neq p' \iff \texttt{color}(p) \neq \texttt{color}(p')) \wedge (\forall p, p' \in t^{\bullet}\ p \neq p' \iff \texttt{color}(p) \neq \texttt{color}(p'))$, i.e., for every transition t, input places of t have distinct colors. The same rule holds for output places of t.

3   Event Logs

Definition 3 (Event, Trace, Event Log). Let $\mathfrak{D}$ be a finite set of data domains, let Σ be a set of colors defined over $\mathfrak{D}$, and let $\mathcal{A}$ be a finite set of activities. An event is a pair $e = (a, R(e))$ s.t. $a \in A$ and $R(e)$ is a set where $\forall r \in R(e), r \in \texttt{C}$ and $\texttt{C} \in \Sigma$. Each element r in $R(e)$ represents an object involved in the execution of activity a in event e. A trace $\sigma = \langle e_1, ..., e_m \rangle$, $m \geq 1$, is a finite sequence of events. An event log L is a multiset of traces.

We denote as $\texttt{color}(r)$ the color of element $r \in R(e)$ in event e. For each object $r = (r^{(1)}, ..., r^{(n)})$ in an event $e = (a, R(e))$, its components $r^{(1)}, ..., r^{(n)}$ represent the state of r after the execution of a. We assume that the first component of r, $r^{(1)}$, is the *object identifier* which cannot be modified; $\texttt{id}(r) = r^{(1)}$ denotes the identifier of r. We consider that objects in a trace can be distinguished. $R(\sigma)$ denotes the set of distinct object identifiers in a trace σ, e.g., for Table 1, $R(\sigma) = \{\texttt{b1}, \texttt{s1}, \texttt{s2}\}$. Let $r = (r^{(1)}, ..., r^{(n)})$ be an object. For

Table 1. A trace σ of an event log, corresponding to a run in a trading system.

event (e)	activity (a)	objects $(R(e))$
e_1	submit buy order	(b1, 1, 22.0, 5)
e_2	new buy order	(b1, 1, 22.0, 5)
e_3	submit sell order	(s1, 2, 21.0, 2)
e_4	new sell order	(s1, 2, 21.0, 2)
e_5	new sell order	(s2, 3, 19.0, 1)
e_6	trade2	(b1, 1, 22.0, 4), (s1, 2, 21.0, 0)

$j \in \{1, ..., n\}$, we consider that each attribute $r^{(j)}$ can be accessed using a name. Objects of the same color share the same set of attribute names, e.g., for color OB described in Sect. 2, we consider names $\{\mathtt{id}, \mathtt{tsub}, \mathtt{price}, \mathtt{qty}\}$; we fix a *member access function* #, that given an object $r = (r^{(1)}, ..., r^{(n)})$ and the name of the jth-attribute, it returns $r^{(j)}$, i.e., $\#(r, \mathtt{name}_j) = r^{(j)}$.

For simplicity, we use $\mathtt{name}_j(r)$ instead of $\#(r, \mathtt{name}_j)$, e.g., for $r = $ (b1, 1, 22.0, 5), $\mathtt{tsub}(r) = 1$, $\mathtt{price}(r) = 22.0$, and $\mathtt{qty}(r) = 5$.

Finally, a criterion of *syntactical correctness* must hold for CPNs and event logs that serve as input to the method we propose. Let L be an event log, and let $CP = (P, T, F, \mathtt{color}, \mathcal{E}, \Lambda)$ be a conservative-workflow CPN. We say that L is *syntactically correct* w.r.t. to CP iff, for every trace $\sigma \in L$, each event e in σ is syntactically correct. An event $e = (a, R(e))$ is syntactically correct w.r.t. to CP iff $\exists t \in T : \Lambda(t) = a \wedge \forall p \in \ {}^{\bullet}t \ \exists! r \in R(e) : \mathtt{color}(r) = \mathtt{color}(p) \wedge \forall r \in R(e) \ \exists! p \in \ {}^{\bullet}t : \mathtt{color}(r) = \mathtt{color}(p)$; that is, for every event $(a, R(e))$, there exists a transition t with activity label a, and each input place of t is mapped to exactly one event's object, and similarly each event's object is mapped to exactly one input place of t.

4   Conformance Method

We present a replay-based method to check conformance between a CPN and a trace of an event log. For each event in a trace, the method seeks to execute a model transition labeled with the event's activity, and consumes tokens that correspond to objects involved in the event. As mentioned in Sect. 1, four kinds of deviations can be detected in events: control-flow deviations, priority rule violations, resource corruptions, and non-proper termination of objects.

Algorithm 1 describes the replay method between a trace σ and a conservative workflow CPN whose initial marking is empty. In addition to deviations, the method returns two counters: the number of *token jumps* j, i.e., the number of tokens that are moved to input places of transitions to force their firing, and the number of consumed/produced tokens k. At the start, each source place of the CPN is populated with the trace's distinct objects $R(\sigma)$ according to their color. For each object to insert as a token in a source place, we set its values according to its first occurrence in σ. As an example, let us consider the replay of trace σ in Table 1 on the CPN of Fig. 1: place p_1 is populated with buy orders (b1, 1, 22.0, 5), and p_2 with sell orders (s1, 2, 21.0, 2) and (s2, 3, 19.0, 1). Then, for each event $e = (a, R(e))$ in σ, a transition is selected to fire s.t. $\Lambda(t) = a$.

To fire t, we check for every object $r \in R(e)$ whether its corresponding token in the model $(d_1, ..., d_n)$, $\text{id}(r) = d_1$, is located in input place p of t s.t. $\text{color}(p) = \text{color}(r)$. If the latter is not true for an object r, we look for its corresponding token in other places, which is moved to the input place p of t for tokens of $\text{color}(r)$. In such a case, a *control-flow deviation* is registered and the number of token jumps increases (e.g., Lines 5-10).

Algorithm 1: Object-Centric Replay with CPNs

Input: $CP = (P, T, F, \text{color}, \mathcal{E}, \Lambda)$ — conservative-workflow CPN;
$\quad\quad\quad P_0, P_F \subseteq P$ — non-empty sets of source and sink places;
$\quad\quad\quad \sigma$ — an event log trace;
Output: counter of token jumps (j) and consumed/produced tokens (k);
1 j ← 0; k ← 0;
2 populateSourcePlaces($P_0, R(\sigma)$);
3 **foreach** $e = (a, R(e))$ in σ **do**
4 $\quad$ t ← selectTransition(a);   // $\exists! t \in T \; \Lambda(t) = a$
5 $\quad$ **foreach** r in $R(e)$ **do**
6 $\quad\quad$ **if** $\neg\exists(d_1, ..., d_n) \in M(p) : p \in {}^\bullet t \wedge \text{color}(p) = \text{color}(r) \wedge \text{id}(r) = d_1$ **then**
7 $\quad\quad\quad$ registerDeviation(CONTROL_FLOW);
8 $\quad\quad\quad$ jump(id(r), p);
9 $\quad\quad\quad$ j ← j + 1;
10 $\quad\quad$ **endif**
11 $\quad\quad$ **if** priorityRuleViolation($(d_1, ..., d_n), M(p)$) **then**
12 $\quad\quad\quad$ registerDeviation(RULE_VIOLATION);
13 $\quad\quad$ **endif**
14 $\quad$ **endfor**
15 $\quad$ fire($t, R(e)$);
16 $\quad$ k ← k + $|R(e)|$;
17 $\quad$ **foreach** r in $R(e)$ **do**
18 $\quad\quad$ **let** $d = (d_1, ..., d_n) : d_1 = \text{id}(r) \wedge d \in M(p) \wedge \text{color}(p) = \text{color}(r) \wedge p \in t^\bullet$
19 $\quad\quad$ **if** $d \neq r$ **then**
20 $\quad\quad\quad$ registerDeviation(RESOURCE_CORRUPTED);
21 $\quad\quad\quad$ $d \leftarrow r$;
22 $\quad\quad$ **endif**
23 $\quad$ **endfor**
24 **endfor**
25 **foreach** r in $R(\sigma)$ **do**
26 $\quad$ **if** $\neg\exists(d_1, ..., d_n) \in M(p) : p \in P_F \wedge \text{color}(p) = \text{color}(r) \wedge \text{id}(r) = d_1$ **then**
27 $\quad\quad$ registerDeviation(NONPROPER_TERMINATION);
28 $\quad\quad$ jump(id(r), p);
29 $\quad\quad$ j ← j + 1;
30 $\quad$ **endif**
31 **endfor**
32 consumeAllObjectsFromSinkPlaces($P_F, R(\sigma)$);
33 k ← k + $|R(\sigma)|$;
34 **return** (j, k);

Let us consider again the replay of σ in Table 1 on the CPN of Fig. 1. Let us assume that events $e_1,...,e_4$ were processed with no deviations detected. Now, consider $e_5 = (\texttt{newsellorder}, \{(\texttt{s2}, 3, 19.0, 1)\})$ which implies to fire transition t_4 consuming token with id. s2. In the current model marking, however, s2 is not in place p_4, but in p_2. To execute the model according to e_5, token s_2 jumps to place p_4 as depicted in Fig. 2. This deviation relates to a sell order that was placed in the order book, but that illegally skipped activity submit sell order.

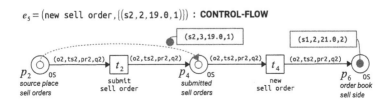

Fig. 2. Control-flow deviation: s2 is not in p_4, so a jump is done to force replay.

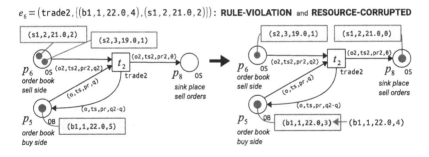

Fig. 3. Example of a priority rule violation and a resource corruption.

Prior to each transition firing, the method checks if each token to consume is the one that must be selected according to a *priority rule*. To this end, we shall assume that input CPNs may have priority rules on some transitions. Let b a selected binding to fire a transition t. We define a priority rule on t as $\Phi(t) = \bigwedge_{\forall p \in \bullet t} \phi_p(M(p), b(\mathcal{E}(p, t)))$, s.t. $b(\mathcal{E}(p, t))$ is the token to consume from input place p, and $\phi_p(M(p), b(\mathcal{E}(p, t)))$ is a priority local rule on p; $\phi_p(M(p), b(\mathcal{E}(p, t)))$ holds if $b(\mathcal{E}(p, t))$ must be consumed before other tokens in $M(p)$. Algorithm 1 checks the truth value of $\Phi(t)$ by checking if the local rule of each input place p of t is violated, i.e., in line 11, function $\texttt{priorityRuleViolation}((d_1, ..., d_n), M(p))$ evaluates to true iff $\Phi(t)$ is defined and $\phi_p(M(p), (d_1, ..., d_n))$ does not hold. If the function returns true, then a *priority rule violation* is registered as token $(d_1, ..., d_n)$ should not have been consumed before other tokens in p. For example, let us assign $\Phi(t) = \phi_{\text{BUY}}(M(p_5), r_1) \wedge \phi_{\text{SELL}}(M(p_6), r_2)$ to transitions t_5, t_6, and t_7 (trade activities) in the CPN of Fig. 1, such that:

$$\phi_{\text{BUY}}(M(p_5), r_1) = \forall_{(\text{o,ts,pr,q}) \in M(p_5)} \text{id}(r_1) \neq \text{o} : (\text{price}(r_1) > \text{pr})$$
$$\vee \, (\text{price}(r_1) = \text{pr} \wedge \text{tsub}(r_1) < \text{ts})$$
$$\phi_{\text{SELL}}(M(p_6), r_2) = \forall_{(\text{o,ts,pr,q}) \in M(p_6)} \text{id}(r_2) \neq \text{o} : (\text{price}(r_2) < \text{pr})$$
$$\vee \, (\text{price}(r_2) = \text{pr} \wedge \text{tsub}(r_2) < \text{ts})$$

where r_1 and r_2 are buy and sell orders to consume; the local rule ϕ_{BUY} on place p_5 states that r_1 must be the order with the highest price (or with the earliest submitted time if other orders have the same price). The local rule ϕ_{SELL} on p_6 is defined similarly, but r_2 must be the order with the lowest price. Let us consider event e_6 in Fig. 3: the rule on p_6, to prioritize sell orders with the lowest price, is violated as order s1 with price 21.0 is consumed before s2 with price 19.0.

After firing a transition according to an event, we search for *resource corruptions*. Specifically, we check if the values of every transferred token are equal to the values of corresponding objects in the event; this detects if a system transformed object attributes as expected, e.g., in Fig. 3, after the trade of 1 stock between b1 and s1, the stock quantity of b1 decreased from 5 to 3; however, event e_6 shows that the b1's stocks changed to 4, indicating that b1 was corrupted; in case of these deviations, values of the corrupted token are updated according to the values of its corresponding object in the event, e.g., in Fig. 3, b1's stocks change to 4.

After replaying a trace, we check *non-proper termination*, that is, whether the system did not fully process all objects. We check if all objects reside in their corresponding sinks. After the replay of the trace in Table 1 on the CPN of Fig. 1, orders b1 and s2 did not arrive at their sinks. These are orders that were not fully handled by the trading system. For these deviations, the method moves these tokens at their sinks, increasing the counter of token jumps j. When all tokens are in the sinks, they are consumed by the "environment", and the counter of transfers k increases by the number of tokens consumed. Finally, the ratio $1 - \text{j/k}$ can be used as a fitness metric to measure the extent to which a system (as observed in the trace) complies with the CPN, e.g., if the result of such ratio is 1, then all behavior observed in the trace complied with the model.

5 Prototype and Experiments

We developed a software prototype[1] of the method proposed using SNAKES [15], a Python library for simulating CPNs. We aimed at detecting deviations within a subset of order books in a real trading system. We considered order books with only *day limit orders*, orders that trade stocks at a fixed price, and that must trade or cancel by the end of a day. The orders considered are not amended after their submission. The system expected behavior is described by the CPN of Fig. 1. The method takes as input the CPN of Fig. 1 and a log where traces relate to the handling of order books during a day. The log was extracted from a set of Financial Information Exchange (FIX) protocol messages [8].

---

[1] https://github.com/jcarrasquel/hse-uamc-conformance-checking.

The messages were exchanged by users and the system during a day, informing activities executed and the status of orders. The set consists of 552935 FIX messages, whereas the log obtained from such set consists of 73 traces (order books) and 2259 events, with a mean of 30.94 events per trace. A fragment of the deviations file computed by the method is shown in Fig. 4. The file lists deviations detected in events of different traces of the input log. Each line describes precise information of a deviation in the real system: the trace (order book), event number, timestamp, and activity where the error occurred, the object affected, the kind of deviation detected, and an automatically generated description. In this experiment, most of the deviations relate to corruption of orders when executing trades: the prices of some orders changed upon the execution of trades, e.g., in event 1781 the price of the order with id. bSovX changed from 105 to 100 after trading, and such transformation is not described in the CPN. Thus, this information about deviations can be used by experts to confirm if this is a failure in the system, or instead the model should be slightly refined.

TRACE	EVENT	TIMESTAMP	ACTIVITY	OBJECT	DEV.	DEVIATION DESCRIPTION
1488058	1781	05:52:58.18	trade2	bSovX	RC	resource has event-state: ('b00d0PhqYSovX' 1550491266 100.0 100) ,but model-state is: ('b00d0PhqYSovX' 1550491266 105.0 100)
1488058	1782	05:52:58.18	trade1	bSovX	RC	resource has event-state: ('b00d0PhqYSovX' 1550491266 101.0 0) ,but model-state is: ('b00d0PhqYSovX' 1550491266 100.0 0)
1488061	1792	05:53:23.38	trade1	sSowK	RV	resource with id: s00d0PhqYSowK did not have priority ,over other resources in the same place.
1488061	1792	05:53:23.38	trade1	sSowK	RC	resource has event-state: ('s00d0PhqYSowK' 1550490938 101.0 0) ,but model-state is: ('s00d0PhqYSowK' 1550490938 101.0 -100)
1488061	1792	05:53:23.38	trade1	bSowJ	RC	resource has event-state: ('b00d0PhqYSowJ' 1550490919 101.0 0) ,but model-state is: ('b00d0PhqYSowJ' 1550490919 105.0 100)
1488061	1793	05:53:23.38	trade2	bSowJ	CF	resource with id: b00d0PhqYSowJ was not in place p5 but in p7
1488061	1793	05:53:23.38	trade2	bSowJ	RC	resource has event-state: ('b00d0PhqYSowJ' 1550490919 105.0 100) ,but model-state is: ('b00d0PhqYSowJ' 1550490919 101.0 -100)
1488061	1793	05:53:23.38	trade2	sSowL	RC	resource has event-state: ('s00d0PhqYSowL' 1550490947 105.0 0) ,but model-state is: ('s00d0PhqYSowL' 1550490947 100.0 0)
1488061	end	-	-	bSowJ	NT	resource with id: b00d0PhqYSowJ was not in final location p7 but in p5
1488062	1803	05:53:31.38	trade2	bSowN	RC	resource has event-state: ('b00d0PhqYSowN' 1550490899 100.0 100) ,but model-state is: ('b00d0PhqYSowN' 1550490899 105.0 100)
1488062	1804	05:53:31.38	trade1	bSowN	RC	resource has event-state: ('b00d0PhqYSowN' 1550490899 101.0 0) ,but model-state is: ('b00d0PhqYSowN' 1550490899 100.0 0)
9088012	end	-	-	bmkq9	NT	resource with id: b00d0PiS3mkq9 was not in final location p7 but in p5
9088012	end	-	-	smkqA	NT	resource with id: s00d0PiS3mkqA was not in final location p8 but in p6
9088015	end	-	-	sSSZd	NT	resource with id: s00d0Pi88SSZd was not in final location p8 but in p6

Fig. 4. Fragment of deviations detected (DEV): resource corruptions (RC), priority rule violations (RV), control-flow deviations (CF), non-proper termination (NT).

In a second experiment, we show how information obtained during replay, about token jumps and transfers, can be used to enhance an input CPN for visualizing deviations. Using SNAKES, we built a model representing a trading system, similar to the CPN of Fig. 1, but with some undesired behavior that shall be uncovered as control-flow deviations: orders may skip activities submit buy order and submit sell order, e.g., this may represent malicious users submitting unverified orders via back-doors. Also, activity new sell order may lead some orders to a deadlock. As input for our method, we consider the model of Fig. 1 and an artificial event log, that records the system's behavior. The log was generated by our solution, running the CPN that represents the faulty system. The log consists of 100 traces and 4497 events, with an average of 44.97

events per trace. In each trace, there is an average of 10 buy orders and 10 sell orders.

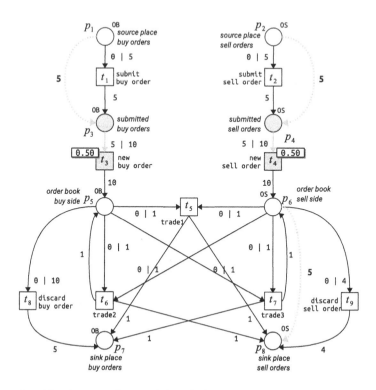

Fig. 5. Specification model extended with diagnostics computed by our method.

Upon the execution of the method, control-flow deviations are detected and reveal the undesired behavior previously described. When detecting such deviations, tokens jump between places via unforeseen model paths in order to continue the replay. Information about token jumps in each place of the CPN, as well as token transfers are registered by our solution. Figure 5 illustrates how such information is used to enhance the input CPN model. Dotted lines represent token jumps related to the deviations mentioned: jumps from p_1 to p_3, and from p_2 to p_4 are from orders that illegally skipped activities **submit buy order** and **submit sell order**. Also, jumps from p_6 to p_8 relate to orders that got locked after executing **new sell order**. The method detects such locked orders when checking non-proper termination. Input arcs and dotted lines indicate the (rounded) average number of transferred/jumped tokens, considering all log traces. The software prototype tracks the proportion of token transfers/jumps flowing through model components. *Local conformance metrics* are computed using such proportions to measure how deviations affect precise system parts. For example, **new buy order** has a measure of 0.5, meaning that 5 out of 10 objects processed by the activity complied with the model path. We refer to [6] for formal definitions and a further discussion about these local measures.

6   Conclusions

In this paper, we presented a conformance method to search for deviations in trading systems. Different deviations are detected by replaying a system's trace on a CPN. We validated the management of orders in a real system and revealed precise deviations. Another experiment showed how conformance diagnostics can be added to a CPN to display control-flow deviations. A direction for further research may study how to visualize more complex deviation patterns.

References

1. van der Aalst, W.: Process Mining: Data Science in Action, 2nd edn. Springer, Heidelberg (2016). https://doi.org/10.1007/978-3-662-49851-4
2. Carmona, J., van Dongen, B., Solti, A., Weidlich, M.: Conformance Checking: Relating Processes and Models, 1st edn. Springer, Cham (2018). https://doi.org/10.1007/978-3-319-99414-7
3. Carrasquel, J.C., Lomazova, I.A.: Modelling and validation of trading and multi-agent systems: an approach based on process mining and petri nets. In: van Dongen, B., Claes, J. (eds.) Proceedings of the ICPM Doctoral Consortium. CEUR, vol. 2432 (2019)
4. Carrasquel, J.C., Lomazova, I.A., Itkin, I.L.: Towards a formal modelling of order-driven trading systems using petri nets: a multi-agent approach. In: Lomazova, I.A., Kalenkova, A., Yavorsky, R. (eds.) Modeling and Analysis of Complex Systems and Processes (MACSPro). CEUR, vol. 2478 (2019)
5. Carrasquel, J.C., Lomazova, I.A., Rivkin, A.: Modeling trading systems using petri net extensions. In: Köhler-Bussmeier, M., Kindler, E., Rölke, H. (eds.) International Workshop on Petri Nets and Software Engineering (PNSE). CEUR, vol. 2651 (2020)
6. Carrasquel, J.C., Mecheraoui, K.: Object-centric replay-based conformance checking: unveiling desire lines and local deviations. Model. Anal. Inf. Syst. **28**(2), 146–168 (2021)
7. Carrasquel, J.C., Mecheraoui, K., Lomazova, I.A.: Checking conformance between colored petri nets and event logs. In: van der Aalst, W.M.P., et al. (eds.) AIST 2020. LNCS, vol. 12602, pp. 435–452. Springer, Cham (2021). https://doi.org/10.1007/978-3-030-72610-2_33
8. FIX Community - Standards: https://www.fixtrading.org/standards/
9. Harris, L.: Trading and Exchanges: Market Microstructure for Practitioners. Oxford University Press, Oxford (2003)
10. Itkin, I., et al.: User-assisted log analysis for quality control of distributed fintech applications. In: IEEE International Conference On Artificial Intelligence Testing (AITest), pp. 45–51. IEEE (2019)
11. Jensen, K., Kristensen, L.M.: Coloured Petri Nets. Springer, Heidelberg (2009). https://doi.org/10.1007/b95112
12. Mannhardt, F., Leoni, de, M., Reijers, H., van der Aalst, W.: Balanced multi-perspective checking of process conformance. Computer **98**, 407–437 (2015)

13. Murata, T.: Petri nets: properties, analysis and applications. Proc. IEEE **77**(4), 541–580 (1989)
14. Rozinat, A., van der Aalst, W.: Conformance checking of processes based on monitoring real behavior. Inf. Syst. **33**(1), 64–95 (2008)
15. SNAKES: a flexible high-level petri net library. https://snakes.ibisc.univ-evry.fr/

SPIDER: Specification-Based Integration Defect Revealer

Vladislav Feofilaktov[1,2] and Vladimir Itsykson[1,2(✉)]

[1] Peter the Great St. Petersburg Polytechnic University, St. Petersburg, Russia
vlad@icc.spbstu.ru
[2] JetBrains Research, St. Petersburg, Russia

Abstract. Modern software design practice implies widespread use in the development of ready-made components, usually designed as external libraries. The undoubted advantages of reusing third-party code can be offset by integration errors that appear in the developed software. The reason for the appearance of such errors is mainly due to misunderstanding or incomplete understanding by the programmer of the details of external libraries such as an internal structure and the subtleties of functioning. The documentation provided with the libraries is often very sparse and describes only the main intended scenarios for the interaction of the program and the library. In this paper, we propose the approach based on the use of formal library specifications, which allows detecting integration errors using static analysis methods. To do this, the external library is described using the LibSL specification language, the resulting description is translated into the internal data structures of the KEX analyzer. The execution of the incorrect scenarios of library usage, such as the incorrect sequence of method calls or the violation of the API function contract, is marked in the program model with special built-in functions of the KEX analyzer. Later, when analyzing the program, KEX becomes able to detect integration errors, since incorrect library usage scenarios are diagnosed as calling marked functions. The proposed approach is implemented as SPIDER (SPecification-based Integration Defect Revealer), which is an extension of the Kex analyzer and has proven its efficiency by detecting integration errors of different classes on several special-made projects, as well as on several projects taken from open repositories.

Keywords: formal library specification · integration error detection · static analysis

1 Introduction

Modern software is usually not designed from scratch. In most cases, when designing software, the developer actively uses external components, implemented, most often, as libraries. This approach has obvious advantages: you can reduce design and development time by reusing other people's solutions that have successfully proven themselves in other projects. However, in the case of using large libraries with the complex internal structure and behavior, integration errors may appear. They are caused by the developer's

© Springer Nature Switzerland AG 2024
R. Yavorskiy et al. (Eds.): TMPA 2021, CCIS 1559, pp. 107–119, 2024.
https://doi.org/10.1007/978-3-031-50423-5_10

misunderstanding or incomplete understanding of the features of the library organization or misunderstanding of the scenarios for working with it. This misunderstanding can be caused by the missing or incomplete documentation accompanying the library, the small number of use cases, and the informal nature of the existing documentation. Integration errors can be quite non-trivial, and the developer needs to spend a significant amount of time to find them.

This article describes the approach developed by the authors that automates the detection of integration errors in a program with external libraries. The approach is based on the use of formal library specifications to describe the behavior of libraries and library functions. To specify valid library usage scenarios, we use LibSL specification language [1, 2] which represents the library as a system of interacting extended finite state machines (EFSM). Based on the mentioned specifications, the enlarged model of library functions is built, capable of detecting errors in using the library. This model is fed to the input of the static analyzer together with the source code of the analyzed application. The static analyzer (we use the KEX analyzer for it [3]) combines the program model and the synthesized library model for joint analysis. At the same time, the library model is formed in such a way that library usage errors (integration errors) are detected by standard analyzer algorithms. The developed approach was implemented as an extension of KEX static analyzer and successfully tested on several Java projects.

The rest of the paper is organized as follows. The Sect. 2 contains definitions of software integration errors. Section 3 contains short description of LibSL. Section 4 explains the main idea of proposed approach. The Sect. 5 considers the synthesis of library approximation. Section 6 describes the implementation of our approach as a tool called SPIDER. Section 7 acquaints with the evaluation of the developed tool. The Sect. 8 contains a conducted review of the related work. In the conclusion, we present the obtained results and discuss possible future work.

2 Integration Errors

Large-scale software systems consisting of many heterogeneous components, as well as other programs, may contain software errors. Some of these errors have the same nature as the errors of simple programs, while others are caused precisely by the difficulties of integrating components with each other. The reason for the integration errors is that the main program violates the protocol of interaction with the library. The protocol of interaction with the library is the rules for calling individual API functions and valid scenarios for calling various API functions.

In this paper, we will consider the following types of software integration errors: violations of the contracts of library API functions and incorrect order of library API function calls.

In software engineering, function contracts define the preconditions and postconditions of functions in the form of logical assertions. The preconditions specify the assertions that must be true when calling the function. The postconditions specify assertions whose truth is guaranteed by the function if the precondition is fulfilled. Violations of API function contracts in multicomponent programs are usually associated with calling functions with incorrect argument values.

Incorrect order of library API function calls are manifested in the fact that API functions are called on some object not in the sequence, in which it is permissible by valid library usage scenarios. For example, a data transfer operation through a stream is called before the stream attributes are set.

3 Library Specification Language

To specify the structure and behavior of libraries in this work, we used the previously developed LibSL language [1, 2, 5]. LibSL is designed to describe the structure of the library, the signature and the enlarged behavior of API functions, as well as to set valid scenarios for using the library. The library and its components are represented by the system of interacting extended finite state machines. The main elements of the specification are presented in Listing 1.

```
libsl "1.0.0";
library Computer version "1.0.0";
types {
  Computer (spider.computer.Computer);
  OS (spider.computer.OS);
  OSName (string);
  Int(int32);
}

automaton spider.computer.Computer : Computer {
  initstate Downed;
  state Boot;
  state OSSelected;
  state OSLoaded;
  finishstate Closed;

  var isMemoryInit: bool = false;
  var isOsLoaded: bool = false;

  shift Downed -> Booted(boot);
  shift Boot -> OSSelected(selectOS);
  shift OSSelected -> OSLoaded(loadOS);
  shift any -> Closed(shutdown);

  fun boot()
    requires isMemoryNotInit: !isMemoryInit;
  {
    isMemoryInit = true;
  }
  fun selectOS(osName: OSName);
  fun setBootPartition(part: Int)
    requires partitionLimits: part >= 0 & part < 16;
  fun loadOS()
    requires isMemoryInit: isMemoryInit;
    requires isOsNotLoaded: !isOsLoaded;
  {
    isOsLoaded = true;
  }
  fun shutdown() {
    isOsLoaded = false;
    isMemoryInit = false;
  }
}
```

Listing 1. Example of LibSL specification

The example contains a fragment of the test library specification and consists of the following descriptions:

- library automaton (*automaton* keyword);
- state of the automaton (*state*, *initstate* and *finishstate* keywords);
- automaton transitions (*shift* keyword);
- automaton internal variables (*var* keyword);

- signatures of library API functions (*fun* keyword) and their aggregated behavior.
- precondition for functions (*requires* keyword);
- annotated semantic types (*types* keyword).

It is assumed that to find possible integration errors, the developer will create a specification of the libraries used exploiting the capabilities of the LibSL language.

4   Main Idea

The main idea of integration error detection proposed in this article is to use formal library specifications to synthesize approximations of the behavior of API library functions capable of detecting violations of the library usage protocol. The mentioned approximations are embedded in the code of the testing program in parallel with the source libraries. The resulting code is the input of a static analyzer. The task of detecting integration errors is reduced to solving the problem of the reachability of the approximation code that diagnoses the error.

To achieve the goal of the research, the following tasks are solved:

- definition of integration errors classes detected in the work;
- development of the approximation model code, which can detect all classes of selected integration errors;
- development of the model code generator to integrate error detector into the internal model of the KEX static analyzer;
- development of a new work mode of the KEX static analyzer, which allows analyzing libraries.

The peculiarity of the proposed approach is to combine the library code and the synthesized model approximation code inside the program model. Meanwhile, the model approximation code does not affect the behavior of the source program in any way. Such a solution allows, on the one hand, preserving the original behavior of the testing program, and, on the other hand, detecting a violation of the specification.

The high-level approach scheme is shown in Fig. 1. The input of the analyzer is supplied with the source program, the library, and an approximation of the "ideal" behavior of the library synthesized based on the specification. The static analyzer processes input artifacts together and generates an error report. Information from the library and its specification is used for the most detailed diagnosis of errors found. Diagnostic message contains information about the type of the error and its location.

5   Synthesis of Library Approximation

The key idea of the proposed approach is to create an "ideal" approximation of the library behavior based on the specification, which can be used as an oracle to check the correctness of the joint work of the application and the library. In the first version of our approach, the approximation was built as a program code in the Java language, in which all the functions of the source library were generated with the same signatures, but with artificial bodies, in which transitions of automata from one state to another

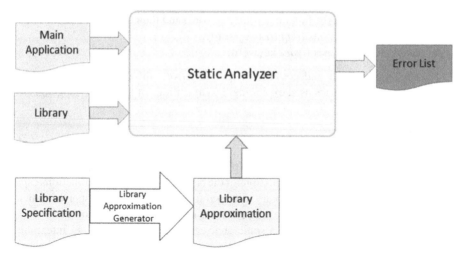

Fig. 1. High-level approach scheme

were simulated and checks of contracts and correctness of states were embedded. In the current version, we have abandoned code generation in Java and create approximations immediately in the form of the internal representation of the static analyzer by instrumenting the internal representation of the original library function. This makes the synthesis process more optimal. However, in this section, for ease of understanding the synthesis process, we will operate in terms of elements of the Java language.

Creating an approximation consists of several components. Firstly, based on the automata available in the specification, data structures are created that store the necessary attributes of automata, such as states and internal variables and so on. Secondly, for each API function of the library, a similar function is built in approximation, having the same signature, and the body of which solves the following tasks:

- checking the correctness of the current state of the automaton and signaling an integration errors;
- changing the current state of the automaton;
- checking contract preconditions at the beginning of the function and signaling an integration error in case of violation;
- checking contracts postconditions after the completion of the function and signaling an integration error in case of a violation.

The detection of integration errors is implemented by embedding specialized internal calls of the static analyzer (intrinsic) into the approximation code, the reachability of which in the program indicates an existing integration error. Additional parameters of these calls allow localizing the error location and getting its additional attributes.

6 Implementation

We implemented the developed approach as a pilot tool, which we called SPIDER (SPECIFICATION-based Integration Defect Revealer). The tool is designed to analyze Java programs using external libraries. Figure 2 shows the architecture of the developed tool, detailing the approach scheme, which is shown in Fig. 1.

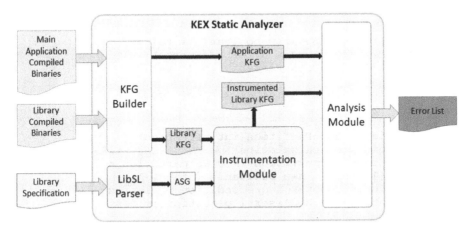

Fig. 2. SPIDER Architecture

The input to the tool is the source program, library and specification. Since there may be no source code for external libraries, the tool accepts the compiled bytecode of the library as the input. For unification, the main application is also submitted to the input in the form of compiled bytecode.

As an analyzer we use the static analyzer KEX [3]. This is a powerful and extendable analyzer that uses SMT-solvers to process a code analysis of JVM bytecode (as a result, it can analyze code in many JVM languages, like Java, Kotlin, Scala, etc.). KEX uses a special internal representation of JVM programs called KFG, which is essentially a variant of the SSA model implementation. For building KFG KEX uses the library named kfg[1] to represent and to instrument JVM bytecode. Both KFG for the main application and for the library are built using the KFG Builder Module, then the KFG graph is used by the Analysis Module. Library specification is converted to an abstract semantic graph (ASG) in LibSL Parser[2]. The ASG represents information about automata, data types, variables, etc. Instrumentation Module modified library KFG aims to insert library approximation behavior into library model. Analysis Module starts the analysis using the built main application KFG and instrumented library KFG. It converts the program into Predicate State representation [4] and uses z3 SMT-solver for defect detection. Instrumentation Module and Analysis Module were developed as KEX extensions.

Let us consider SPIDER in detail. The kfg library allows the manipulation of JVM bytecode on a higher level. It allows instrumenting automata in original code classes.

---

[1] https://github.com/vorpal-research/kfg.

[2] https://github.com/vorpal-research/libsl.

We put a state transition code in specified methods. A simple example of such transition obtained by processing of specification from Listing 1 is shown in Listing 2.

```
public void selectOS(String name) {
  if (this.$KEX$INSTRUMENTED$STATE == 2) {
    // State transition code
    this.$KEX$INSTRUMENTED$STATE = 3;
  }
  else {
    boolean[] var16 = new boolean[] { false };
    // intrinsic denotes a forbidden state
    AssertIntrinsics.kexAssert("id2", var16);
  }
  ... // location of original method's code
}

public void setBootPartition(int partition) {
  // precondition calculation
  boolean temp1 = partition >= 0 && partition < 16;
  boolean[] temp2 = new boolean[] { temp1 };
  // intrinsic denotes a precondition violation
  AssertIntrinsics.kexAssert("partitionLimits", temp2);
}
```

Listing 2. Fragment of instrumented code

The example shows two main concepts of SPIDER: automaton state with its transition code and contracts. Contracts are implemented as Boolean variables, the value of which is calculated according to the predicate. The result is passed as a parameter to the internal KEX intrinsic function. Automaton state transitions are implemented as three statements: current state check, new state assignment and intrinsic function call. The Analysis Module finds the library API function calls and checks their conditions. If the condition can be false then intrinsic call is reachable, and the error occurs.

The current version of SPIDER has a limitation. Contracts of functions cannot describe the requirements for complex data types, such as arrays and collections (for example, their size and content). We are planning to fix it later.

7 Evaluation

To evaluate our approach, we conducted a series of experiments. For the first experiment, we use a simple artificial library shown in Listing 1. We create a small application that contains all types of integration errors, which can be detected by our approach. The small fragment of this application is shown in Listing 3.

```
// correct library usage
Computer computer1 = new Computer();
computer1.boot();
computer1.setBootPartition(0);
computer1.selectOS("win");
computer1.loadOS();

// wrong sequence of function call
Computer computer2 = new Computer();
computer2.boot();
computer2.loadOS();
computer2.selectOS("linux");
// Error: selectOS called after loadOS

// shift from finish state
Computer computer3 = new Computer();
computer3.shutdown();  // finish state
computer3.boot();
// Error: try to shift from finish state

// precondition violation: partition must be positive
Computer computer4 = new Computer();
computer4.boot();
computer1.setBootPartition(-1);
// Error: contract violation
```

Listing 3. Simple test project

The test library (named Computer) has the eponymous class and all methods shown in the listing, but their implementations are beyond the scope of this paper. We emphasize that in our analysis we could not have the source code of the library, we only need its bytecode. The listing shows the four test cases: a correct library protocol usage, a wrong method call ordering, an erroneous shift from state marked as 'finish' in the specification and a precondition violation. All these cases are covered by the analyzer and errors were successfully detected.

For the second group of experiments we used a well-known library named okHttp[3]. It proposes an elegant way to send HTTP requests. For the evaluation of SPIDER, we used one of the demo projects named OkCurl. The project contains one code file that represents a console application that looks like curl.

We created a specification for okHttp[4] and evaluated SPIDER on it. The results of the evaluation are shown below.

The Listing 4 illustrates the code fragment of OkCurl. We can see a command line argument *connect-timeout* and a variable *connectTimeout* that represents it. The program doesn't validate the argument, so this is the place where an error may occur (e.g. if the value is negative). Our specification covers this case: the error successfully found.

---

[3] https://square.github.io/okhttp/.

[4] https://github.com/vorpal-research/kex/blob/spider/kex-runner/src/test/resources/org/jetbra ins/research/kex/spider/okhttp3.lsl.

```
@Option(names = ["--connect-timeout"],
  description = ["Maximum time allowed for connection"])
var connectTimeout = DEFAULT_TIMEOUT
// ...
if (connectTimeout != DEFAULT_TIMEOUT) {
  // SPIDER detects an error on the next line
  builder.connectTimeout(connectTimeout.toLong(), SECONDS)
}
```

Listing 4. Code fragment of OkCurl

In addition to these errors, we have added our own ones. For example, we commented out the line of code that sets the URL of request. Fragment of the code is shown on the Listing 5. SPIDER successfully found this error.

```
val url = url ?: throw IllegalArgumentException()
// request.url(url) this line was commented out
// SPIDER detects an error on the next line
return request.build()
```

Listing 5. Code fragment with artificial error

Also, all other errors that were added in the evaluation were successfully found by SPIDER. This means, our approach and tool can be used to detect integration errors in applications using real libraries.

8 Related Work

There are many papers devoted to the use of formal specifications for finding errors in complex programs. We will focus on the articles closest to our approach. In our review, we will be interested in the following aspects:

- Which programming languages are the oriented approach?
- Is it possible to specify libraries without having their source code?
- Does the approach allow to create specifications without changing the library itself?
- Does the approach allow describing the behavior of the entire library, and not just individual API functions?
- How accurate and sound is the approach?

Some of the analyzed approaches are focused on the C programming language. Hallam, Chelf, Xii and Engler in [6] propose an approach to finding errors in C programs using checkers. Checkers describe the rules for code fragments in a special Metal language. Metal uses an automaton paradigm to describe correctness checks. It allows you to find violations of known correctness rules and automatically derive such rules from the source code. The limitations of the approach are the strict binding to the C language and the inability to describe the semantics of an entire library. A similar approach is used by Microsoft Research in the SLAM project. [7–10]. The approach uses the Specification Language for Interface Checking (SLIC) to specify the external API and perform static code analysis to verify the correctness of use of the API. SLIC expresses temporal API security requirements, such as the order of function calls, and the goal of the project is to automatically check whether these requirements are met by the client and the API developer. Complex checks can be described imperatively as insertions in the C language. The resulting code written in SLIC is also compiled into C code. The main goal of the SLAM project is to check the correctness of the drivers. The main limitations of the project are the C programming language used and unsafe and uncontrolled imperative inserts. The WYSIWEB project [11] describes the implementation of a tool that uses a C-like language to search the Linux kernel source code for a certain type of errors and API uses.

Some approaches are initially focused on the Java programming language. The main language for the specification of Java programs is the JML (Java Modeling Language) [12]. It allows you to specify class methods in detail in terms of pre- and postconditions, embedding specifications directly into the code in the form of annotating comments. There are projects for implementing static JML-based analyzers, for example, ESC/Java [13], which statically check JML specifications. The limitations of the approach are the inability to annotate external components without affecting their source code, as well as the lack of an explicit mechanism for describing the correct behavior of the entire external library. Reiss in [14] suggests an approach for finding errors in multicomponent Java programs. The authors have developed a CHET system that allows you to check the correctness of the use of components by checking a variety of conditions. CHET is implemented as an interactive tool that allows the programmer to visually monitor the correctness of working with components.

Bierhoff in his dissertation [15] reveals the issues of compliance with API protocols in object-oriented software. Two key entities made it possible to implement the proposed approach: object-oriented types of states defined by means of hierarchical state refinements and access permissions. Ferles, Stephens and Dillig in [16] propose to set API specifications using parameterized context-summary grammars. This approach does not have enough power to set the behavior of complex libraries. A group of researchers from University de Montreal in [17] presented the results of a study of several types of API usage restrictions, as well as their documentation. The authors have developed an algorithm that automatically determines four types of usage restrictions in the API source code.

In the approaches discussed earlier, the specifications were created manually, but there is a group of approaches in which the specifications are extracted from existing programs. Thus, in [18], a method of mining specifications from external components is proposed, followed by static checking of the correctness of the implementation of this specification. The method is very promising, but its significant limitations: the need for the source code of the library, as well as the low accuracy and soundness of the obtained specifications and, as a result, the possible omission of errors or false positives detections. A similar approach to dynamically extracting library usage protocols is offered by Pradel from ETH [19]. Dynamic analysis is used to analyze the instrumented program and extract the automatic specification. It is further refined and can be used to test other programs. The limitations of the method are like the previous one: low completeness and accuracy of the approach.

9 Conclusion

The paper describes the approach developed by the authors to detect integration errors based on the use of formal library specifications in the LibSL language. Formal specifications are used to build approximations of libraries that are used as oracles for the program being analyzed. Based on the approach, the SPIDER tool was developed, implemented as an extension of the KEX static analyzer. Experiments on simple projects with artificial and industrial libraries have shown the fundamental applicability of the approach and the operability of the tool.

The directions of further research are related to the expansion of the apparatus for describing library functions, including support for complex data types; expansion of classes of detected integration errors; support for different modes of joint analysis of libraries and their approximations.

The areas of improvement of the tool are related to overcoming the existing technical limitations of the tool, creating Java Standard Library specifications, conducting more experiments with large-scale industrial projects using popular open libraries.

References

1. Itsykson, V.M.: LibSL: language for specification of software libraries. Programmnaya Ingeneria 9(5), 209–220 (2018)
2. Itsykson, V.M.: Formalism and language tools for specification of the semantics of software libraries. Aut. Control Comp. Sci. **51**, 531–538 (2017). https://doi.org/10.3103/S01464116 17070100
3. Abdullin, A., Akhin, M., Belyaev, M.: Kex at the 2021 SBST Tool Competition. In: 2021 IEEE/ACM 14th International Workshop on Search-Based Software Testing (SBST), pp. 32–33 (2021). https://doi.org/10.1109/SBST52555.2021.00014
4. Akhin M., Belyaev M., Itsykson V. (2017) Borealis Bounded Model Checker: The Coming of Age Story. In: Mazzara M., Meyer B. (eds.) Present and Ulterior Software Engineering, pp. 119–137. Springer, Cham (2017). https://doi.org/10.1007/978-3-319-67425-4_8
5. Itsykson, V.: Partial specifications of libraries: applications in software engineering. In: Kalenkova, A., Lozano, J.A., Yavorskiy, R. (eds.) TMPA 2019. CCIS, vol. 1288, pp. 3–25. Springer, Cham (2021). https://doi.org/10.1007/978-3-030-71472-7_1
6. Hallem, S., Chelf, B., Xie, Y., Engler, D.: A system and language for building system-specific, static analyses. In: SIGPLAN Not. 37, vol. 5, pp. 69–82 (2002). DOI:https://doi.org/10.1145/543552.512539
7. Ball, T., Rajamani, S.K.: The SLAM project: debugging system software via static analysis. In: SIGPLAN Not. 37, vol. 1, pp. 1–3 (2002). https://doi.org/10.1145/565816.503274
8. Ball, T., Rajamani, S.K.: Automatically validating temporal safety properties of interfaces. In: Dwyer, M. (ed.) SPIN 2001. LNCS, vol. 2057, pp. 102–122. Springer, Heidelberg (2001). https://doi.org/10.1007/3-540-45139-0_7
9. Ball, T., Bounimova, E., Levin, V., Kumar, R., Lichtenberg, J.: The Static Driver Verifier Research Platform. CAV (2010)
10. Ball, T., Levin, V., Rajamani, S.K.: A decade of software model checking with SLAM. Commun. ACM **54**(7), 68–76 (2011).https://doi.org/10.1145/1965724.1965743
11. Lawall, J.L. Brunel, J., Palix, N., Hansen, R.R., Stuart, H., Muller, G.: WYSIWIB: a declarative approach to finding API protocols and bugs in Linux code. In: 2009 IEEE/IFIP International Conference on Dependable Systems & Networks, pp. 43-52 (2009). https://doi.org/10.1109/DSN.2009.5270354

12. Leavens, G.T., Baker, A.L., Ruby, C: Preliminary design of JML: a behavioral interface specification language for java. SIGSOFT Softw. Eng. Notes **31**(3), 1–38 (2006). https://doi.org/10.1145/1127878.1127884

13. Flanagan, C., Leino, K.R.M., Lillibridge, M., Nelson, G., Saxe, J.B., Stata, R.: Extended static checking for Java. SIGPLAN Not. **37**(5), 234–245 (2002). https://doi.org/10.1145/543552.512558

14. Reiss, S.P: Specifying and checking component usage. In: Proceedings of the Sixth International Symposium on Automated Analysis-Driven Debugging (AADEBUG'05). Association for Computing Machinery, New York, NY, USA, 13–22 (2005). https://doi.org/10.1145/1085130.1085133

15. Bierhoff, K.: API Protocol Compliance in Object-Oriented Software. PhD thesis, Carnegie Mellon University, School of Computer Science (2009)

16. Ferles, K., Stephens, J., Dillig, I.: Verifying correct usage of context-free API protocols. Proc. ACM Program. Lang. **5**, POPL, Article 17, 30 pages (2021). https://doi.org/10.1145/3434298

17. Pradel, M., Jaspan, C., Aldrich, J., Gross, T.R.: Statically checking API protocol conformance with mined multi-object specifications. In: 2012 34th International Conference on Software Engineering (ICSE), pp. 925–935 (2012). https://doi.org/10.1109/ICSE.2012.6227127

18. Pradel, M.: Dynamically inferring, refining, and checking API usage protocols. In: Proceedings of the 24th ACM SIGPLAN Conference Companion on Object Oriented Programming Systems Languages and Applications (OOPSLA '09). Association for Computing Machinery, New York, NY, USA, pp. 773–774 (2009). https://doi.org/10.1145/1639950.1640008

19. Saied, M.A., Sahraoui, H., Dufour, B.: An observational study on API usage constraints and their documentation. In: 2015 IEEE 22nd International Conference on Software Analysis, Evolution, and Reengineering (SANER), pp. 33–42 (2015). https://doi.org/10.1109/SANER.2015.7081813

Link Graph and Data-Driven Graphs as Complex Networks: Comparative Study

Vasilii A. Gromov$^{(\boxtimes)}$ (iD)

The School of Data Analysis and Artificial Intelligence, HSE University, Moscow 109028, Russian Federation
stroller@rambler.ru

Abstract. The link and data-driven graphs corresponding to the same dataset are studied as complex networks. It appears that a link graph features the majority of complex networks characteristics, whereas the corresponding data-driven graphs feature only part of these characteristics. Some characteristics appear to be more stable, when one moves from a link graph to data-driven graphs and over data-driven graphs, than others. In particular, one observes giant components and power-law community size distributions for most link and data-driven graphs. Also, data-driven graphs usually retain small world property and relatively large values of clustering coefficients, provided the same holds true for the respective link graph. Meanwhile, only the ε-ball neighbourhood graph and the Gabriel graph exhibit power-law degree distributions as their link counterparts do. The assortativity coefficient is essentially corrupted when one moves from a link graph to data graphs. Sometimes, assortativity alters to disassortativity. Among all data-driven graphs considered, the Gabriel graph seems to retain most properties of complex networks.

Keywords: Data-driven graph · proximity graph · complex networks · power-law distributions

1 Introduction

The complex networks [1, 2] prove to be an efficient tool to study and describe most real-world complex systems [3, 4]. Usually, a vertex of any complex network has a large amount of data associated with it; that is particularly true for networks that correspond to social or information structures. Such data, taken collectively, may give an accurate account of the underlying system, alternative to that provided by the complex network itself. To such data, considered independently of the network and its vertices, one may apply any data mining technique. In particular, it is possible to construct various data-driven graphs [5], alternatively referred to as proximity graphs [6]. We should stress that both approaches, with data-driven and with proximity graphs, should be construed as different, but equitable, ways to describe some information system. One assumes that each graph is associated with its own dynamics, roughly corresponding to disease and information spreading for social systems. Hence it appears to be important to study comparatively features of the graphs.

© Springer Nature Switzerland AG 2024
R. Yavorskiy et al. (Eds.): TMPA 2021, CCIS 1559, pp. 120–129, 2024.
https://doi.org/10.1007/978-3-031-50423-5_11

Quite naturally, these graphs must share most features, at least qualitatively. The present paper employs several real-world data sets in order to compare complex networks characteristics for various graphs, both link and data-driven. Namely, the ε-ball neighbourhood graph (ε-ball), the Gabriel graph (GG), the influence graph (IG), the nearest neighbourhood graph (NNG), the relative neighbourhood graph (RNG) [5, 7–9], which all exemplify data-driven graphs.

Looking ahead, a link graph usually shows most features of complex networks, whereas a data-driven graph usually retains only a part of them. It is important to be clear in one's mind that there are two possible explanations for this fact. On the one hand, this may be interpreted to mean that such and such method to construct a data-driven graph is inapplicable for data with a complex network structure. On the other hand, the respective features may not be of fundamental importance for the description of complex networks. Furthermore, it seems to be, that if the features of graphs of both types coincide, then this fact indicates that graphs observe true data structure of the information object. The similarity between results for graphs of both types (for example, between distributions of their communities) defines, in a sense, a measure of the observability of the data structure.

Another raison d'être to study this problem is the large number of problems that involve community detection in linked data, and algorithms designed to solve this problem [10]. The overwhelming majority of such algorithms operate on either an explicit or implicit assumption that it is possible to handle link and data-driven graphs in a unified way. In turn, this implies that both graphs share qualitatively similar structures.

The rest of the paper is organized as follows. The next section reviews recent advances in both data-driven graphs and complex networks. The third section outlines the types of data-driven graphs and complex networks characteristics used for the current analysis. The fourth section discusses a comparative study of complex network characteristics for various graphs of both types. The last section presents conclusions.

2   Related Works

A pressing need to represent raw data, leads to different data-driven graphs and algorithms intended to construct and explore them [11]. Since the performance of many data mining techniques depends heavily on the data-driven graph they use, there is a large number of distinctly different graphs of this kind, based on different assumptions. Qiao et al. [11] comprehensively reviewed the overwhelming majority of state-of-the-art data-driven graph construction techniques. They broadly classify all possible approaches on parameter-free techniques (the minimum spanning tree, the Delaunay triangulation, the Gabriel graph, the relative neighbourhood graph and others), single-parameter techniques (the beta-skeleton, the nearest neighbours graph, the ε-ball neighbourhood graph, the b-matching graph), and techniques that require flexible parameter selection schemes. Aronov et al. [12] consider witness proximity graphs, which are data-driven graphs with the structure determined by two separate sets of points. Sometimes, it is reasonable to generalize classical data-driven graphs in order to define k-graphs. For instance, k-Gabriel graph allows k points within the circle, such that its diameter connects two given points. In these terms, a conventional Gabriel graph is a 0-Gabriel graph [7].

Engineers frequently demand that a graph should satisfy certain constraints. First, the graph must be able to adequately represent complex raw data. For example, a popular minimum spanning tree usually fails. Second, the graph should be robust and insensitive to noise, thereby usually ruling out the Delaunay triangulation. Third, standard demand is that of a symmetric graph. This demand leads one to propose symmetrisation techniques for k-nearest neighbours models and, generally, to post-processing techniques, intended to balance a constructed graph [11]. Sometimes, it is reasonable to demand a connected graph. Another frequent demand is to vary the degree of graph sparsity (please, see [13] and references therein). Certain problems make it necessary to construct a graph inductively, with an increasing dataset [14]. And last but not least, algorithms to construct a given data-driven graph should be efficient. In our opinion, to this conventional list, one should add one more constraint: A graph produced by complex systems should satisfy complex networks constraints.

The constraints in question usually comprise of: a small-world property, a power-law distribution of vertex degrees, presence of a giant component (which is a connected subgraph with the number of vertices of the same order of magnitude with the total number of vertices in the network) and so on [1]. Another important issue is the number and sizes of communities of a complex network [15]. Community sizes for a complex network also follow some power law. Such a network usually exhibits a giant component. Molloy and Reed [16] prove criterion for a giant connected component. Aiello et al. [17] estimate a range for a power exponent of the degree distribution, such that a giant component necessarily exists for any complex network with the degree distribution corresponding to this range. Ding et al. [18] discuss an evolving RNG-graph of a traffic network interpreted as a complex network.

In order to verify that a given graph belongs to complex networks, one should perform a goodness-of-fit test for the degree distribution, the community size distribution, and others, verifying whether or not they obey some power laws. The simplest possible technique, the Hill's method, implies that one fits data in double logarithmic scale linearly [19]. Ibragimov and his colleagues [20] ascertain an adequate expression for a significant interval for a power law exponent estimated by this method. The approach by Clauset et al. [21] employ Kolmogorov-Smirnov (KS-) statistic in order to estimate both a power law exponent and a lower cutoff, which is a lower boundary for observations that fit this power law. It is worth stressing that the method allows one not only to estimate the distribution parameters, but also to test the hypothesis that the sample corresponds to a power-law distribution. Pruessner [22] discusses 'data collapse', another method used to verify whether or not the sample is generated by some power law. Advantageously, the method is able to handle not only a 'true' power-law distribution, but also the one modified by a scaling function. A plot of such modified probability distribution function, usually exhibits a 'hunch' – that is the case for most real-world power-law distributions. The method is also able to test the hypothesis that the sample is generated by a power law. Gromov and Migrina [23] examine application of this method to natural language processes.

3 Materials and Methods to Analyse Data-Driven and Link Graphs

Data-Driven Graphs. In this study, we utilize the following types of data-driven graphs: the ε-ball neighbourhood graph, the Gabriel graph, the influence graph, the nearest neighbourhood graph, and the relative neighbourhood graph. Among them, the ε-ball neighbourhood graph and the nearest neighbourhood graph are single parameter graphs, the three others are parameter free graphs.

To describe graphs, we use the following notation $G = (V, E)$, where $V = \{v_i\}$ is a set vertices, $E = \{e_{ij}\}$ is an adjacency matrix for graph edges, $x(v_i)$ are data associated with a vertex v_i, $D = \{d_{ij}\}$, $d_{ij} = \rho(x(v_i), x(v_j))$ is a distance matrix for the data. The distance is Euclidean in this paper. $N_k(x(v_i))$ stands for a set of k nearest neighbors of $x(v_i)$, $O(x(v_i))$ for a sphere with a centre at $x(v_i)$ and a radius equal to the distance between a point $x(v_i)$ and its nearest neighbor $x(v_j)$: $R = \rho(x(v_i), x(v_j))$, where $x(v_j) \in N_1(x(v_i))$.

The ε-Ball Neighbourhood Graph. Vertices v_i and v_j are connected ($e_{ij} = 1$), if $d_{ij} < \varepsilon$.

The Gabriel Graph. For that model, v_i and v_j are connected, if the hypersphere such that its diameter is an interval connecting $x(v_i)$ and $x(v_j)$ does not contain any other sample points: $e_{ij} = 1$, if $e_{ij} = 1$, if $d_{ij} < \left(d_{ik}^2 + d_{kj}^2\right)^{1/2} \forall k \neq i, j$.

The Influence Graph. For each point, one builds up the hypersphere $O(x(v_i))$, v_i and v_j are connected, if their hyperspheres are intersected: $e_{ij} = 1$, if $O(x(v_i)) \cap O(x(v_j)) \neq \varnothing$.

The (k-)Nearest Neighbourhood Graph. Any vertex is connected to its k nearest neighbors: $e_{ij} = 1$, if $x(v_j) \in N_k(x(v_i))$.

The Relative Neighbourhood Graph. Two points are connected, if the intersection of the two hyperspheres with centres at these points and radii equal to the distance between the points does not contain any other sample points: $e_{ij} = 1$, $d_{ij} < \max\{d_{ik}, d_{jk}\} \forall k \neq i, j$. To construct the graph, we use the algorithm by O'Rourke [24]. Toussaint [25] proved that MST $\subset$ RNG $\subset$ GG $\subset$ DT.

Complex Networks Characteristics. In order to compare various graphs as complex networks, we use the following complex networks characteristics: the degree distribution, the community size distribution, the clustering coefficient distribution, the graph diameter, and assortativity coefficient. For the respective definitions, please refer to [1]. It is worth noting that these characteristics collectively makes it possible to ascertain a type of a complex network one deals with. For each empirical distribution, we test whether it follows a normal or a power law. Then we calculate, if applicable, a mean; for power-law distributions it may appear to be infinite.

Goodness-of-Fit Tests for a Power-Law Distribution. We use the approach proposed by Clauset et al. [21] to test the statistical hypothesis in question; it is grounded on the Kolmogorov-Smirnov (KS) criterion. The method not only evaluates a power law exponent, but also cut off the smallest elements of the sample that usually do not fit a power law. Actually, one estimates the power exponent α and calculates this statistic for each value of the lower cutoff x_{min}. Then the values of α and x_{min} that achieve minimum of the KS-statistic are chosen as the estimates. In order to test whether a sample follows a power law (to perform a goodness-of-fit test), Clauset et al. [21] propose to generate a large number of artificial sample sets from the power law with the values of both a power exponent α and a lower cutoff x_{min} that equal to their estimates obtained in the way discussed above. For each artificial set, one then calculates the KS-statistic just as for the original sample set. Finally, the statistic for the goodness-of-fit test is the number of the KS-statistic larger than the one for the original sample set. Clauset et al. [21] propose to reject the null hypothesis that the sample in question follows a power law, if the respective proportion is less than 10%.

In order to detect communities in the graphs [15], we employ the label propagation algorithm [26]; advantageously, the algorithm does not require knowledge of the number of clusters in advance. The algorithm [26] implies that each node is initialized with a unique label, and each node for each iteration of the algorithm adopts a label that a maximum number of its neighbors have, with ties broken uniformly randomly. As the labels propagate through the network in this manner, densely connected groups of nodes form a consensus on their labels. At the end of the propagation process, nodes having the same labels are grouped together as one community.

4 A Comparative Study of Link and Data-Driven Graphs

Datasets Used. The first dataset, Six Degrees of Francis Bacon (SDFB), belongs to digital library Folger Shakespeare [27]. The dataset contains information about circles of friends for Frenchmen of the XVII and XVIII centuries. Two persons are considered to be acquainted, if letters between them have survived, or one has mentioned another one in some historical document. The network consists of 15801 vertices (persons) and 171408 edges (acquaintances). Besides that, for every person, we have information about their name, sex, title (if any), trade, dates of birth and death, and the documents in which he or she has been mentioned. These data are used to construct data-driven graphs.

The second dataset belongs to the Stanford University complex networks collection [28]. It contains information about goods that are available at the Amazon site. The network consists of 548552 vertices (goods and comments on them) and 987942 edges. To construct data-driven graphs, we employ the following data for each vertex (good): a sales-rank, its internal popularity rating; list of goods frequently bought with it; detailed information about the category it belongs to; users' comments on the good. All frequent words of the English language were removed from the comments before the analysis.

The third dataset belongs to the Aminer collection [29]. It includes information about Twitter users' subscriptions and actions. The graphs here consist of 112416 vertices (users) and 308927 tweets. For all presented values, the normalized p-value does not exceed 0.001 for power-law distributions and 0.1 for normal distributions. As discussed above, a goodness of fit (GoF) statistic that exceeds 0.1, suggests a power-law distribution [21].

Link Graphs Characteristics. The complex networks characteristics, outlined in the previous section, were first employed to explore link graphs of the three datasets discussed above.

SDFB link graph appears to be weakly disassortative. Its assortativity coefficient equals to -0.08 (if Pearson correlation coefficient is used), -0.08 (Spearman), and -0.06 (Kendall). Two other graphs appear to be assortative. For the Amazon link graph, the respective values are $0.04, 0.07, 0.05$; for the Twitter link graph, $0.365, 0.447, 0.412$.

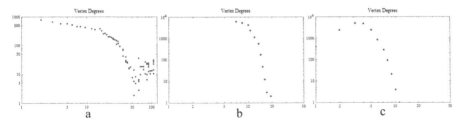

Fig. 1. The degree distributions for the SDFB link graph in the double logarithmic scale.

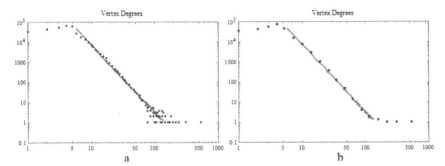

Fig. 2. The degree distributions for the Amazon link graph in the double logarithmic scale, before (a) and after (b) the binning; the red dots represent the distribution with estimated power exponent, the blue ones the raw data.

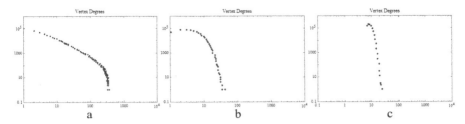

Fig. 3. The degree distributions for the Twitter link graph in the double logarithmic scale.

The degree distributions for all the three link graphs follow power law distributions. By way of illustration, Fig. 2 exhibits the degree distributions for the Amazon link graph in the double logarithmic scale, before and after the binning; the large red dots represent the distribution with an estimated power exponent, the small blue ones the raw data.

The distributions were tested for normality, and the hypotheses were rejected. The data appear to be consistent with power-law distributions. Namely, the SDFB link graph features power exponent $\alpha = 2.8$ with the lower cutoff $x_{min} = 15$. Goodness-of-fit statistic for this hypothesis equals to 0.42. For the Amazon link graph these qualities amount to 3.18, 75, and 0.88, respectively; for the Twitter link graph 3.34, 19, and 0.62. The graph diameters are equal to 9, 12, and 11 respectively. This allows one to draw the conclusion that all three graphs feature small-world property. Furthermore, all three graphs possess giant components, and the community sizes follow power-law distributions with exponents 2.11, 2.97, and 2.28, respectively. The features discussed above make it possible neighbourhood graph (a), the nearest neighbourhood graph (b) to conclude that the link graphs may be construed as complex networks.

Data-Driven Graphs Characteristics. The method outlined above leads to quite different results for data-driven graphs corresponding to the datasets in question. For data-driven graphs corresponding to the Six Degrees of Francis Bacon, the assortativity coefficients are as follows (the first value is the coefficient, calculated using Pearson correlation coefficient, the second one Spearman correlation coefficient, the third one Kendall correlation coefficient): for the ε-ball neighbourhood graph, 0.98, 0.96, and 0.84; for the Gabriel graph, 0.36, 0.37, and 0.27; for the influence graph, 0.59, 0.47, and 0.4; for the nearest neighbourhood graph, 0.12, 0.12, and 0.1; for the relative neighbourhood graph, 0.19, 0.12, and 0.17. For Amazon data graphs: 0.9, 0.93, and 0.78 (ε-ball); 0.41, 0.44, and 0.38 (GG); 0.4, 0.46, and 0.34 (IG); 0.13, 0.12, and 0.09 (NNG); 0.2, 0.19, and 0.16 (RNG). For the Twitter data graphs: 0.95, 0.95, and 0.87 (ε-ball); 0.35, 0.32, and 0.3 (GG); 0.41, 0.48, and 0.36 (IG); 0.13, 0.12, and 0.09 (NNG); 0.17, 0.18, and 0.14 (RNG). It is quite obvious that the assortativity coefficient changes drastically when the link graphs are replaced by the data-driven ones; sometimes, assortativity alters to disassortativity. It is worth stressing that assortative coefficients are rather close to each other for various datasets. It seems that their values are determined not by a dataset, but rather by the type of a data-driven graph.

For all three datasets and for all data-driven graphs, the degree distributions are tested for normality, and whether samples are consistent with a power law. The latter is one of the most important 'fingerprints' of complex networks. It appears that not all data-driven graphs exhibit power law distribution of their vertices. Namely, only the ε-ball neighbourhood graph and the Gabriel graph follow a power law; the influence graph, the nearest neighbourhood graph, and the relative neighbourhood graph follow a normal distribution instead. Moreover, even for the graphs that keep following a power law, an exponent changes from the values that yield finite mathematical expectations, to those that yield infinite ones. In particular, for the SDFB dataset, it switches from 2.8 to 1.49 and 1.4; for the Amazon dataset, from 3.18 to 1.72 and 1.6; for the Twitter dataset, from 3.34 to 1.53 and 1.36. Besides that, for the ε-ball neighbourhood graph, the exponents depend on ε. All PDFs here show hunches, typical for most real-world power laws; the hunches are usually attributed to what is known as scaling functions [22]. Meanwhile, PDFs for the respective link graph do not show the hunches in the double logarithmic scale (Fig. 1). Figures 2 and 3 display the degree PDFs for the data-driven graphs corresponding to the Amazon and Twitter datasets. Table 1 summarizes discussed results.

Table 1. Complex networks and Their Characteristics

DataSet	SDBF				Amazon				Twitter			
Graph	Ast	Deg	Com	Dia	Ast	Deg	Com	Dia	Ast	Deg	Com	Dia
Link	−.08	2.8	2.11	9	0.04	3.18	2.97	12	0.365	3.34	2.28	11
ε-ball	0.98	1.49	–	10	0.9	1.72	–	11	0.95	1.53	–	12
GG	0.36	1.4	–	9	0.41	1.6	–	12	0.35	1.36	–	11
IG	0.59	–	–	11	0.4	–	–	10	0.41	–	–	12
NNG	0.12	–	–	9	0.13	–	–	11	0.13	–	–	12
RNG	0.2	–	–	10	0.2	–	–	10	0.17	–	–	12

Ast stands for assortativity coefficient (Pearson); Deg, for the power exponent for degree distribution; Com, the power exponent for community size; Dia, for a graph diameter.

Small world property appears to be inherent to some extent, to all data-driven graphs. Besides that, all the data-driven graphs exhibit relatively large values of average clustering coefficients. Interestingly, the estimates for average clustering coefficients of link and data-driven graphs demonstrate a satisfactory agreement.

5 Conclusions

Using three various data sets (Six Degrees of Francis Bacon, which contains information about circles of friends for Frenchmen of XVII and XVIII; Amazon, which contains information about goods sold by an eponymous company; Twitter, which contains information about subscriptions of its Twitter users) we examine the respective link and data-driven graphs as complex networks. The link graphs feature the majority of characteristics of complex networks, whereas the corresponding data-driven graphs feature only part of these characteristics, depending on data-driven graph type. On the other hand, some characteristics appear to be more stable, when one moves over data-driven graphs, than others.

In particular, one observes giant components and community size power-law distributions for most link and data-driven graphs. Moreover, the power exponents of the respective distribution for link and data-driven graphs are in good agreement. Also, data-driven graphs usually retain small world property and relatively large values of clustering coefficients, provided the same holds true for the respective link graph.

Meanwhile, a power-law degree distribution is exhibited by the ε-ball neighbourhood graph and the Gabriel graph only, as their link counterparts do. The degree distributions for other types of data-driven graphs appear to be normal. Even for the data-driven graph types that retain this property, the value of the power exponent crosses the border between exponents that yield finite mathematical expectations and those that yield infinite.

In turn, the assortativity coefficient is essentially corrupted when one moves from a link graph to data graphs. Sometimes, assortativity alters to disassortativity. It seems that values of the assortativity coefficients are determined not by a dataset, but rather by the type of a data-driven graph.

Among all data-driven graphs considered, the Gabriel graph seems to retain most properties of complex networks.

Acknowledgments. The author is deeply indebted to Mr. Joel Cumberland, HSE, for the manuscript proof-reading and language editing.

Funding. The article was prepared within the framework of the HSE University Basic Research Program, HSE University, Moscow, Russian Federation.

Data Sharing and Data Accessibility. Data sources are presented in references.

Conflict of Interest. The authors declare that there is no conflict of interest regarding the publication of this paper.

References

1. Barrat, A., Barthelemy, M., Vespignani, A.: Dynamical Processes on Complex Networks. Cambridge University Press, Cambridge (2008)
2. Erdos, P., Renyi, A.: On random graphs. Publicationes Mathematicae **6**, 290–297 (1959)
3. Albert, R., Jeong, H., Barabasi, A.L.: Diameter of the world-wide web. Nature **401**(6749), 130–131 (1999)
4. Barabási, A.L., Albert, R.: Emergence of scaling in random networks. Science **286**(5439), 509–512 (1999)
5. Vathy-Fogarassy, Á., Abonyi, J.: Graph-Based Clustering and Data Visualization Algorithms. Springer, New York (2013). https://doi.org/10.1007/978-1-4471-5158-6
6. Mathieson, L., Moscato, P.: An introduction to proximity graphs. In: Moscato, P., de Vries, N.J. (eds.) Business and Consumer Analytics: New Ideas, pp. 213–233. Springer, Cham (2019). https://doi.org/10.1007/978-3-030-06222-4_4
7. Bose, P., et al.: Proximity graphs: E, δ, Δ, χ and ω. Int. J. Comput. Geom. Appl. **22**(05), 439–469 (2012)
8. Mitchell, J.S.B., Mulzer, W.: Proximity algorithms, In Handbook of discrete and computational geometry. In: Goodman, J.E., O'Rourke, J. (eds.) Discrete and Computational Geometry, pp. 849–874. CRC Press LLC, Boca Raton (2004)
9. Carreira-Perpinán, M.A., Zemel, R.S.: Proximity graphs for clustering and manifold learning. Adv. Neural. Inf. Process. Syst. **17**, 225–232 (2005)
10. Aggarwal, C.C., Reddy, C.K.: Data Clustering Algorithms and Applications. Taylor and Francis Group, London (2014)
11. Qiao, L., Zhang, L., Chen, S., Shen, D.: Data-driven graph construction and graph learning: a review. Neurocomputing **312**, 336–351 (2018)
12. Aronov, B., Dulieu, M., Hurtado, F.: Mutual witness proximity graphs. Inf. Proc. Lett. **114**(10), 519–523 (2014)
13. Dornaika, F., Weng, L., Jin, Z.: Structured sparse graphs using manifold constraints for visual data analysis. Neurocomputing **315**, 107–114 (2018)
14. Dornaika, F., Dahbi, R., Bosaghzadeh, A., Ruichek, Y.: Efficient dynamic graph construction for inductive semi-supervised learning. Neural Netw. **94**, 192–203 (2017)
15. Fortunato, S., Hric, D.: Community detection in networks: a user guide. Phys. Rep. **659**, 1–44 (2016)

16. Molloy, M., Reed, B.: The size of the giant component of a random graph with a given degree sequence. Comb. Probab. Comput. **7**(3), 295–305 (1998)
17. Aiello, W., Chung, F., Lu, L.: A random graph model for power law graphs. Exp. Math. **10**(1), 53–56 (2001)
18. Ding, J.X., Qin, R.K., Guo, N., Long, J.C.: Urban road network growth model based on RNG proximity graph and angle restriction. Nonlinear Dyn. **96**(4), 2281–2292 (2019)
19. Resnick, S.I.: Heavy-Tail Phenomena: Probabilistic and Statistical Modeling. Springer, New York (2007). https://doi.org/10.1007/978-0-387-45024-7
20. Ibragimov, M., Ibragimov, R., Walden, J.: Heavy-Tailed Distributions and Robustness in Economics and Finance, vol. 214. Springer, New York (2015). https://doi.org/10.1007/978-3-319-16877-7
21. Clauset, A., Shalizi, C.R., Newman, M.E.: Power-law distributions in empirical data. SIAM Rev. **51**(4), 661–703 (2009)
22. Pruessner, G.: Self-Organized Criticality. Cambridge University Press, Cambridge (2012)
23. Gromov, V.A., Migrina, A.M.: A language as a self-organized critical system. Complexity **2017** (2017)
24. O'Rourke, J.: Computing the relative neighborhood graph in the L1 and L∞ metrics. Pattern Recogn. **15**(3), 189–192 (1982)
25. Toussaint, G.T.: The relative neighbourhood graph of a finite planar set. Pattern Recogn. **12**(4), 261–268 (1980)
26. Raghavan, U.N., Albert, R., Kumara, S.: Near linear time algorithm to detect community structures in large-scale networks. Phys. Rev. E **76**(3), 036106 (2007)
27. Folger Shakespeare Library's digital collections. http://collections.folger.edu/. Accessed 20 Sept 2021
28. Stanford Large Network Dataset Collection. http://snap.stanford.edu/data/. Accessed 20 Sept 2021
29. Twitter-Dynamic-Net Dataset. https://aminer.org/data-sna. Accessed 20 Sept 2021

An Approach to Creating a Synthetic Financial Transactions Dataset Based on an NDA-Protected Dataset

Luba Konnova[1]([✉]), Yuri Silenok[1], Dmitry Fomin[1], Daria Degtiarenko[1], Ksenia Vorontsova[1], Andrey Novikov[2], and Egor Kolesnikov[2]

[1] Exactpro Systems Limited, London, UK
{luba.konnova,yuri.silenok,dmitry.fomin,daria.degtyarenko,
ksenia.vorontsova}@exactpro.com
[2] Syndata.io, Moscow, Russia
{andreyn,egork}@syndata.io
http://exactpro.com

Abstract. This paper outlines an experiment in building an obfuscated version of a proprietary financial transactions dataset. As per industry requirements, no data from the original dataset should find its way to third parties, so all the fields, including banks, customers (including geographic locations) and particular transactions, were generated artificially. However, we set our goal to keeping as many distributions and correlations from the original dataset as possible, with adjustable levels of introduced noise in each of the fields: geography, bank-to-bank transaction flows and distributions of volumes/numbers of transactions in various subsections of the dataset.

The article could be of use to anyone who may want to produce a publishable dataset, e.g. for the alternative data market, where it's essential to keep the structure and correlations of a proprietary non-disclosed original dataset.

Keywords: Financial transactions · Data obfuscation · Synthetic data set · Data generation

1 Introduction

The alternative data market is a promising opportunity for many businesses, including data owners - that can take advantage of additional revenue streams - on one side, and data analysts - that bring real or close-to-real data from outside sources to produce better predictive analytics for businesses they affiliate with - on the other side.

The financial domain, however, introduces a certain level of security-related restriction. While analysts can reasonably benefit from understanding the general structure of monetary flows with different slices like volumes, currencies, countries and even correlations, no data of any given company should be compromised in any way. To honor this requirement, the task of producing a shareable dataset is essentially not *obfuscation*, but *synthesis*.

R. Yavorskiy et al. (Eds.): TMPA 2021, CCIS 1559, pp. 130–141, 2024.
https://doi.org/10.1007/978-3-031-50423-5_12

This article describes our experiment of producing a synthetic shareable dataset from proprietary data provided by a leading international financial transaction support party. We share our insights - gained from a limited-time engagement with the data owner - and experiments with the dataset.

In further sections, we elaborate probable business requirements for this dataset and the process of its generation, outline the process of generation and describe possible enhancements to the algorithm. Although only initial parts of the experiment are described, and this work is still to be developed, this article may be of interest to anyone willing to produce a synthetic dataset out of a proprietary one, while keeping both the privacy of the original data, and its value for reasonable analysis by third parties.

2   An Outlook on the Data and Business Task Clarification

The original dataset consisted of around 400,000 transactions that were provided with the following data (partially NANs):

- Bank codes (BICs) of the originating and receiving banks;
- Beneficiary (receiving) customer, including account number and address;
- Ordering (paying) customer, including account number and address;
- Additional information, including bank fees, transaction IDs, and some other fields (see details in section *Exploratory Data Analysis*).

While the general setting of the task is to make a dataset publicly shareable (possibly, on the open data market) to any party, we motivated our research by the idea that certain parties may be interested in certain slices of the data, for example:

- Governments and municipalities may be interested in having very precise geographic data to analyze the business volumes generated by particular territory-based businesses.
- Central banks and Forex trading entities may be interested in precise data per currency and the smallest differences in distributions of transaction amounts, but, probably, do not need much precision in geography.
- Banking regulators and global market researchers may benefit from the understanding of flows between major banks.

Other potential customers may have different requirements for the dataset. To reflect this demand, it would be beneficial to not only produce a single dataset, but a technology to generate datasets with different levels of precision in different directions. While datasets with more introduced noise may be shared in open repositories, datasets with more precise data in certain directions may only be sold in over-the-counter deals with certain NDA levels.

Any generating algorithm implementing this idea should offer a number of numeric parameters that define the structure of the obfuscation. A possible business scenario based on this algorithm should define personal and NDA-level restriction on producing datasets with precision higher than certain levels.

3   Literature Review

Data obfuscation techniques always include three components: data randomization, data anonymization, and data swapping.

Data randomization aims to prevent subsequent data recovery through repetitive queries (e.g. to a database).

Data anonymization is implemented via classifying data into intervals and replacing the values in each interval with newly generated values. In this case, it is easy enough to preserve the statistical value of the information, which is important for further application of the data in machine learning.

Data swapping consists in mixing values in a separate field.

With this, a good obfuscation method should be irreversible, so that sensitive data could not be revealed and/or harmed [1]. We followed these approaches in developing our solution.

Various methods can be used to obfuscate transaction data while preserving the statistics, important to machine learning. In finance and insurance, the Monte Carlo method is widely used for this purpose. It is convenient because it allows you to preserve important statistical indicators without much effort. However, banks and insurance companies mostly use it to simulate unexpected occurrences, as an auxiliary method in the decision-making process [2]. In our work, the Monte Carlo method was applied to preserve the confidentiality of the data.

Thomas Blumensath and Michael E. Davies compared various methods of time series approximation in [3]. From the ones that were reviewed, the Monte-Carlo method with Gibbs sampling showed the best results. Since a sequence of transactions can be represented as a time series, we followed this way and applied the Monte Carlo method to generate not only the values of transactions, but also their affiliation with specific end clients (i.e. attributing packs of transactions to the same generated client entity) and geographies.

Following the abovementioned papers, our research presents a case study where these methods are applied to a specific field with stringent requirements from both the credibility and security perspectives, keeping in mind high value of data to potential users, but also high risks of disclosing potentially sensitive commercial information on a large scale.

4   Exploratory Data Analysis

The analysed dataset contains around 400 thousand SWIFT MT103 Single Customer Credit Transfer messages [4]. Table 1 lists all attributes as available. As a result of the analysis, it was discovered:

- how many unique Senders/Receivers there are;
- which columns are blank;
- which columns are obfuscated;
- how column values interrelate;

- how transaction volumes are distributed per Sender, per Sender/Receiver, per Sender/Receiver currency;
- how Sender/Receiver charges are populated;
- how Ordering Customer/Beneficiary Customer are distributed per Sender/Receiver, geography of their distribution.

It was discovered that Sender/Receiver, Ordering Customer/Beneficiary Customer had already been obfuscated. So, we didn't have to think of the logic of obfuscating BICs.

Mathematical graphs have been chosen to visualize the dataset, with nodes representing Sender/Receiver, edges representing transaction amounts and currencies.

No correlation between Interbank Settled Account and Sender's or Receiver's Charges was discovered. Interbank Settled Amount is always equal to Instructed Amount in the database. This fact leaves us with a single numeric figure - amount of transaction - to analyse and generate.

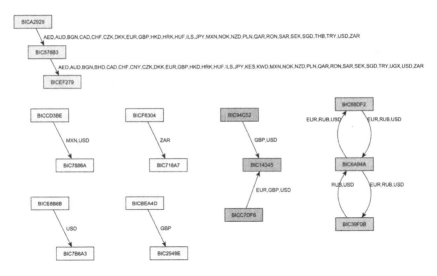

Fig. 1. Transaction flows between banks.

The structure of the transaction flow from the initial data is a disconnected directed graph with 17 nodes, as shown in Fig. 1. We can distinguish between different types of connections between banks by direction (unidirectional and bidirectional connections), the set of currencies sent along each edge, the number of sites in each component. The three banks shown at the top of the figure have the greatest variety of currencies, but the number of transactions between them is not so high. It is worth noting that about 60% of the total number of transactions were sent between the BIC68DF2-BIC6A94A pair.

Table 1. Dataset Fields.

Column	Field Name	Required Parsing	Blank
UETR	Unique End-to-End Transaction Reference		
Message Type			
Sender			
Receiver			
20	Sender's Reference		
23B	Bank Operation Code		
32A	Value Date/Currency/Interbank Settled Amount	y	
33B	Currency/Instructed Amount	y	
36	Exchange Rate		y
50A	Ordering Customer	y	
50F		y	
50K		y	
52A	Ordering Institution		
56A	Intermediary Institution		y
57A	Account With Institution		
59F	Beneficiary Customer	y	
70	Remittance Information		y
71A	Details of Charges		
71F	Sender's Charges	y	
71G	Receiver's Charges	y	

The distributions of transaction amounts between each pair also had their own characteristics. The users of some banks sent transactions with volumes close to a uniform distribution, the transaction volumes of users of other banks tended to have an exponential distribution, as shown in Fig. 2.

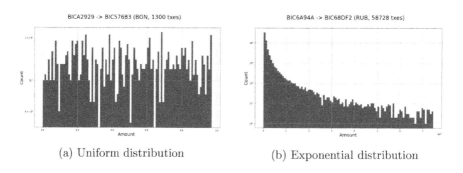

(a) Uniform distribution   (b) Exponential distribution

Fig. 2. Different types of sent amounts.

The most common situation is where the ordering customer sent only 1 transaction as in Fig. 3a. There is a clear inverse relationship between the number of users in each bin and the number of transactions sent by the users. With beneficiaries, the picture is slightly different, which is shown in Fig. 3b. There is a minor increase around the 20 transactions mark, with the maximum of 41 transactions received by one customer.

Concerning the geography to be analysed in the dataset, Ordering/Beneficiary Customers have countries and cities specified in the 50, 50F fields. As per our observations, streets and client names, sender/receiver BICs were obfuscated in the original dataset. So, Ordering/beneficiary geographic client distributions were built. Figure 4 shows the Ordering clients distribution on the map.

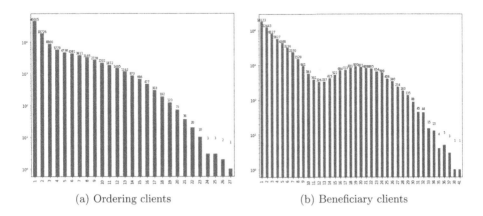

(a) Ordering clients   (b) Beneficiary clients

Fig. 3. Number of transactions sent by one client distribution.

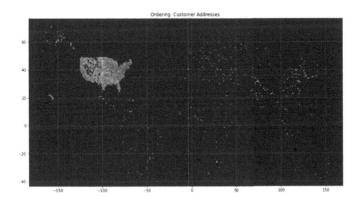

Fig. 4. Ordering customers location, colors code Sender banks.

5   The Dataset Generation Process

We generate the dataset in a three-step process (Fig. 5).

First, we create the graph of Sender and Receiver banks and flows between them marked by currencies.

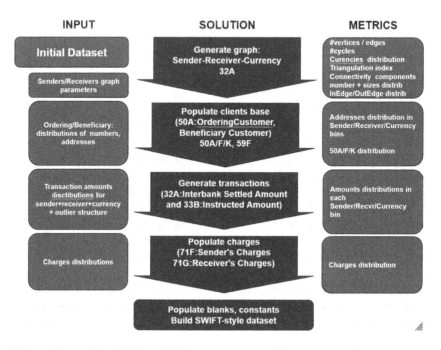

Fig. 5. Generation pipeline. Field names given in MT103 protocol conventions.

Second, we work inside each of the Sender-Receiver-Currency containers to generate transactions with numbers, amounts and distributions by paying/receiving parties that are similar to the original dataset. At this point, we copy the geography information from similar parties in the original dataset.

The third stage is changing the end customer names and introducing noise to geographies.

The final post-processing after the generation process includes adding bank charges and converting the dataset to a shareable table.

5.1   Generating Sender-Receiver-Currency Graph

At the first stage, we replicate the banks and currencies structure of the original dataset, as depicted in Fig. 1, and continue the generation process within each Sender-Receiver-Currency container.

This approach is quite straightforward, as it keeps this structure untouched, which is meaningful in many use cases. However, in further iterations of our research, we aim to explore several opportunities to add an obfuscation layer to this process by adding the following:

- **Change the banks.** Since it's a simple obfuscation, a certain percentage of transactions can be randomly re-plugged from one bank to another. Some banking entities can be mapped 'many-to-one', this making de-obfuscation practically impossible. Even high levels of noise of this kind are acceptable for customers looking for precise information on amounts and customers, but not banks.
- **Change the currencies, while recalculating the amounts per currency exchange rates**. This adds another layer of obfuscation to keep the bank names undisclosed.
- **Generate the graph, while keeping the essential structural parameters.** A graph generation algorithm can be applied to generate a graph with given parameters. For example, a graph with a certain number of vertices, edges and connectivity components could be generated, and then iteratively mutated in a genetic algorithm to bring its metrics close enough to the original graph. In our intuition, the following parameters may be preserved: numbers of nodes and edges, triangulation index, number of connectivity components.
- **Scaling the graph** while keeping the abovementioned parameters, except for the numbers of nodes and edges.

5.2   Transactions

We perform all of the following generations inside each of the Sender-Receiver-Currency containers. Although this approach is somewhat contradictory to the fact that some clients work with different banks and send transactions in different currencies, this allows us to keep the correlations between the structure of the banking graph and end client/transaction flows, which is important for more local analysis. The drawback of a separate generation may be addressed by identifying different generated customers at the post-processing stage, while adhering to the same distributions of clients working simultaneously with different banks and currencies, as in the original dataset, with a technique similar to the one described below in the Generating Transaction Volumes subsection.

Generating Ordering and Beneficiary Clients. We start generating transactions from populating two tables, one for Ordering (paying) clients, and the other with Beneficiary (receiving) clients, each containing the following columns:

- Number of transactions
- Mean amount of a transaction

First, we gather this information from the initial dataset.

Second, we use the common PCA-based method of generating a multidimensional random variable with a known distribution, as described, for example, in [5]. In particular, we leverage PCA to decorrelate our random values and use specific amounts of random value pairs, build a randomly generated two-dimensional dataset with a uniform distribution, and then inverse-transform them with the same PCA. If we need to scale the number of transactions or their amounts, we generate a scaled number of points before doing the reverse PCA or scale each transaction amount as the final step.

As a result of this operation, we have two synthetic sets of Senders and Receivers. Then we add the geography information for each customer, copying it from the most similar customer (in terms of the overall volume and number of transactions). The geography is obfuscated at further stages of the generation process.

Generating Transaction Volumes. Up to this point, we have bound the synthesis with a specific tuple of Sender (bank), Receiver (bank) and currency, and generated lists of Ordering and Beneficiary clients, with target numbers of transactions and mean volumes.

As a next step, we generate transaction amounts, aiming to keep the same distribution as in the original Sender/Receiver/Currency container, not linking them to Ordering clients or Beneficiaries for now.

To do this, we split all transactions into logarithmic bins (e.g., 0–10, 10–100, 100–1000), and generate new transaction volumes as uniform distributions of the same number of values within the respective bins. The number of bins is a parameter of approximation (the higher it is, the closer the generated distribution will be to the original).

Thus, we get a set of transaction volumes, with the same number of transactions as in the original dataset (multiplied by the scale factor, if needed), their statistical distribution is generated by a piecewise linear distribution function.

This technique could be further improved, taking into account that, in the original dataset, values were distributed exponentially, so the generation algorithm can also generate exponentially distributed values instead of the uniformly distributed ones.

Linking Transactions to Clients. As the final step of the transaction generation process, we link the Ordering and Receiving customer sets on the one hand, and a set of transaction volumes on the other, both generated as explained above.

We do this iteratively for each transaction volume.

We take the next transaction volume V that we want to distribute, randomly choose a sender, using the number of transactions that each sender has to send as the relative probability. If the chosen sender's average transaction volume does not match V (it is much higher or much lower than V, with a user-defined threshold on the relative difference), then we take a different sender and repeat this up to 10 times. If none are found again, we give the transaction to the last sender. When the sender is found, we use the same logic to choose a recipient.

This allows us to expect the structure of volumes and numbers of transactions to be distributed similarly to the original dataset within each Sender-Receiver-Currency container.

This finishes our generation process, and we only need to obfuscate the geographic information, at this step copied from the original dataset. An example of generated clients, amounts and geographies is depicted in Fig. 6.

Ordering customers				
ID	Number of transactions	Average transaction amount	Sum Amount	Location
1	20	100	2000	Vladimir, Russia
2	10	1500	15000	Kazan, Russia
3	5	100	500	Samara, Russia
4	2	5000	10000	Ekaterinburg, Russia

Synthetic ordering customers						Obfuscated location
ID	Number of transactions	Average transaction amount	Sum Amount	Location		Obfuscated location
1	3	3300	9900	Ekaterinburg, Russia		Chelyabinsk, Russia
2	12	175	2100	Vladimir, Russia		Ryazan, Russia
3	3	240	720	Samara, Russia		Tolyatti, Russia
4	18	750	13500	Kazan, Russia		Cheboksary, Russia
5	20	740	14800	Kazan, Russia		Cheboksary, Russia
6	4	120	480	Samara, Russia		Tolyatti, Russia
7	8	225	1800	Vladimir, Russia		Ryazan, Russia
8	4	2850	11400	Ekaterinburg, Russia		Chelyabinsk, Russia

Fig. 6. Example of generated customers.

5.3   Obfuscating Geographies and Client Names

In this chapter, we outline the process of geographies and names obfuscation.

Transactions contain information about the address of the beneficiary and ordering customers. The result of obfuscating such data implies replacing the original set of cities with new ones, so that the clients' geographic locations remain approximately the same as in the original dataset, but become less precise.

In the initial dataset, addresses were given as a record of Name/Street/City /Country. Consequently, our first step was to find the geographic coordinates (latitude and longitude) of each address (country + city).

To do this, we used one of the online services that provide an API to get geographic coordinates based on an address. The advantage of this technique is the ability to process a chunk of, for example, 100 addresses at once. This allows us to quickly process all the unique values. However, usually such services require a key that has a limit on the monthly number of requests (paid keys have a larger number of transactions). It is also worth paying attention to the fact that the data received from an online service can contain multiple results for one city (possibly, from different countries with same city name), that need to be reviewed and filtered.

Whenever an API did not deliver satisfactory results for any reason (e.g. none of the results fell to the necessary country), we used the *geopy* Python library. It can be used without restrictions, but its use is time-consuming, as each address is processed by a separate call.

Now that we have found the coordinates of each location from the original dataset, we need to change the address, while keeping it "not so far" from the original location (where "not so far" should be a user-defined parameter) to keep the geography-related correlations.

First, the world map was divided into sectors of a certain granularity, each sector is defined by a latitude from/to and longitude from/to values. We worked with 360 sectors for longitude and 720 for latitude, with 360° of latitude and 180° of longitude evenly distributed among the sectors, so that each sector was no more than 55 × 55 km.

For each sector, we populated a list of cities consisting of cities located in this sector from the original dataset, and a user-defined number of randomly picked cities within the same sector from a publicly available dataset.

Finally, to obfuscate the client's geography, we changed its city to a randomly picked city within the same sector as the original one. Then we used Python's *faker* module to generate the name and the rest of the address (street, postal code).

The two parameters (number of sectors and number of newly introduced cities) regulate the level of precision in the geographic data.

With this process and techniques, we obtained a fully synthetic dataset, while adhering to distributions, correlations and geographies existing in the original dataset.

The distribution for the generated data is demonstrated in Fig. 7. If compared to the distribution above in Fig. 4, this map is missing some points. This is because several addresses could have been assigned to the same user in the original dataset. In real-world data, this is usually impossible.

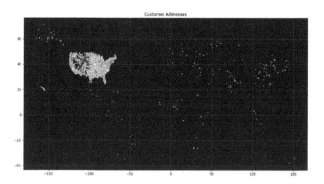

Fig. 7. Synthetically generated ordering customers locations, color codes indicate Sender banks.

6   Conclusion and Future Work

Many questions are to be answered in further iterations of this research, the main ones featuring:

- What metrics are preserved by the process of this kind, and to what extent the random nature of the generation process allows to control their deviation from the original ones?
- Is there a way to keep all the pairwise correlations between key parameters - such as the banking graph, geographies, distributions of numbers of transactions and volumes - ideally preserved without compromising their security?
- What should be regarded as business-appropriate use of the generation and obfuscation techniques? How does one safely protect data from reverse engineering and, at the same time, keep the required characteristics?

Answering all these important questions is the target for the future research journey. However, taking into account the fast-growing market of alternative data sources and potential value that could be delivered by using synthetically generated data that retains the essential structure of the original dataset for the interested conscientious parties, we consider any improvement in this direction as valuable.

References

1. Bakken, D., Parameswaran, R., Blough, D.: Data obfuscation: anonymity and desensitization of usable data sets. In: IEEE Security and Privacy (2004)
2. Herzog, T., Lord, G.: Applications of Monte Carlo Methods to Finance and Insurance. ACTEX Publications Inc, Winsted, Connecticut (2002)
3. Blumensath, T., Davies, M.: Monte Carlo methods for adaptive sparse approximations of time-series. In: IEEE Transactions on Signal Processing (2007)
4. SWIFT. Knowledge Centre. Category 1 - Customer Payments and Cheques - Message Reference Guide. https://www2.swift.com/knowledgecentre/publications/us1m_20180720?topic=aia.htm#mt103/
5. Correlated Variables in Monte-Carlo Simulations. https://towardsdatascience.com/correlated-variables-in-monte-carlo-simulations-19266fb1cf29/

Optic Flow Approximated by a Homogeneous, Three-Dimensional Point Renewal Process

D. V. Dubinin[1] , A. I. Kochegurov[2] , E. A. Kochegurova[2] ,
and V. E. Geringer[3(⊠)]

[1] Tomsk State University of Control Systems and Radioelectronics, Prospect Lenina 40, 634050
Tomsk, Russia
dmitrii.v.dubinin@tusur.ru

[2] National Research Tomsk Polytechnic University, Lenin Avenue 30, 634050 Tomsk, Russia
kaicc@tpu.ru

[3] Baden-Wuerttemberg Cooperative State University (DHBW) Ravensburg, Fallenbrunnen 2,
88045 Friedrichshafen, Germany
geringer@DHBW-Ravensburg.de

Abstract. The paper describes a mechanism for modeling an optical flow as a random vector field – closed areas on the image plane with certain brightness and dynamics of changes in the vector field. The optical flow is formed by a homogeneous, three-dimensional point renewal process. The characteristics of the vector field on the image plane of the resulting optical flow are interconnected by the Palm's formulas. The type of the constituent elements of the vector field (the alphabet, which determines the morphology of the field on the image plane) is chosen randomly. The proposed approach will produce various types of interconnected digital sequences of images with horizontal, vertical and diagonal elements; create the prerequisites for efficient and flexible motion analysis on digital video sequences; make it possible to use the probabilistic factor in researching image processing algorithms and comparing the algorithms based on a detailed factor analysis.

Keywords: Stochastic Modelling · Renewal Process · Optical Flow · Comparison of Algorithms · Image Processing

1 Introduction

Advances in digital information technology made it possible to create highly efficient systems than can analyze, process and transmit optical information. Hence, much recent research is aimed at creating and testing new image processing algorithms. However, testing the algorithms has been disadvantaged by the use of real images as reference images. On the one hand, this approach makes it possible to customize the created algorithms for a specific subject area, but on the other hand, it makes it difficult to assess the quality of the algorithms, to refine and compare the algorithms in various application fields.

R. Yavorskiy et al. (Eds.): TMPA 2021, CCIS 1559, pp. 142–148, 2024.
https://doi.org/10.1007/978-3-031-50423-5_13

One possible solution is to develop a mathematical apparatus to analyze the algorithms under certain, strictly controlled conditions and create prerequisites for factor analysis. Then the key point is to construct random multi-dimensional dynamic vector fields (temperature, change, brightness fields of the earth, atmosphere, ocean, etc.) that are used for modeling. This makes it possible to introduce a probabilistic factor into the modeling, and thereby detail and generalize the subject of research.

2 General Approaches and Modeling Techniques

An adequate mathematical model that can be used to synthesize a numerical model of the experiment, prepare and control the initial data is of great importance in stochastic modeling. In other words, it is necessary to create prerequisites for efficient preparation of a directed experiment aimed to maintain the statistical reliability of experiment results and achieve the maximum accuracy of the experiment estimates with the minimum number of modeling iterations.

There exist a number of methods for modeling random fields. In general, all field models can be divided into two classes [1]. The models of the first class describe fields with continuous distributions. This class includes Gaussian and Markov random fields [2–4], which are often constructed using either spectral transformations or shaping filters [5, 6]. However, the visual structure of such fields does not correspond to the pronounced contour structures of piecewise constant real images. Meanwhile, the outgoing point of the specificity of a subject area – taking account of physical processes, sensor dynamics, data presentation and processing algorithms – is of particular importance in modeling. It is known that real optical images can be represented as brightness fields, which are close to piecewise constant functions of two variables, i.e. consist of regions with similar brightness and regions separated from each other by sharp boundaries. In this regard, the models of the second class are of particular interest as they describe the decomposition of the fields into constituent parts or regions. Such models include models of a collection of objects against a background [1] and mosaic models [7, 8], including the mosaics formed by a family of straight or curved lines and the models where points are grouped around random centers [9].

This paper describes a mechanism for modeling an optical flow as a random vector field – closed regions on the image plane with certain brightness and dynamics of changes in the vector field between frames. A sequence of images on a plane, hereafter referred to as an optical flow, was formed by selecting complex 3D elements of the vector field. The characteristics of the vector field on the image plane were interconnected by the Palm's formulas [7, 8]. The type of the constituent elements of the vector field (the alphabet) and the frequency of their occurrence determined the a-priory morphology of the field on the image plane. In other words, the optical flow was formed by a homogeneous, three-dimensional point renewal process [10]. This made it possible to control the characteristics of the generated field on the image plane: morphology, probabilistic and spectral properties [11]. The proposed approach summarized previous research on modeling mosaic reference images [10–13]. Previous approaches to the construction of optical flows failed to construct the morphology of a contour image with various types of elements, which limited the modeled brightness fields and possible applications of mathematical generation mechanisms.

3 Problem Formalization

The following requirements and necessary conditions should be met to create an optical flow as a random vector field on the image plane approximated by a three-dimensional point renewal flow.

In the process of modeling, it is necessary to obtain $I(x, y, t)$ – a random, scalar, piecewise constant function of the brightness field of two variables that depends on the discrete time t. X is a finite subset on the image plane where I is defined as $I(x, y, t)$: $S(t) = \{S_1(t), S_2(t), ..., S_K(t)\}$, where $K = |S(t)|$ is the number of subsets for a certain discrete time, $S(t) = \{S_1(t), S_2(t), ..., S_K(t)\}$ has the meaning of K connected, piecewise linear subsets on the image plane $Z'(t)$ that are formed on the basis of a random vector field. Piecewise linear subsets $S(t)$ have certain properties and are filled with random brightness based on the homogeneity predicate LP.

Besides, four basic requirements should be met:

1. The vector field that defines the boundaries of piecewise linear subsets $S(t) = \{S_1(t), S_2(t), ..., S_K(t)\}$ should be constructed on the basis of a three-dimensional point renewal flow, which in turn should guarantees the introduction of a probabilistic factor and the closedness of the regional boundaries on the image plane.
2. Each point on the image plane should relate to a certain region $Z'(t) = \bigcup\limits_{i=1}^{K} S_i(t)$.
3. The resulting set of piecewise linear subsets on the image plane $S(t) = \{S_1(t), S_2(t), ..., S_K(t)\}$ should be connected and should meet the condition $S_i(t) \cap S_j(t) = \{\varnothing\}$ $\forall i \neq j$.
4. The following condition of homogeneity of an individual subset should hold from the point of view of the homogeneity predicate LP: $LP(S_i(t)) = true$ $\forall i$.

4 Contour Model

The analysis of images obtained by real systems based on spatial sensors using time sampling in telecommunication channels showed that they contain contour lines that can be considered rectilinear in sufficiently small fragments. Therefore, object boundaries can be represented by line segments oriented horizontally, vertically and diagonally relative to the sampling grid when forming reference sequences of images in multi-dimensional space-time grids.

The model of object boundaries and their vector description was based on a homogeneous, single-level three-dimensional point renewal flow. This made it possible to introduce a probabilistic factor into the conditions of the experiment and obtain a stable mechanism to create a vector description of the contour structure of a reference image sequence and construct an optical flow. The continuity of the obtained boundaries of the regions on the image plane $Z'(t)$ and the change in the position of the vector description of the region structure $S(t)$ at $Z'(t) \to Z'(t + 1)$ of no more than one resolution point of the sampling grid are guaranteed by the Markov property of the renewal flow.

Considering the 3D neighborhood Z (see Fig. 1), it should be noted that the boundaries of the regions can in general be formed by rays in the directions ($a_1, b_1, c_1, d_1, e_1; a_2, b_2, c_2, d_2, e_2; a_3, b_3, c_3, d_3, e_3, f_3, g_3, h_3, z_6$) emanating from the center of the neighborhood $\mathbf{Z}$. The indexes define the side of the 3D neighborhood and were borrowed from a traditional dice built according to the classical scheme "1-2-3-4-5-6" where the sum of the numbers on the opposite sides is 7. It can be seen from Fig. 1 that the geometry of forming the optical flow can be expressed through a left-handed three-dimensional Cartesian coordinate system. The image plane of the optical flow corresponds to the generally accepted orientation of the coordinate axes (the $\mathbf{Y}$ axis directed downward) that is used to present and process images. In our case, the $\mathbf{Z}$ axis describes the time component of the optical flow and will subsequently be denoted by the letter $\mathbf{T}$.

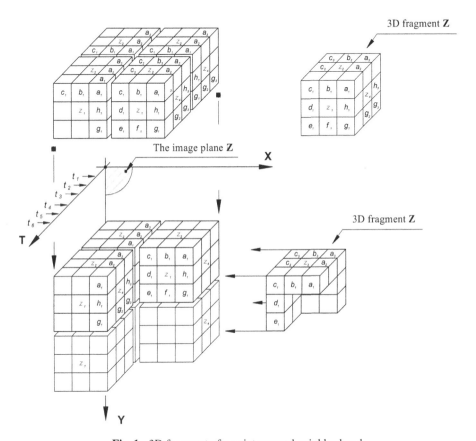

Fig. 1. 3D fragment of a point renewal neighborhood.

At $\{i = 1, 2, 3\}$, a_i, b_i, c_i, d_i, e_i, f_i, g_i, hi take the values "0" or "1" and mean the absence or presence of the corresponding contour ray.

An alphabet of 32 elements can be used to simply demonstrate the operation of the contour structure formation mechanism. Some elements are shown in Fig. 2. The elements of the alphabet were formed based on two conditions:

1. The shear rate from one time sample to the next time sample on the image plane should not exceed one point.

2. The velocity vector for a certain time point t on the image plane should not change its direction and should be determined only in the vertical or horizontal direction.

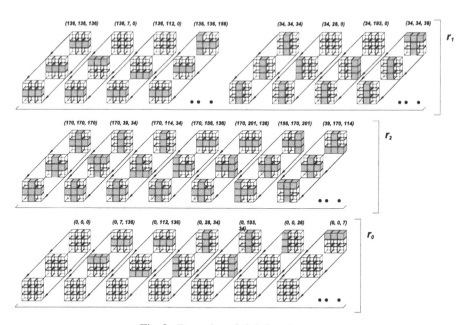

Fig. 2. Formation of alphabet elements.

While maintaining the acceptability of the classification of the alphabet elements, we proposed to describe individual letters of the alphabet by a sequence of three decimal code values, e.g. $\{0; 0; 0\}$ described a letter with no contour rays inside the region (see Fig. 2). Each decimal value described the value of a 3×3 neighborhood on the image plane, and a letter summarized the three values. In turn, the decimal code values were determined by the formula:

$$N_j = a_j 2^0 + b_j 2^1 + c_j 2^2 + d_j 2^3 + e_j 2^4 + f_j 2^5 + g_j 2^6 + h_j 2^7,$$ where j – described the section number in the 3D neighborhood of the alphabet letter (see Fig. 3).

The basic alphabet used to construct a random optical flow consisted of the following letters: $L_1 = [\{136, 136, 136\}, \{136, 7, 0\}, \{136, 112, 0\}, \{136, 136, 201\}, \{136, 136, 156\}, \{112, 136, 7\}, \{7, 136, 112\}, \{34, 34, 34\}, \{34, 28, 0\}, \{34, 193, 0\}, \{34, 34, 114\}, \{34, 34, 39\}, \{28, 34, 193\}, \{193, 34, 28\}, \{170, 170, 170\}, \{170, 39, 34\}, \{170, 114, 34\}, \{170, 156, 136\}, \{170, 201, 136\}, \{156, 170, 201\}, \{39, 170, 114\}, \{201, 170, 156\}, \{114, 170, 39\}, \{0, 0, 0\}, \{0, 7, 136\}, \{0, 112, 136\}, \{0, 28, 34\}, \{0, 193, 34\}, \{0, 0, 28\}, \{0, 0, 7\}, \{0, 0, 193\}, \{0, 0, 112\}]$. The contours were constructed with the following values of the final probabilities: $r_0 = 0{,}49, r_1 = 0{,}42, r_2 = 0{,}09$; an additional generality of alphabet letters, e.g. $L_+ = [\{170, 199, 0\}, \{170, 124, 0\}, \{17, 160, 64\}, \{17, 10, 4\}, ...]$, was introduced by constructing the diagonal components of the image contour structure.

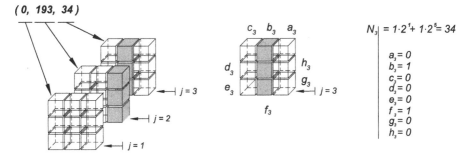

Fig. 3. The structure of the neighborhood description for a single letter of the alphabet.

5 Mechanism for Obtaining the Contour Structure of the Field

An optical flow was constructed as a random vector field using a set of basic 3D elements called a construction alphabet (see Fig. 2). The elements were arranged in a random sequence based on a system of conditional probabilities. Changes in the final probabilities and introduction of additional alphabet elements into the groups made it possible to create various types of contour grids (from the simplest rectangular gids to very complex ornaments) on the image plane. The properties of the contour image were determined by the probabilities $P(a_i, b_i, c_i, d_i, e_i, f_i, g_i, h_i)$ at $i = 1, 2$ and 3.

When modeling the optical flow based on the alphabet L_1, all letters were divided into 3 groups with the final probabilities r_0, r_1, r_2, where r_0 was the probability of occurrence of structural elements $\{0, 0, 0\}$, $\{0, 7, 136\}$, $\{0, 112, 136\}$, $\{0, 28, 34\}$, $\{0, 193, 34\}$, $\{0, 0, 28\}$, $\{0, 0, 7\}$, $\{0, 0, 193\}$, $\{0, 0, 112\}$ r_1 was the probability of occurrence of elements $\{136, 136, 136\}$, $\{136, 7, 0\}$, $\{136, 112, 0\}$, $\{136, 136, 201\}$, $\{136, 136, 156\}$, $\{112, 136, 7\}$, $\{7, 136, 112\}$, $\{34, 34, 34\}$, $\{34, 28, 0\}$, $\{34, 193, 34\}$, $\{34, 34, 114\}$, $\{34, 34, 39\}$, $\{28, 34, 193\}$, $\{193, 34, 28\}$, r_2 was the probability of occurrence of elements $\{170, 170, 10\}$, $\{170, 39, 34\}$, $\{170, 114, 34\}$, $\{170, 156, 136\}$, $\{170, 201, 136\}$, $\{156, 170, 201\}$, $\{39, 170, 114\}$, $\{201, 170, 156\}$, $\{114, 170, 39\}$ and their sum $r_0 + r_1 + r_2 = 1$.

The conditional probabilities $P(\vec{v}_1/\vec{v}_2)$ obtained from the formula of the total probability [7] were used in constructing contours:

$$P(\vec{v}_1/\vec{v}_2) = \frac{P(\vec{v}_1 \| \vec{v}_2)}{\sum_{v_1} P(\vec{v}_1 \| \vec{v}_2)},$$

where vector v_1 was defined from $[h_1, f_1, g_1, z_1, \ h_2, f_2, g_2, z, \ h_3, f_3, g_3, z_6]$ and vector v_2 was defined as $[a_1, b_1, c_1, d_1, e_1; a_2, b_2, c_2, d_2, e_2; a_3, b_3, c_3, d_3, e_3, f_3, g_3, h_3, z_6]$.

6 Conclusion

The proposed technique for modeling random optical flows approximated by a homogeneous, single-level 3D point renewal flow can be used to check and tune image processing methods. It will serve the basis for high-quality algorithms for searching and localizing boundaries, segmentation and skeletonization of images, tracking object behavior in images. The technique is of particular interest in creating new, objective systems to assess the performance of systems for processing and transmitting optical information as a whole. The formation of a random optical flow will make it possible to search for optimal conditions when choosing significant factors, to evaluate and refine the constants of theoretical models and algorithms. It will make it possible to eliminate or reduce systematic errors and their displacement during field studies. It will further allow the assessment of not only the variance of the estimated parameters, but also the parameters of the environment accompanying the experiment.

Acknowledgement. We are deeply indepbted to our family members for their patience, friendly support and assistance.

References

1. Kashkin, V.B., Sukhinin, A.I.: Remote sensing of the Earth from space. Digital Image Processing: A Tutorial. - Logos, p. 264 (2001)
2. Glazov, G.N., Kostevich, A.G., Shelupanov, A.A. (eds.) Modelirovanie diskretnykh gaussovykh sluchainykh polei [Gaussian random discrete field modelling]. Intellektual'nye sistemy v upravlenii, konstruirovanii i obrazovanii, Iss. 2, Tomsk, STT, pp. 19–27 (2002)
3. Domínguez, E., Lage-Castellanos, A., Mulet, R.: Random field Ising model in two dimensions: Bethe approximation, cluster variational method and message passing algorithms. J. Stat. Mech. Theory Exp. (7), 1–23 (2015)
4. Krasheninnikov, V.R., Mikeyev, R.R., Tishkin, V.V.: Synthesis of a wave model of a multidimensional random field with a given correlation function. Bull. Samara Sci. Center Russ. Acad. Sci. **16**(6–2), 474–478 (2014)
5. Balter, B.M., Balter, D.B., Egorov, V.V., et al.: Methods of imitating modeling of hyperspectral images of the earth's surface. Earth Res. Space **5**, 21–29 (2007)
6. Chen, C.H., Pau, L.F., Wang, P.S.P. (eds.) The Handbook of Pattern Recognition and Computer Vision, 2nd edn., pp. 207–248. World Scientific Publishing Co. (1998)
7. Buimov, A.G.: On the statistics of palm fields. Avtometriya **6**, 13–18 (1981)
8. Sergeev, V.V., Soifer, V.A.: Image simulation model and data compression method, automatic control and computer sciences. **3**, 76–78 (1978)
9. Kaufman, L., Rousseeuw, P.J.: Finding Groups in Data: An Introduction to Cluster Analysis, p. 344. Wiley, New York (2009)
10. Dubinin, D., Geringer, V., Kochegurov, A., Reif, K.: Ein stochastischer Algorithmus zur Bildgenerierung durch einen zweidimensionalen Markoff-Erneuerungsprozess. Oldenbourg Wissenschaftsverlag, In: at- Automatisierungstechnik, Band 62 (Heft 1), pp. 57–64 (2014)
11. Geringer, V., Dubinin, D., Kochegurov, A.: On the statistics of space-time signals created by a two-dimensional Markov renewal process. Bull. Tomsk Polytechnic University Tomsk **321**(5), 194–198 (2012)
12. Geringer, V., Dubinin, D., Kochegurov, A., Reif, K.: Bundled software for simulation modeling. In: Proceedings of the International Symposium on Signals, Circuits and Systems (ISSCS 2013), Romania, Iasi, IEEE Catalog Number: CFP13816-CDR, pp. 1–4. ISSCS Press (2013)
13. Dubinin, D.V., Geringer, V.E., Kochegurov, A.I., Rayf, K.: An efficient method to evaluate the performance of edge detection techniques by a two-dimensional Semi-Markov model. In: Proceedings of the IEEE Symposium Series on Computational Intelligence - 4 IEEE Symposium on Computational Intelligence in Control and Automation (SSCI - CICA 2014), no. 7013248, pp. 1–7 (2014)

Fair Mutual Exclusion for N Processes

Yousra Hafidi[iD], Jeroen J. A. Keiren[(✉)][iD], and Jan Friso Groote[iD]

Eindhoven University of Technology, Eindhoven, The Netherlands
{y.hafidi,j.j.a.keiren,j.f.groote}@tue.nl

Abstract. Peterson's mutual exclusion algorithm for two processes has been generalized to N processes in various ways. As far as we know, no such generalization is starvation free without making any fairness assumptions. In this paper, we study the generalization of Peterson's algorithm to N processes using a tournament tree. Using the mCRL2 language and toolset we prove that it is not starvation free unless weak fairness assumptions are incorporated. Inspired by the counterexample for starvation freedom, we propose a fair N-process generalization of Peterson's algorithm. We use model checking to show that our new algorithm is correct for small N. For arbitrary N, model checking is infeasible due to the state space explosion problem, and instead, we present a general proof that, for $N \geq 4$, when a process requests access to the critical section, other processes can enter first at most $(N-1)(N-2)$ times.

Keywords: Mutual exclusion · Peterson's algorithm · Starvation freedom · mCRL2 · Model-checking

1 Introduction

Peterson's algorithm [20] is a classic, widely studied mutual exclusion algorithm for two processes. It satisfies all requirements desired from a mutual exclusion algorithm, e.g., mutual exclusion, starvation freedom, and bounded overtaking.

Peterson's algorithm can be generalized to N processes using a tournament tree [21]. The tournament tree is a binary tree in which each of the leafs is assigned (at most) two processes that want to gain access to the critical section. In each node of the tree, two processes compete using Peterson's algorithm for two processes. The winner moves up in the tournament tree. Ultimately, the process that wins in the root of the tree gets access to the critical section.

This generalization is known to satisfy mutual exclusion. However, the situation for starvation freedom is less clear. Fokkink argues the algorithm satisfies starvation freedom [9], but is not explicit about the assumptions needed for this. Others argue that starvation freedom is not satisfied [22], and that tournament tree solutions never satisfy bounded overtaking [1,15].

To ensure starvation freedom, it turns out (weak) fairness assumptions are required. In particular, if a process is in a state where it can continuously execute a particular statement, it will eventually be allowed to execute said statement. To the best of our knowledge there is no generalization of Peterson's algorithm to N processes that does not require fairness to ensure starvation freedom.

© Springer Nature Switzerland AG 2024
R. Yavorskiy et al. (Eds.): TMPA 2021, CCIS 1559, pp. 149–160, 2024.
https://doi.org/10.1007/978-3-031-50423-5_14

Contributions. We create an mCRL2 model [12] of the generalization of Peterson's algorithm to N processes using tournament trees, based on [9]. We specify the most important requirements using the first order modal mu-calculus [10], and verify them using the mCRL2 toolset [3] for instances with $N \leq 5$. It is shown that the algorithm satisfies mutual exclusion[1]. However, it is not starvation free. We present a counterexample illustrating that, when a process requests access to the critical section, a process in a different subtree can repeatedly request, and get, access to its critical section, preventing progress of the first process.

We propose a fair N-process mutual exclusion algorithm that introduces dependencies between the progress of all processes in order to rule out such counterexamples. Using model checking we verify that this algorithm is starvation free. Furthermore, we verify that it satisfies bounded overtaking for $N \leq 5$. Due to the state space explosion problem, the verification times are prohibitive for larger N. We therefore, additionally, prove a general bound of $(N-1)(N-2)$ on the number of overtakes for $N \geq 4$ processes. Detailed proofs have been omitted due to space restrictions, and can be found in [13].

Related Work. The mutual exclusion problem was first described around 1960. For two processes, the main challenge is to break the tie when both processes want to access their critical section. The first solution for this problem was Dekker's algorithm [6], that uses a nested loop to break this tie. The desire to eliminate this loop led to a series of algorithms [7,16,20]. Peterson's algorithm [20] is a well-known solution without nested loop. It uses one shared variable per process to indicate the request to enter the critical section, and a single variable shared among all processes to break the tie. Mutual exclusion algorithms for N processes were first studied in [5]. Many solutions use tournament trees [21]. An alternative generalization of Peterson's algorithm uses a filter lock [20].

Correctness of Peterson's algorithm, even for two processes, is subtle and depends on the assumptions on the environment. For instance, it requires that shared variables are atomic, which can be deemed unrealistic as this requires a mutual exclusion algorithm in the operating system [8]. In other cases, fairness is required [2], which may rule out realistic behavior [8].

Model checkers are commonly used to verify the correctness of mutual exclusion algorithms [11,18]. They have also been used for performance evaluation of mutual exclusion algorithms [19], and to verify such algorithms in a timed setting [4]. The state space explosion problem limits model checking to instances with a few processes. Theorem provers can be used to verify arbitrary numbers of processes. Isabelle/HOL, e.g., was used to verify Peterson's algorithm [17].

Structure. The remainder of this paper is organized as follows. Section 2 introduces the necessary background. Peterson's algorithm for N processes and its model and verification are described in Sect. 3. In Sect. 4, the fair N-process mutual exclusion algorithm is described. The paper is concluded in Sect. 5.

---

[1] Similarly, it can be verified that every process can always eventually request access to the critical section. We leave out its verification in view of space.

2 Preliminaries

In this section we present the most important concepts of mCRL2 and the modal mu-calculus that we use in this paper to model and verify Peterson's algorithm.

mCRL2 Specifications. The mCRL2 language [12] is a process algebra with data. It supports common data types such as Booleans $\mathbb{B}$, and numeric data types such as natural numbers $\mathbb{N}$ and their typical operations out of the box. Additional abstract data types and operations can be defined as needed.

The behavior of a system is described using processes. The basic building block of a process is a (parameterized) action, e.g., $a_s(42)$. Process $x \cdot y$ describes the sequential composition of processes x and y, where first x and then y is executed. The choice between x and y is denoted using alternative composition $x + y$. Named processes can be defined using equations, and carry parameters, e.g. $P(n : \mathbb{N}) = a(n) \cdot P(n + 1)$, where $P(0)$ is the process that performs $a(0) \cdot a(1) \cdot a(2) \cdot \cdots$. Within a process, the sum-operator offers a generalized alternative composition over data, e.g., $\sum_{n : \mathbb{N}} a_r(n)$ is equivalent to the process $a_r(0) + a_r(1) + \cdots$. A process can be restricted using the conditional operator $c \rightarrow x \diamond y$, where c is a Boolean expression describing the condition. The process x is executed when c is true, else y is executed.

Processes x and y can be executed in parallel, using parallel composition $x \parallel y$. For actions a_s and a_r, $a_s \parallel a_r$ is equivalent to $a_s \cdot a_r + a_r \cdot a_s + a_s | a_r$, where $a_s | a_r$ denotes the simultaneous occurrence of a_s and a_r. Using communication operator $\Gamma_{\{a_s | a_r \rightarrow a_c\}}$ we express that processes synchronize on actions a_s and a_r, which results in action a_c. This can be used to model that one process sends a value along a_s, and the other process receives that same value along a_r, resulting in handshaking communications a_c. For instance $\Gamma_{\{a_s | a_r \rightarrow a_c\}}(a_s \parallel a_r) = a_s \cdot a_r + a_r \cdot a_s + a_c$. If we want to enforce synchronization, since we are not interested in unsuccessful communication using a_s and a_r, we use the allow operator $\nabla_{\{a_c\}}$. For instance, $\nabla_{\{a_c\}}(\Gamma_{\{a_s | a_r \rightarrow a_c\}}(a_s \parallel a_r)) = a_c$.

Modal μ-Calculus. The first order modal μ-calculus is a temporal logic that extends Hennessy-Milner logic (HML) [14] with fixed points and data. Besides the standard boolean connectives $\neg$, $\wedge$, and $\vee$, it includes the modalities $[R]\Phi$ and $\langle R \rangle \Phi$ and the least (resp. greatest) fixed point operator μ (resp. ν). We write *true* inside the modalities to represent the set of all actions, so, e.g., $\langle true \rangle true$ holds if an action is possible from the current state, whereas $[true]false$ holds if no action is possible. We can specify that, from the initial state, actions other than a are not possible using $[\bar{a}]false$. R represents a regular formula. For instance, property $\langle true^* \cdot a \rangle true$ holds in a state if there is a path to a state in which the action a can be done. $[R]\Phi$ holds in a state if all paths characterized by R end up in a state satisfying Φ.

Using fixed points, we can express that action a must inevitably occur within a finite number of steps using $\mu X.([\bar{a}]X \wedge \langle true \rangle true)$.

To support using data, the μ-calculus also includes quantifiers $\forall$ and $\exists$. For a detailed description see [12].

3   Peterson's Algorithm for $N > 2$ Processes

Peterson's algorithm [20] can be generalized to more than two processes using a tournament tree [21]. We follow the description of the algorithm from [9], and first introduce the tournament tree, then describe the algorithm, and finally describe the model and its verification using mCRL2 [3,12].

3.1   Tournament Trees

Given N processes that compete for the critical section, a tournament tree is a binary tree with at least $\lceil \frac{N}{2} \rceil$ leaves. We identify the nodes with a number. The root has number 0, and all other nodes n have parent $p(n) = \lceil \frac{n}{2} \rceil - 1$. Each process is associated to either the left (denoted 0) or right (1) side of a node in the tree. At any time, at most one process is associated to every side of a node. The processes associated to internal nodes are the winners of the tournament in the left and right subtrees, respectively. The initial position of process i, i.e., when it is in its non-critical section and has not yet requested access to its critical section, is on side $s = init\_side(i)$ of node $n = init\_node_N(i)$, defined as follows.

$$init\_node_N(i) = 2^{\log_2 \lceil \frac{N}{2} \rceil} - 1 + \lfloor \tfrac{i}{2} \rfloor$$
$$init\_side(i) = i \mod 2$$

Example 1. The tournament tree for $N = 3$, with processes $0 \le i < 3$ is used as a running example throughout this paper. It is shown on the right.

The tournament tree has root node 0, with left child 1 and right child 2. Processes $i = 0$ and $i = 1$ are initially associated with the left and right side of node 1, respectively. Process $i = 2$ is at the left side of node 2.

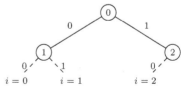

3.2   Algorithm

In Peterson's mutual exclusion algorithm for N processes [21], each process that competes for access to its critical section repeatedly executes Peterson's algorithm for two processes [20] in different nodes in the tournament tree.

If process i is currently at side s of node n it competes with the process at side $1 - s$ using Algorithm 1. At most one process is allowed to move up to the parent of node n, $p(n)$. Peterson's algorithm in node n is executed using shared variables $flag_n[0]$, $flag_n[1]$ to indicate whether the left (resp. right) process wants to move up in the tree. A third shared variable, $wait_n$, is used to break the tie in case both processes want to move up. If $wait_n = i$ process $1 - i$ has priority and is allowed to move up first, or enter the critical section in case $n = 0$.

A process indicates it wants to access the critical section, and move up in the tree, by setting its flag to *true*. By setting $wait_n$ to itself, it allows the other

---

Algorithm 1: $Peterson(i, n, s, N)$

Input: $i, n, s, N \colon \mathbb{N}$; i is the id of the process, process i is currently at side s of node n in the tree, and N is the number of processes.

1 non-critical section;
2 $flag_n[s] \leftarrow true$;
3 $wait_n \leftarrow s$;
4 **while** $flag_n[1 - s]$ **and** $wait_n = s$ **do**
5 $\quad$ {}
6 **end**
7 **if** $n = 0$ **then**
8 $\quad$ enter the critical section;
9 $\quad$ leave the critical section;
10 **else**
11 $\quad$ $Peterson(i, \lceil \frac{n}{2} \rceil - 1, (n + 1) \mod 2, N)$;
12 **end**
13 $flag_n[s] \leftarrow false$;
14 **if** $n = init\_node_N(t)$ **then**
15 $\quad$ $Peterson(i, init\_node_N(i), init\_side(i), N)$
16 **end**

---

process to go first in case that process already executed lines 1–2. If the other process has not set its flag, or arrived at line 3 last (i.e., $wait_n = 1 - i$), process i can move up in the tree, and execute the algorithm again in the parent of node n. If the algorithm is executed in the root and process i is allowed to progress, it enters the critical section. Upon leaving the critical section it resets all flags (in all nodes) it previously set to $true$ back to $false$, moving down in the tree to its initial position. Once the flag in the initial node is set to $false$, process i repeats the algorithm, and it can request access to the critical section again if needed.

3.3 mCRL2 Encoding

Our model is a generalization of the model for two processes from [11], and reduces to that model when $N = 2$. Hence we only discuss the main ideas[2].

As in [11], shared variables are modelled as separate processes. For instance, $flag_n[s]$ is modelled as follows.

$$Flag(n \colon \mathbb{N}, s \colon \mathbb{N}, v \colon \mathbb{B}) = \sum_{v' \colon \mathbb{B}} set\_flag_r(n, s, v') \cdot Flag(v = v')$$
$$+ get\_flag_s(n, s, v) \cdot Flag()$$

Here v records the current value, set_flag_r specifies writing a new value v' into the shared variable, and get_flag_s describes the action of sending the current value. The other shared variables are modelled analogously.

---

[2] See https://gitlab.tue.nl/y.hafidi/petersonspapermodels.git for the full model.

This is used in Peterson's algorithm, for process i, on side s of node n.

$Peterson(i: \mathbb{N}, n: \mathbb{N}, s: \mathbb{N}) =$
$\quad set\_flag_s(n, s, true) \cdot$
$\quad set\_wait_s(n, s) \cdot$
$\quad (get\_flag_r(n, 1 - s, false) + get\_wait_r(n, 1 - s)) \cdot$
$\quad ((n = 0) \rightarrow enter(i) \cdot leave(i)$
$\qquad\qquad \diamond Peterson(n = \lceil \frac{n}{2} \rceil - 1, s = (n + 1) \mod 2)) \cdot$
$\quad ((n = init\_node_N(i)) \rightarrow set\_flag_s(n, s, false) \cdot$
$\qquad\qquad\qquad Peterson(n = init\_node_N(i), s = init\_side(i)))$
$\qquad\quad \diamond set\_flag_s(n, s, false)$

The process follows the description in Algorithm 1. First, the *flag* and *wait* variables are set. To model the busy-waiting loop, we rely on communicating actions that block as long as one of the communication partners cannot take part. In particular, $get\_flag_r(n, 1 - s, false)$ can only be executed when also $get\_flag_s(n, 1 - s, false)$ executes, i.e., the process can only take a step if the corresponding shared variable $flag_n[s]$ is *false*. If the process was executing in the root of the tournament tree, i.e., $n = 0$, it enters and leaves the critical section. Otherwise, it recursively executes the algorithm in the parent node in the tree. Once the process has left the critical section, it will reset all flags to *false*, and once it reaches its initial node, the process repeats.

To describe a particular instance of Peterson's for N processes, N copies of *Peterson* and processes for all shared variables in each of the tree nodes are put in parallel. The communication operator Γ is used to specify synchronization between, e.g., set_flag_s and set_flag_r. Synchronization is enforced using ∇.

Example 2. For our running example with $N = 3$, the initialization is as follows.

$\nabla_{\{enter, leave, get\_flag, set\_flag, get\_wait, set\_wait\}}($
$\quad \Gamma_{\{get\_flag_s | get\_flag_r \rightarrow get\_flag, set\_flag_s | set\_flag_r \rightarrow set\_flag,}$
$\qquad {get\_wait_s | get\_wait_r \rightarrow get\_wait, set\_wait_s | set\_wait_r \rightarrow set\_wait\}}($
$\qquad Peterson(0, init\_node_3(0), init\_side(0)) \parallel$
$\qquad Peterson(1, init\_node_3(1), init\_side(1)) \parallel$
$\qquad Peterson(2, init\_node_3(2), init\_side(2)) \parallel$
$\qquad Flag(0, 0, false) \parallel Flag(0, 1, false) \parallel Wait(0, 0) \parallel$
$\qquad Flag(1, 0, false) \parallel Flag(1, 1, false) \parallel Wait(1, 0) \parallel$
$\qquad Flag(2, 0, false) \parallel Flag(2, 1, false) \parallel Wait(2, 0)))$

3.4   Requirements

In this paper, we restrict ourselves to the verification of the three requirements described below. These requirements are generally desirable for a mutual exclusion algorithm. It is well-known they hold for Peterson's algorithm for two processes. They were formalized in the mu-calculus and verified in [11].

Mutual Exclusion. At any time at most one process can be in the critical section. This is formalized by saying that, invariantly, there are no two consecutive enters without an intermediate leave.

$$[true^* \cdot (\exists_{i_1 : \mathbb{N}} enter(id_1)) \cdot \overline{(\exists_{i_2 : \mathbb{N}} leave(id_2))}^* \cdot (\exists_{i_3 : \mathbb{N}} enter(id_3))] false$$

Starvation Freedom. If a process requests access to the critical section, it is allowed to enter within a finite number of steps. The least fixed point in the formula ensures that, after requesting access to the critical section, actions other than $enter(i)$ can only be taken a finite number of times, before $enter(i)$ is taken.

$$[true^*] \forall_{i : \mathbb{N}} (i < N \implies$$
$$[set\_flag(init\_node_N(i), init\_side(i), true)] (\mu X . \overline{[enter(i)]} X \wedge \langle true \rangle true))$$

Bounded Overtaking. When process i requests access to the critical section, other processes enter the critical section at most B times before process i enters.

$$[true^*] \forall_{i : \mathbb{N}} (i < N \implies$$
$$[set\_flag(init\_node_N(i), init\_side(i), true)] (\nu Y(n : \mathbb{N} = 0) \cdot (n \leq B) \wedge$$
$$[enter(i)] Y(n) \wedge$$
$$[\exists_{i' : \mathbb{N}} i' \neq i \wedge enter(i')] Y(n + 1)$$

The formula says that for every process i, if it requests access to the critical section, every enter action other than $enter(i)$ increments parameter n of the greatest fixed point. If the condition $n \leq B$ is violated, then the formula is false.

3.5 Verification

We verified Peterson's algorithm for N processes using the mCRL2 toolset [3] for $N \in \{3, 4, 5\}$.

Experiments were run on a system running Ubuntu Server 18.04 LTS with 4 x Intel(R) Xeon(R) Gold 6136 CPU @ 3.00 GHz (96 processors) and 3 TB of RAM. All experiments are restricted to a single processor core, with a timeout of 4 h.

The results are shown in Table 1. For all values of N, mutual exclusion is satisfied. However, starvation freedom (and hence also bounded overtaking) is not satisfied. We explain why this is the case using our running example.

Table 1. Verification results for Peterson's algorithm for N processes.

N	Mutual exclusion		Starvation freedom	
	Time	Result	Time	Result
3	0.34	✓	0.37	Y
4	1.41	✓	0.93	Y
5	139.76	✓	34.74	Y

Example 3. We show the counterexample for $N = 3$ by listing steps executed by each of the processes in Fig. 1. The counterexample shows that process 0 requests access to the critical section ($flag_1[0] := true$), but never enters. Instead, process 2 accesses its critical section infinitely many times, by setting its flag in node 2 immediately after finishing the execution of the algorithm. Until process 0 sets $flag_0[0]$ to $true$, it can always be overtaken by process 2.

$i = 0$	$i = 1$	$i = 2$
$flag_1[0] := true$		
$wait_1 := 0$		
$flag_1[1] = false$		
	$flag_1[1] := true$	
	$wait_1 := 1$	
		$flag_2[0] := true$
		$wait_2 := 0$
		$flag_2[1] = false$
		$flag_0[1] := true$
		$wait_0 := 1$
		$flag_0[0] = false$
		enter CS
		leave CS
		$flag_0[1] := false$
		$flag_2[0] := false$
		/* repeat */

Fig. 1. Counterexample for starvation freedom ($N = 3$)

One could argue this counterexample is unfair. In particular, process 0 continuously wants to set $flag_0[0]$ to *true*, but never gets the chance to do so because process 2 always takes priority. Indeed, if we assume weak fairness, the algorithm is starvation free, but does not satisfy bounded overtaking. However, we also recall that Peterson's algorithm for two processes is starvation free without requiring fairness assumptions. The reason for this is that mutual dependency between the two processes based on their *wait* variables forces progress. This observation inspires our fair algorithm in the next section.

4   Fair N-Process Mutual Exclusion Algorithm

We modify Peterson's algorithm for N processes such that any process that requests access to the critical section is eventually forced into its critical section by all other processes. The main idea is that, each time when a process leaves its critical section, it will wait for another process, t, in a cyclic way.

We first introduce some notation. The sibling of process i ($0 \leq i < N$) is the process j that shares the same initial node in the tournament tree if such process exists, and it is undefined otherwise.

$$sibling_N(i) = \begin{cases} j & \text{if } 0 \leq j < N \text{ s.t. } j \neq i \text{ and } init\_node_N(j) = init\_node_N(i) \\ \bot & \text{if for all } 0 \leq j < N \text{ s.t. } j \neq i, init\_node_N(j) \neq init\_node_N(i) \end{cases}$$

If process i is waiting on process t, it will next wait for process $next_N(t, i)$.

$$next_N(t, i) = \begin{cases} (t+1) \mod N & \text{if } init\_node_N((t+1) \mod N) \neq \\ & init\_node_N(i) \\ next_N((t+1) \mod N, i) & \text{otherwise} \end{cases}$$

The sibling of i is skipped, as it will be forced to progress based on the properties of the two-process Peterson's algorithm executed in the shared initial node.

Algorithm 2: *PetersonFair*(i, n, s, N, t)

Input: i, n, s, N, t: $\mathbb{N}$; $(\dots)$ t is the process on which i waits after it has left the critical section.

13 $\vdots$
14 **if** $n = init\_node_N(t)$ **then**
15 $\quad$ **while** $flag_{init\_node_N(t)}[init\_side(t)]$ **do**
16 $\quad\quad$ | {}
17 $\quad$ **end**
18 $\quad$ *PetersonFair*$(i, init\_node_N(i), init\_side(i), N, next_N(t, i))$
19 **end**

The modifications required to make the algorithm fair are shown in Algorithm 2. An additional parameter t is added to keep track of the process on which the algorithm will wait. The recursive call on line 10 passes this parameter on unchanged. Lines 14–16 are changed such that, upon leaving its critical section, process i blocks waiting for process t as long as process t has set its flag in its initial node in the tournament tree. Once the flag becomes false, process i is allowed to proceed as usual, while waiting for $next_N(t, i)$ after it leaves the critical section the next time. If process t has set its flag, and has not yet entered the critical section, eventually the algorithm will end up in a situation where all processes are waiting for t, and t is forced to progress into its critical section.

4.1   mCRL2 Encoding

The mCRL2 model of the improved algorithm is mostly analogous to the model of Algorithm 1. Parameter t is added. Other than that, only the last conditional in the process needs to be changed. Once process i has set the flag to *false* in its initial node upon leaving the critical section, it blocks until the flag of process t in the corresponding initial node is *false*. We use the same construct for modelling a busy-waiting loop as before.

$PetersonFair(i: \mathbb{N}, n: \mathbb{N}, s: \mathbb{N}, t: \mathbb{N}) =$

$\quad\vdots$

$\quad((n = init\_node_N(i))$
$\quad\quad \rightarrow (set\_flag\_s(n, s, false)\cdot$
$\quad\quad\quad get\_flag\_r(init\_node_N(t), init\_side(t), false)\cdot$
$\quad\quad\quad PetersonFair(n = init\_node_N(i), s = init\_side(i), t = next_N(t)))$
$\quad\quad \diamond set\_flag\_s(n, s, false))$

4.2   Verification

Using the same setup as in Sect. 3.5 we have verified Algorithm 2. The results are shown in Table 2, where 'to' denotes a timeout. We include the results for bounded overtaking, where B is the lowest bound for which the property holds.

Table 2. Verification results for the fair mutual exclusion algorithm for N processes.

N	Mutual exclusion		Starvation freedom		Bounded overtaking		
	Time	Result	Time	Result	Time	Result	B
3	0.82	✓	1.94	✓	2.70	✓	4
4	42.03	✓	164.01	✓	352.82	✓	6
5	to	N/A	to	N/A	to	N/A	12

From Table 2 we can observe that all of the properties are satisfied for all values of N that we verified. Furthermore, the verification time grows rapidly, in fact, much more so than for the original algorithm. This is due to the different combinations of processes on which each process can be waiting. For $N = 5$ verification times out, meaning it already requires over 4 h.

4.3 Analysis

Due to the state space explosion problem, we are unable to verify correctness of the algorithm for arbitrary values of N using model checking. That Peterson's algorithm for N processes satisfies mutual exclusion is well-known. As the guarding mechanism for the critical section remains unaltered in our proposed algorithm, mutual exclusion is preserved. We therefore give a manual proof of an upper bound on the number of times a process can be overtaken. Starvation freedom follows immediately from this.

We first characterize $overtakes_N(j)$, which is the number of times a process j can be overtaken by any other process, once it has requested access to the critical section. The number of times process i can overtake j, denoted $overtake_N(i, j)$, is bounded by the number of different values parameter t of i can have until the value of t becomes j, since at that point process i is blocked until j has left (and thus entered) its critical section. This is specified as follows.

Definition 1. *Let N be the number of processes, and $0 \le i, j < N$. Then*

$$overtakes_N(j) = \sum_{i=0}^{N-1} overtake_N(i, j)$$

$$overtake_N(i, j) = \begin{cases} 0 & \text{if } i = j \\ 2 & \text{if } i = sibling_N(j) \\ |\{next_N(t, i) \mid 0 \le t < N\}| & \text{otherwise} \end{cases}$$

The key observation now is that $overtakes_N(j)$ characterizes the number of times process j can be overtaken in Algorithm 2. This follows from the structure of the algorithm and the definition of $next_N$, and is formalized as follows.

Lemma 1. *Let N be the number of processes. If process j requests access to its critical section, Algorithm 2 guarantees that other processes enter their critical section at most $overtakes_N(j)$ times before process i enters its critical section.*

Now that we have established a link between the algorithm and $overtakes_N$, we can focus on the latter definition to determine the bound on the number of overtakes. Following the case distinction in Definition 1, the exact number of times process i can be overtaken depends on whether i has a sibling, and whether all processes have a sibling. This results in the following property.

Lemma 2. *Let $N > 2$ and $0 \le i < N$. Then*

$$overtakes_N(i) = \begin{cases} 2 + (N-2)^2 & \text{if } sibling_N(i) \ne \bot \text{ and } N \text{ is even} \\ 3 + (N-2)^2 & \text{if } sibling_N(i) \ne \bot \text{ and } N \text{ is odd} \\ (N-1)(N-2) & \text{otherwise (i.e. } sibling_N(i) = \bot) \end{cases}$$

Observe that for all i, $overtakes_N(0) \ge overtakes_N(i)$ if $N = 3$, and otherwise $overtakes_N(N-1) \ge overtakes_N(i)$. Hence, to determine the bound for a given N, we either need to consider the number of times process 0 or process $N-1$ gets overtaken. From this and Lemmas 1 and 2 we get the following bound.

Theorem 1. *Let $N \ge 4$ be the number of processes. If a process requests access to its critical section, then other processes enter their critical section at most $(N-1)(N-2)$ times before this process enters its critical section.*

So, Algorithm 2 satisfies bounded overtaking. Using Lemma 2, in case $N = 3$, the bound is 4.

5   Conclusion

We studied the generalization of Peterson's algorithm to N processes using a tournament tree. Using the mCRL2 language and toolset we showed that the algorithm is not starvation free if no additional fairness assumptions are imposed. We propose a fair mutual exclusion algorithm for N processes. Using the mCRL2 model checker we verified that for small N the algorithm is starvation free, and, in fact, satisfies bounded overtaking. For the general case, when $N \ge 4$, we additionally present a proof that the bound is $(N-1)(N-2)$.

Acknowledgements. This work was supported partially by the MACHINAIDE project (ITEA3, No. 18030).

References

1. Alagarsamy, K.: A mutual exclusion algorithm with optimally bounded bypasses. Inf. Process. Lett. **96**(1), 36–40 (2005). https://doi.org/10.1016/j.ipl.2005.05.015
2. Bouwman, M., Luttik, B., Willemse, T.A.C.: Off-the-shelf automated analysis of liveness properties for just paths. Acta Inform. **57**(3), 551–590 (2020). https://doi.org/10.1007/s00236-020-00371-w
3. Bunte, O., et al.: The mCRL2 toolset for analysing concurrent systems. In: Vojnar, T., Zhang, L. (eds.) TACAS 2019. LNCS, vol. 11428, pp. 21–39. Springer, Cham (2019). https://doi.org/10.1007/978-3-030-17465-1_2

4. Cicirelli, F., Nigro, L., Sciammarella, P.F.: Model checking mutual exclusion algorithms using UPPAAL. In: Silhavy, R., Senkerik, R., Oplatkova, Z.K., Silhavy, P., Prokopova, Z. (eds.) Software Engineering Perspectives and Application in Intelligent Systems. AISC, vol. 465, pp. 203–215. Springer, Cham (2016). https://doi.org/10.1007/978-3-319-33622-0_19

5. Dijkstra, E.W.: Solution of a problem in concurrent programming control. Commun. ACM **8**(9), 569 (1965). https://doi.org/10.1145/365559.365617

6. Dijkstra, E.W.: Over de sequentialiteit van procesbeschrijvingen. Technical report. EWD-35 (Undated, 1962 or 1963)

7. Doran, R., Thomas, L.: Variants of the software solution to mutual exclusion. Inf. Process. Lett. **10**(4), 206–208 (1980). https://doi.org/10.1016/0020-0190(80)90141-6

8. Dyseryn, V., van Glabbeek, R., Höfner, P.: Analysing mutual exclusion using process algebra with signals. EPTCS **255**, 18–34 (2017). https://doi.org/10.4204/EPTCS.255.2

9. Fokkink, W.: Distributed Algorithms: An Intuitive Approach. The MIT Press, Cambridge (2013)

10. Groote, J.F., Willemse, T.A.C.: Model-checking processes with data. SCICO **56**(3), 251–273 (2005). https://doi.org/10.1016/j.scico.2004.08.002

11. Groote, J.F., Keiren, J.J.A.: Tutorial: designing distributed software in mCRL2. In: Peters, K., Willemse, T.A.C. (eds.) FORTE 2021. LNCS, vol. 12719, pp. 226–243. Springer, Cham (2021). https://doi.org/10.1007/978-3-030-78089-0_15

12. Groote, J.F., Mousavi, M.R.: Modeling and Analysis of Communicating Systems. The MIT Press, Cambridge (2014)

13. Hafidi, Y., Keiren, J.J.A., Groote, J.F.: Fair mutual exclusion for n processes (extended version) (2021). https://doi.org/10.48550/arXiv.2111.02251

14. Hennessy, M., Milner, R.: Algebraic laws for nondeterminism and concurrency. J. ACM **32**(1), 137–161 (1985). https://doi.org/10.1145/2455.2460

15. Hesselink, W.H.: Tournaments for mutual exclusion: verification and concurrent complexity. FAOC **29**(5), 833–852 (2017). https://doi.org/10.1007/s00165-016-0407-x

16. Holt, R.C., Graham, G.S. Lazowska, E.D., Scott, M.A.: Structured Concurrent Programming with Operating Systems Applications, vol. 2937. Addison-Wesley (1978)

17. Ji, X., Song, L.: Mutual exclusion verification of Peterson's solution in Isabelle/HOL. In: TSA 2016, pp. 81–86 (2016). https://doi.org/10.1109/TSA.2016.22

18. Long, S.G., Yang, H.W.: Modelling Peterson mutual exclusion algorithm in DVE language and verifying LTL properties. In: AMM, vol. 577, pp. 1012–1016 (2014). https://doi.org/10.4028/www.scientific.net/amm.577.1012

19. Mateescu, R., Serwe, W.: Model checking and performance evaluation with CADP illustrated on shared-memory mutual exclusion protocols. SCICO **78**(7), 843–861 (2013). https://doi.org/10.1016/j.scico.2012.01.003

20. Peterson, G.L.: Myths about the mutual exclusion problem. Inf. Process. Lett. **12**(3), 115–116 (1981). https://doi.org/10.1016/0020-0190(81)90106-X

21. Peterson, G.L., Fischer, M.J.: Economical solutions for the critical section problem in a distributed system (extended abstract). In: STOC 2077, pp. 91–97. ACM (1977). https://doi.org/10.1145/800105.803398

22. Raynal, M.: Concurrent Programming: Algorithms, Principles, and Foundations. Springer, Heidelberg (2013). https://doi.org/10.1007/978-3-642-32027-9

Data Stream Processing in Reconciliation Testing: Industrial Experience

Iosif Itkin[1] ![ORCID], Elena Treshcheva[2]([envelope]) ![ORCID], Alexey Yermolayev[1],
Nikolay Dorofeev[1], and Stanislav Glushkov[1]

[1] Exactpro Systems Limited, London, UK
{iosif.itkin,alexey.yermolayev,nikolay.dorofeev,
stanislav.glushkov}@exactpro.com
[2] Exactpro Systems LLC, Cincinnati, USA
elena.treshcheva@exactpro.com

Abstract. The paper focuses on a research area encompassing tools and methods of reconciliation testing, an approach to software testing that relies on the data reconciliation concept. The importance of such a test approach is steadily increasing across different knowledge domains, triggered by growing data volumes and overall complexity of present-day software systems. The paper describes a software implementation created as part of the authors' industrial experience in data stream processing for the task of reconciliation testing of complex financial technology systems. The described solution is a Python-based component of an open-source test automation framework built as a Kubernetes-based microservices platform. The paper outlines the advantages and disadvantages of the approach as well as compares it to existing state-of-the-art solutions for data stream analysis and reconciliation.

Keywords: software testing · test automation · data reconciliation · data stream processing · dynamic verification · th2 test automation framework

1 Introduction

Across different knowledge domains relying on information technology, data reconciliation remains an important task. The problem of matching records associated with the same entity but represented in different datasets is typical for systems dealing with data flows between multiple components of a complex platform or between different systems connected to each other. The focus of the data reconciliation task is accuracy and consistency of information received from different channels or via different protocols. In financial technology, data reconciliation is crucial for market data dissemination, electronic trading, clearing and settlement, asset management, and other areas of financial technology that involve matching data across different sources [1].

With processing power rapidly increasing over the past years, the data volumes being processed by modern technology platforms are also growing at a fast

R. Yavorskiy et al. (Eds.): TMPA 2021, CCIS 1559, pp. 161–174, 2024.
https://doi.org/10.1007/978-3-031-50423-5_15

pace. At the same time, the high availability requirement for mission-critical systems triggers the demand in highly accurate and high-performance monitoring. Both trends create new challenges for existing data reconciliation approaches, requiring new data reconciliation tools with higher throughput and real-time processing capabilities.

In this context, data reconciliation for complex financial systems generating massive data arrays is no longer a simple field-matching task. An effective data reconciliation approach needs to not only satisfy the data accuracy requirement, but also be fit for the task of the rule-based processing of large volumes of real-time data. This industrial need can be addressed by the stream processing paradigm that shifted the task from querying stationary data towards dynamic queries against real-time data [2].

The capability of real-time data processing is a crucial functionality for a test automation solution, especially for one targeted at reconciliation testing for complex transactional systems lying in the core of global capital markets. In this paper, we detail and reflect on the industrial experience of implementation of such a functionality through development of *check2recon*, a real-time data reconciliation module of an open-source microservices-based test automation suite called th2 [3].

The paper is organized as follows. Section 2 provides an overview of published research related to the problem of real-time data processing and reconciliation testing as well as outlines the business context and testing tools developed as precursors of the described solution. Section 3 explains the tool's architecture, main capabilities, and role in the automated testing workflow within the th2 framework. Section 4 compares the *check2recon* solution to alternative state-of-the-art instruments and contains the lessons learned as a result of *check2recon*'s application to the real-world data reconciliation tasks. Section 5 concludes the paper.

2 Related Work

2.1 Data Reconciliation

Research papers cite the task of data reconciliation as very important across multiple knowledge domains, with known applications spanning from finance [1] to chemical engineering [4], from telecommunications [5,6] to social networks [7]. With the general goal of the task being rule-based processing and matching of database records, its most common application areas are finding duplicates or errors in data, entity identification, data accuracy/consistency checks.

As far as we can judge based on analysis of research literature, the approaches to data reconciliation vary depending on the following parameters:

– data model,
– data format,
– matching type,
– matching procedure.

Data Model: First of all, the approaches differ depending on whether reconciliation checks are performed against persistent or continuously changing (modified or appended) data: a stored data set is appropriate for the case of same queries being performed repeatedly against rarely updated data, whereas the tasks involving significant and constant - often, real-time - changes of data are most likely supported by the data stream model, e.g. [8,9].

Data Format: As per [9], the items in a database can be represented as "tuples, either typed or untyped; records, organized as sets of key-value pairs; objects, as in object-oriented languages or databases; or XML documents". By its essence, the data can vary from e.g. string or numeric values to graph representations consisting of nodes and links (relations).

Matching Type: Data reconciliation task is typically a matching one, to a certain extent. Scholars distinguish several algorithms used to identify similar data in two or more different sources. The most straightforward method is exact matching, also called a 'basic field matching algorithm' [10], that is looking for exact (full or partial) matches. This approach is typical for the tasks of data consistency/accuracy checks or finding duplicates. Another matching approach allows for more variation and is based on recursive field matching [10], using the recursive structure of the fields and represented by several matching patterns between data strings and substrings. Yet another approach, the one allowing for similarity of data rather than exact match, is approximate matching [10]. This method relies on mathematical approximations and can be implemented through machine learning techniques. The examples of this matching method being applied are tasks around identifying measurement errors, alignment between related protein or DNA sequences, or various tasks of matching unstructured or multi-parameter data (e.g. social network reconciliation or user de-anonymization) [6,7,10].

Matching Procedure: There are two types of queries/requests used for data processing: SQL-like vs. programmatic [11,12]. SQL-like queries are the most known type, used in traditional relational databases. In case of a static database, it is an ordinary, a.k.a. one-time, SQL query. If the database is a dynamic one, it is to be approached with Streaming SQL query [9,13]. In contrast to SQL-like queries, programmatic ones are implemented using custom APIs with requests being run against custom data stores/structures. Programmatic approach is applicable for both static and dynamic data models. Some sources also mention the term of continuous queries [8,14–16], representing fixed queries run repeatedly against continuously updated data flows, i.e. against both old and new data. A special case of dynamic queries is streaming queries, when both data and queries have continuous nature and the matching procedure suggests their reconciliation against each other [14].

To perform efficient data reconciliation in the financial services industry, where data plays an increasingly important role, it is crucial to have a tool allowing for most challenging combinations of the above data characteristics: the ideal instrument should be fit for the task of processing constantly updated large volumes of multi-format financial information, and be able to perform matching procedures based on complex rules. Over the past several years, these challenges have been being solved by a relatively new field of stream processing.

2.2 Stream Processing

The need of real-time processing of continuously flowing data stimulated the shift from traditional data base management systems towards a new generation of tools, collectively referred to as 'information flow processing' systems [9], i.e. the systems specifically built as tools aimed at dynamic information processing as opposed to querying against persistent data.

The data stream concept is defined, for example, in [17]: "A data stream is a real-time, continuous, ordered (explicitly by timestamp or implicitly by arrival time) sequence of items". Data stream processing relies on the concept of continuous queries against data flows, which in its turn relies on the windowing concept. Types of windows are covered in [11–13,18,19].

There are lots of instruments available, both proprietary and open-source, for working with streaming data, which is by no means a very important enhancement for complex high-load software systems of the present day. An overview of these tools allows to distinguish two types of them: the tools aimed at stream data integration and the tools for stream analytics [11,12].

Stream data integration technologies allow us to connect stream producers and stream consumers according to our needs. Apache Kafka [20,21] should be named as one of the most common stream data integration software, with production applications across many companies and diverse industrial sectors. The tool proposes a number of APIs (including the core ones: Admin API, Producer API, Consumer API, Kafka Streams API, and Kafka Connect API) to control streams [22]. Other examples of stream data integration solutions include, for example, Flume [23], Kinesis [24], and some other instruments (see more examples in [19]).

If the stream data integration tools are used to manage the data flows, the stream analytics solutions are developed to process these data applying certain user-defined algorithms. Again, this field is also quite diverse in terms of available instruments.

For example, Apache Kafka can provide certain processing functionality supported by the Streams API, but it is quite lightweight and is limited to raw input data consumption from Kafka topics and its subsequent aggregation, enrichment, or other transformation into new topics for further consumption or follow-up processing [22].

Apache Flink provides data stream analytics via the DataStream API [25], the tool also has a capability of comparing events from different streams by key. Apart from being able to analyse and process real-time streaming data, Apache Flink is also capable of processing finite data sets (i.e. batch processing) using the DataSet API [26].

Yet another solution, Apache Spark [27], also supports real-time streaming data analytics through joining two streams by key, and is capable of working in batch mode as well as through interactive queries [28].

Esper by EsperTech can provide both data stream integration and stream analytics functionality with the stream joining capability [29].

Most recent advances in the area of data stream processing are reflected in [19]. The paper concentrates on events processing and provides an overview of the research in the area as well as of the industrial solutions aimed at the task. Also, the authors propose a classification of these systems based on their key functionalities (e.g. query language, supported query types, window types, etc.) as well as non-functional characteristics, such as scalability and performance.

A number of proprietary tools are described by G. Cugola and A. Margara, who propose a classification of stream processing solutions, capturing the variety of their "system architecture, data model, rule model, and rule language" [9].

Thus, different aspects of rule-based analysis and reconciliation of real-time or near-real-time data flows appear to be quite heavily researched and implemented in the present-day tools. All of them create a very diverse external industrial context for our streaming data reconciliation task. However, this context cannot be considered fully outlined without taking into account the preceding experience with the company's internal software implementations related to the task.

2.3   Business Context of the Solution

The development of *check2recon* builds upon the team's experience of development of test automation tools targeted at solving similar problems. In this section, we will provide an overview of the solution's precursors tackling the tasks of data streaming, data analysis and reconciliation as part of the testing approaches used in multiple client projects over the years. The industrial domain covered by this experience is functional and non-functional testing of trading platforms used in major stock exchanges.

Over the years the company built several tools addressing one or several aspects of the stream processing and data reconciliation task. In particular, this paper gives an overview of the TVR, Shsha, Minirobots, NFA Analyzer, and MD Analyzer (a.k.a. Bookchecker) test harnesses.

TVR. TVR is the company's historic proprietary implementation of the reconciliation testing approach. Functionally, it appears to be the closest one to the idea of the *check2recon* solution, which is the subject of this research paper. The tool's name - TVR - is an abbreviation standing for *Trade VeRification*. TVR is a passive post-transactional testing tool which allows to verify results obtained during both functional and non-functional testing of trading systems. Its main purpose is performing the checks around trading logic rules and the consistency of message flows, without actively interfering with the system under test.

The *data model* behind this reconciliation tool is persistent one: the checks are performed against static arrays of previously captured test execution data.

The tool works with various *data formats* as it deals with message flows via diverse protocols and APIs. The *matching type* behind TVR is exact and recursive field matching, and, as for the tool's underlying *matching procedure*, it uses programmatic queries and requests.

This tool reconciles all available order entry flows against each other and against reference data. Functional tests created with TVR cover wide range of testing scenarios allowing for the diversity of parameters and their combinations to be matched during the reconciliation checks (financial instruments structure, trade order details, redundant or absent messages, order life cycle events). Non-functional tests can cover quite tricky random matching scenarios, verifying system's performance and failover capabilities along with correctness and consistency of its behavior during these tests.

Shsha. Shsha is a post-transactional passive testing tool [30] which allows for testing backend of trading platforms, market data, post-trade, and market surveillance systems without interacting with them. Shsha is also used for compliance-related tasks, providing evidence for audit and regulatory reporting, as well as for client on-boarding and certification. For these tasks, it leverages built-in groups of SQL-based scenarios covering regulatory or client connectivity requirements issued by supervisory bodies and exchanges, correspondingly [31].

Data reconciliation process supported by the Shsha tool relies on the persistent *data model*, it works with database objects *data format* supporting various industry-standard and proprietary protocols, uses exact and recursive field *matching types* and SQL queries in the core of its *matching procedure*.

From the functional point of view, the tool is capable of reading the wire and log files and extracting data from them. It parses captured message flows, storing each message as a database table entry where each column corresponds to a particular message field. After the messages are parsed and saved as database objects, Shsha runs checks against them to find data discrepancies and identify system behaviour patterns. The tool has a user-friendly GUI allowing to display logs and create summarized reports.

Minirobots. The Minirobots testing tool is aimed at finding defects lying at the confluence of functional and non-functional testing [32]. At the core of its functionality there is an idea of simulation of trading behaviour similar to that one of real traders on the electronic trading venue. By reproducing certain trading algorithms, the tool allows for testing the behaviour of both trading platforms and market participants. Depending on testing needs, each of the robots can act independently or jointly executing a particular trading strategy or simply replaying a stored list of orders [33].

Each of the Minirobots components is developed as a simulator of trading activity according to a particular trading strategy, so it is crucial for it to be able to assess current market conditions and react in line with its algorithm and in a timely manner - hence, it is the only one out of the company's internal solutions that is aimed at real-time data processing, i.e. the *data model* behind this tool suggests working with continuously changing data. The tool is not aimed at data reconciliation, so the notions of *data format*, *matching type* and *matching procedure* are not applicable to Minirobots as part of data matching process overview.

From the stream processing perspective, there are a number of characteristics contributing to Minirobots being an interesting example in the context of real-time data stream analytics. First of all, the tool is relatively fast - capable of processing lots of data and sending hundreds and thousands of messages (depending on the algorithm complexity) with a millisecond precision. Another important point is the tool's multi-threading capability: Minirobots support many trading flows, including market data, through multiple simultaneous heterogeneous connections supporting various industry-standard and proprietary protocols. The tool is capable of concurrent emulation of multiple participants as well as real-time adaptation of its trading strategy outlined in the algorithms.

NFA Analyzer. NFA Analyzer is the company's proprietary testing tool developed specifically for the regulatory reporting use case involving data reconciliation according to the XML schema definitions issued by the National Futures Association (NFA). The tool processes previously captured API flows of order entries and market data and, based on that data, generates an XML file with an NFA report. The parameters and values in this report are then reconciled against the data in the corresponding XML file generated by the system under test.

NFA Analyzer is a passive post-transactional tool, thus, its *data model* is static/persistent. The tool supports various industry-standard and proprietary protocols, meaning that it is quite versatile in terms of *data format*. Similarly to TVR, the *matching type* of NFA Analyzer allows for exact and recursive field matching, and its *matching procedure* is based on programmatic queries that are quite flexible in their configuration (can contain conditional operators, variables, loops, etc.).

MD Analyzer/Bookchecker. MD (stands for "market data") Analyzer, also known as Bookchecker, is a tool for building instrument books (according to the logic of order book construction in a ticker plant system) based on market data and then reconciling them with the data flow from the ticker plant system under test according to programmed rules [34].

The tool receives data flows sent from exchanges via a UDP-based quote dissemination protocol, consuming them through MListener program that allows for recovery in the case of lost packet data. A special agglutination component is used to merge real-time data flow with the restored market information ensuring real-time data completeness and consistency. Thus, the Bookchecker tool operates through a continuous *data model* consuming both real-time and near real-time recovered data. As for the tool's *data format*, it works with JSON files, providing the advantages of lightness/compactness, higher processing speed, human readability, flexibility and cross-platform applicability. The tool uses exact *matching type* and is based on programmatic queries as a *matching procedure.*

Each of the tools described in this subsection addresses a software testing task within a specific use case - hence the variability in the approaches to data processing and/or reconciliation.

Some of the tools (Minirobots, Bookchecker) support dynamic processing of continuous data streams, most of them perform data reconciliation either with SQL (Shsha) or programmatic (TVR, NFA Analyzer, Bookchecker) queries. While specific features of the tools are just enough to perform testing within a certain business area, they have limitations that do not allow for their application to other software testing tasks.

Since reconciliation per se is one of the typical software testing tasks, it is important that a test automation solution be able to address it ubiquitously for different use cases and technology environments.

Thus, it would be methodologically feasible to design a test automation solution in such a way that the data reconciliation functionality is implemented as a component capable of working with both static and dynamic data, omnivorous in relation to data formats and types, and flexible in terms of customization of data consumption time frames and validation rules. To avoid any potential test artifacts affecting the system under test, the reconciliation module is seen as a passive testing tool - capturing and analyzing data flow from the system under test without sending anything back. Needless to say, the performance requirements for such a component should correspond to those of a present-day technology platforms to be tested. Conceptually, the requirements for such a passive testing approach implementation are very similar to the characteristics and functionality of market surveillance systems [35].

3   Data Reconciliation Module *check2recon*

check2recon is one of the components, or 'boxes' of th2, a Kubernetes-based framework for functional and nonfunctional testing of complex distributed transactional systems, especially those used by financial market infrastructures. This module is implemented as a Kubernetes pod and is supported by a set of comparison rules.

The purpose of *check2recon* is to compare several event streams, implementing the original idea of the comparison of actual messages against expected ones in order to detect discrepancies and explore their reasons. In addition to direct comparison, *check2recon* can mark-up the messages with notes signalling about potential problems.

Before use, *check2recon* should be configured to adapt to the user's purposes. For this, a custom configuration should be defined for the Kubernetes pod: the configuration parameters include a maximum number of stored events, cache size, events sending interval. Also, in the same configuration file, it is possible to define the name of the box to be displayed in the th2 report, a GUI for tracking the th2 events.

For each *check2recon* box, several checking rules can be defined along with timeout values and unique names for each rule. The name of the rule serves as an identifier in GUI. Timeout is the time interval between receiving and deleting the message captured from the RabbitMQ message broker: for reconciliation testing, it is important to have this possibility to compare messages received with a sufficient offset.

The rules that govern the reconciliation logic are implemented through separate files containing the definition of the 'Rule' class. The working principle behind this class is as follows:

– For each rule, there are the 'get' functions - the 'getters' - associated with the rule name, description and other attributes to displayed in the GUI.
– Message groups to compare are described in a corresponding special getter, allowing you to define a group name and type. Group types are available as part of the *check2recon* package. At the moment, there are two group types:
  1. the type 'Single' is assigned to define a certain group as allowing messages in this group to have unique hashes (i.e. keys) only - in case of an incoming message with an existing hash, the new message replaces the old one that is already in this group;
  2. the type 'Multiple' means that the corresponding message group can store several messages with the same hash (Fig. 1).

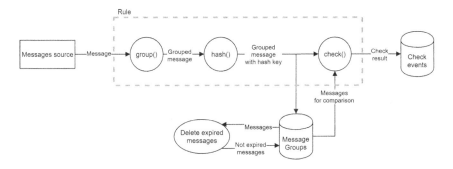

Fig. 1. Data flow diagram of the *check2recon* component

– The 'Group', 'Hash', and 'Check' methods in the 'Rule' class are responsible for messages processing, which is performed sequentially from 'Group' to 'Hash' to 'Check' for each and every incoming message.
  • The 'Group' method analyses message using an algorithm written by the user and sets the message group ID, which will subsequently used for allocating the message to an appropriate group.
  • The 'Hash' method generates the hash key for the message to be processed by the JOIN query. The hash key is similar to a composite key in relational databases and depends on one or several fields of the message. The fields dependant on the hash key are defined by the user in the

method implementation. If values in all these fields are the same for any two messages, the final hash keys of such messages will also be equal.

- The 'Check' method is used to compare a given message with all messages from different groups having the same hash key. By its nature, the underlying programmatic query is not very different from SQL-like JOINs: if we expanded the scope of the 'Check' method to include many messages instead of just one, comparing two groups would be similar to performing the JOIN operation of two tables on their equal hash keys (Fig. 2).

– After the comparison, the 'Check' method generates an event with the reconciliation result, depending on the logic defined by the rule written by the user. After that the original message is available for comparison with upcoming messages until its pre-defined timeout (i.e. during the message's "lifespan", as per the terminology in [9]).

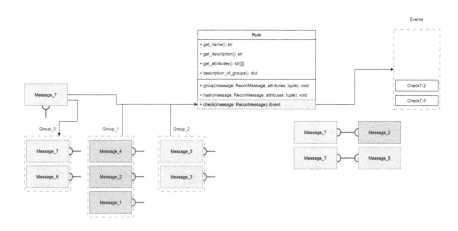

Fig. 2. The 'Check' method of the *check2recon* module

4   Discussion and Lessons Learned

Our industrial experience illustrates an attempt to incorporate a data reconciliation module into a complex microservices-based architecture of a bigger test automation framework.

Reflecting on the results of the implementation, the place of this approach among existing solutions can be described using the framework proposed above in the Subsect. 2.1.

The *check2recon* module supports both persistent and streaming *data models*. It was developed to make the streaming analysis and does it successfully. At the same time, the th2 framework can be configured to read the stored system's flows. This means that check2recon can be considered both as a passive testing tool and a data stream analysis module. At the same time, for the better fault tolerance it would be great to use hybrid approach. When the message flow is too big to be processed in streaming mode, the tool could start storing the unprocessed messages above the queue and continue analysis with a minor delay. Further, when the message flow becomes weaker and the queue is completely processed, it could get back to real-time streaming analysis again. Currently, this feature, planned along with a seamless switch between the two modes, is under development.

The tool allows for the *data format* to be highly customizable: strategically oriented on data-driven capabilities, th2 is designed to store and process the data in a unified format, even if original protocols of data flows are different.

The *matching type* used in the module for data reconciliation is completely configurable by rules. We could configure to work few rules simultaneously.

As for the *matching procedure*, we followed the programmatic approach developing a custom API for advanced processing based on user-defined logic. At the same time, the approach also demonstrates a certain similarity to SQL-like query structures: for example, to reconcile values in discrete parts of messages, hash is used as a composite key for message identification and search.

Commenting on the implementation of the module, the choice of Python as a programming language underpinning the solution has both advantages and drawbacks. On a plus side, the implementation benefits from simplicity and flexibility, it is also easy to use due to Python's popularity and relatively low entry threshold, which is an important detail from the perspective of a user. The disadvantages of the implementation include the limitation of using it in a single-threaded mode only and relatively low performance.

This module was developed as a proof of concept for streaming analysis via th2. To a certain extent, this experiment proved to be a success, providing the team with advanced rule-based reconciliation capabilities suitable for working with continuous message flows. The solution has been successfully implemented in real client projects and satisfies current software testing needs. At the same time, *matching procedure* can barely be considered a viable solution in the perspective. Comparison of the tool with most present-day applications for data stream analysis shows that it is not the most efficient implementation of the reconciliation testing approach. In particular, one of the closest alternatives could be the Apache Flink solution, which provides the data analytics capability via its DataStreamAPI (also, a custom one). Apache Flink is made for Java and Scala, it also supports PyFlink (Python API for Apache Flink). Moreover, according to its non-functional characteristics (e.g. provided in [19]), it should be faster and more productive.

5   Conclusion

The paper presents an industrial experience around an implementation of the data reconciliation approach applied to streaming data flows generated by high-performance technology platforms within major-scale financial market infrastructures. This experience is described in the context of the state-of-the-art tools and approaches developed within the conceptual area of data stream processing. An additional context is provided in the form of internally developed precursors of the described solution.

Reflecting upon this industrial example, the following insights are worth highlighting.

First, the idea of such a component contributes to the development of the software testing professional domain. It is important to incorporate such generalized solution for finding discrepancies in data flows into any testing approach. Its implementation as a microservice component of a bigger test automation framework illustrates the idea of creating a reconciliation testing component that is positioned as a centralized checking mechanism, connected to other components and intercommunicating with them. Additionally, the solution helps to emphasize the importance of an approach allowing for near-realtime monitoring for potential problems without a significant delay that is typical for post-transactional passive testing tools.

Second, as the described test automation framework is an open-source solution, it is important to share every single component's implementation results with a community of developers and testers. The contribution here is provided by outlining the lessons learnt and conclusions made from the comparison of this custom-made component against existing tools.

Finally, the description of the experience contributes to obtaining a clearer vision on the task, helping to create a roadmap for the future improvements of the data reconciliation component within a bigger software testing framework.

References

1. Kriger, A.-M., Pochukalina, A., Isaev, V.: Reconciliation testing aspects of trading systems software failures. In: Preliminary Proceedings of the 8th SpringSummer Young Researchers' Colloquium on Software Engineering (SYRCoSE 2014) (2014)
2. Basak, A., Venkataraman, K., Murphy, R., Singh, M.: Stream Analytics with Microsoft Azure: Real-Time Data Processing for Quick Insights Using Azure Stream Analytics. Packt Publishing Ltd. (2017)
3. Exactpro Systems Limited. th2. Licensed under Apache-2.0 License (2021). https://github.com/th2-net
4. Crowe, C.: Data reconciliation-progress and challenges. J. Process Control **6**, 89–98 (1996)
5. Caruso, F., Cochinwala, M., Ganapathy, U., Lalk, G., Missier, P.: Telcordia's database reconciliation and data quality analysis tool. In: VLDB, pp. 615–618 (2000)
6. Cochinwala, M., Kurien, V., Lalk, G., Shasha, D.: Efficient data reconciliation. Inf. Sci. **137**(1–4), 1–15 (2001)
7. Korula, N., Lattanzi, S.: An efficient reconciliation algorithm for social networks. Proc. VLDB Endow. **7**(5), 377–388 (2014)
8. Babu, S., Widom, J.: Continuous queries over data streams. ACM SIGMOD Rec. **30**(3), 109–120 (2001)
9. Cugola, G., Margara, A.: Processing flows of information: from data stream to complex event processing. ACM Comput. Surv. **44**(3) (2012). https://doi.org/10.1145/2187671.2187677

10. Monge, A.E., Elkan, C., et al.: The field matching problem: algorithms and applications. In: KDD, vol. 2, pp. 267–270 (1996)
11. JeeConf. Stream Processing - Concepts and Frameworks (Guido Schmutz, Switzerland) (2019). https://youtu.be/vFshGQ2ndeg
12. Schmutz, G.: Stream Processing - Concepts and Frameworks (2019). https://www.slideshare.net/gschmutz/stream-processing-concepts-and-frameworks-142484653
13. Babcock, B., Babu, S., Datar, M., Motwani, R., Widom, J.: Models and issues in data stream systems. In: Proceedings of the Twenty-First ACM SIGMOD-SIGACT-SIGART Symposium on Principles of Database Systems, pp. 1–16 (2002)
14. Chandrasekaran, S., Franklin, M.J.: PSoup: a system for streaming queries over streaming data. VLDB J. Int. J. Very Large Data Bases **12**(2), 140–156 (2003)
15. Wei, Y., Son, S.H., Stankovic, J.A.: RTSTREAM: real-time query processing for data streams. In: Ninth IEEE International Symposium on Object and Component-Oriented Real-Time Distributed Computing (ISORC 2006), pp. 10–pp. IEEE (2006)
16. Law, Y.-N., Wang, H., Zaniolo, C.: Relational languages and data models for continuous queries on sequences and data streams. ACM Trans. Database Syst. (TODS) **36**(2), 1–32 (2011)
17. Golab, L., Özsu, M.T.: Processing sliding window multi-joins in continuous queries over data streams. In: Proceedings VLDB Conference, pp. 500–511. Elsevier (2003)
18. Patroumpas, K., Sellis, T.: Window specification over data streams. In: Grust, T., et al. (eds.) EDBT 2006. LNCS, vol. 4254, pp. 445–464. Springer, Heidelberg (2006). https://doi.org/10.1007/11896548_35
19. Dayarathna, M., Perera, S.: Recent advancements in event processing. ACM Comput. Surv. (CSUR) **51**(2), 1–36 (2018)
20. Apache Software Foundation. Apache Kafka. Licensed under Apache-2.0 License (2017). https://kafka.apache.org/
21. Kreps, J., Narkhede, N., Rao, J., et al.: Kafka: a distributed messaging system for log processing. In: Proceedings of the NetDB, vol. 11, pp. 1–7 (2011)
22. Apache Software Foundation. Apache Kafka Documentation (2017). https://kafka.apache.org/documentation/
23. Apache Software Foundation. Welcome to Apache Flume - Apache Flume. https://flume.apache.org/
24. Apache Software Foundation. AWS 2 Kinesis: Apache Camel. https://camel.apache.org/components/3.7.x/aws2-kinesis-component.html
25. Apache Software Foundation. Apache Flink: Stateful Computations over Data Streams. https://flink.apache.org/
26. Carbone, P., Katsifodimos, A., Ewen, S., Markl, V., Haridi, S., Tzoumas, K.: Apache flink: stream and batch processing in a single engine. Bull. IEEE Comput. Soc. Tech. Committee Data Eng. **36**(4) (2015)
27. Apache Software Foundation. Spark Streaming - Spark 3.1.2 Documentation. https://spark.apache.org/docs/latest/streaming-programming-guide.html
28. Zaharia, M., et al.: Apache spark: a unified engine for big data processing. Commun. ACM **59**(11) (2016)
29. EsperTech Inc., Esper - EsperTech. https://www.espertech.com/esper/
30. Shsha - Client Onboarding and Test Coverage Verification Tool. https://exactpro.com/test-tools/shsha
31. Alekseenko, A.N., Averina, A.A., Sharov, D.S., Protsenko, P.A., Itkin, I.L.: Usage of passive testing tools for certification of trading systems clients. Sistemy i Sredstva Informatiki [Syst. Means Inform.] **24**(2), 83–98 (2014)

32. Minirobots - Realistic Market Agents Simulation for Testing Purposes. https://exactpro.com/test-tools/minirobots

33. Sukhov, A., Ushakov, E., Leonchik, V., Itkin, I., Lukina, A.: Reference test harness for algorithmic trading platforms. Univ. Sci. J. S. Petersburg Univ. Consortium **19**, 69–82 (2016)

34. Bulda, A., Orlova, M.: Dynamic verification of input and output data streams for market data aggregation and quote dissemination systems (Ticker Plant). In: Proceedings of the International Research Conference Tools and Methods of Program Analysis (TMPA) (2015)

35. Matveeva, A., Antonov, N., Itkin, I.: Characteristics of testing tools that can be leveraged in the industrial operation of trading systems [Osobennosti instrumentov dlya testirovaniya, primenimykh pri promyshlennoy ekspluatatsii treydingovykh sistem]. In: Tools & Methods of Program Analysis TMPA-2013, pp. 189–200 (2013). (in Russian)

Short Papers

Detection of Flying Objects Using the YOLOv4 Convolutional Neural Network

Semen Tkachev$^{(\boxtimes)}$ ⓘ and Nikolay Markov ⓘ

School of Computer Science and Robotics, Tomsk Polytechnic University, 30, Lenin Avenue, Tomsk 634050, Russia
{sat12,markovng}@tpu.ru

Abstract. The efficiency of the YOLOv4 convolutional neural network (CNN) in detection of objects moving in airspace is investigated. Video materials of two classes of flying objects (FO) were used as the initial data for training and testing of the CNN: helicopter-type unmanned aerial vehicles and gliders. Video materials were obtained in the optical and infrared (IR) wavelength ranges. Datasets are formed from them in the form of a set of images. Large-scale studies of the detection efficiency of the YOLOv4 CNN on such images have been conducted. It is shown that the accuracy of detection of FO in optical images is higher than in images obtained in the IR wavelength range.

Keywords: YOLOv4 convolutional neural network · researching of the efficiency of detection of flying objects · helicopter-type unmanned aerial vehicles · gliders

1 Introduction

The most important task in airspace control is the task of localization and classification of FO: various manned and unmanned aerial vehicles, birds, etc. For this, appropriate systems for analysis of data obtained in the optical, IR and other wavelength ranges are being created [1]. The radar systems of detection of FO are the most widely used. However, in recent years, images of FO obtained in the optical and IR wavelength ranges have been increasingly analyzed. In order to detect FO in such images, computer vision systems based on modern CNN are being created [2].

The article examines the efficiency of the YOLOv4 CNN in detection of two classes of FO in images. Such FO are recognized both in optical images and in images obtained in the IR wavelength range.

2 Architecture of the YOLOv4 CNN

There are two types of CNN architectures for object detection in images: one-stage and two-stage detectors (Fig. 1). One-stage detectors are capable to detect objects without using a preliminary stage. In contrast, two-stage detectors use a preliminary stage in which important areas in space are detected and then they are classified to see if an object has been detected in these areas. The advantage of one-stage detectors is that they are able to make predictions quickly, which allows them to be used in real time.

© Springer Nature Switzerland AG 2024
R. Yavorskiy et al. (Eds.): TMPA 2021, CCIS 1559, pp. 177–182, 2024.
https://doi.org/10.1007/978-3-031-50423-5_16

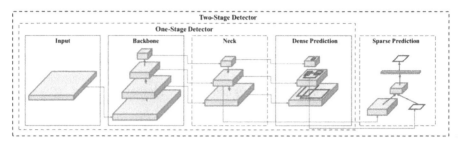

Fig. 1. One-stage and two-stage detectors

The studied YOLOv4 CNN refers to one-stage detectors and consists of blocks [3]: Input – source images; Backbone (used to build a deeper CNN in order to improve its accuracy) – this block uses CSPDarknet53 [4]; Neck (used to obtain richer spatial and semantic information) – this block uses SPP [5] for additional layers and PAN for path aggregation; Dense Prediction (used to determine the coordinates of the bounding boxes along with the confidence score for the class) – this block uses the YOLOv3 CNN.

Compared to the previous versions of the YOLO CNNs, the YOLOv4 CNN uses new methods and tools; therefore, it is a more efficient CNN for object detection than the previous CNNs of this class. Therefore, the average detection accuracy – mAP (mean Average Precision) metric – increased with its help from 57.9% to 65.7% compared to the YOLOv3 CNN.

3 Researching of the Efficiency of Detection of Flying Objects in Images

3.1 Preparation of Datasets and Software Implementation of the YOLOv4 CNN

To research the efficiency of the YOLOv4 CNN in solving the problems of detection of FO, datasets were marked and prepared based on video materials of FO of two classes: helicopter-type unmanned aerial vehicles and gliders. The size of the dataset of each class is about 5000 images of which one half is optical images and other half is images obtained in the IR wavelength range. To obtain such number of images of FO, preliminary data augmentation was performed using operations of variability of positioning and image size; operations of obtaining vertically and horizontally inverted images; operations of obtaining images rotated at a certain angle, etc.

For training of the YOLOv4 CNN 80% of the volume of these datasets were used and for testing/researching of the YOLOv4 CNN – 20%. For software implementation of the YOLOv4 CNN the Python programming language, the PyTorch framework and the Google Colab development environment were used. Training of the CNN and testing/researching of its efficiency were performed on a Tesla T4 processor.

3.2 Results of Detection of Flying Objects in Images

When testing of the trained YOLOv4 CNN and researching of its efficiency on optical and IR images the following parameters of the CNN were changed: input image size

$(416 \times 416, 512 \times 512, 608 \times 608$ pixels), mini-batch size $(4, 8)$ and activation function (Leaky ReLU, Mish). When training and testing of the YOLOv4 CNN the following parameters were unchanged: number of epochs (equals to 200), learning rate (equals to 0.001) and the Adam algorithm was used as an optimizer.

Figure 2 shows, as an example, the results of detection of FO for each of the classes in optical images and in images obtained in the IR wavelength range.

a)   b)

Fig. 2. Results of detection of FO in optical images and in images obtained in the IR wavelength range: a) helicopter-type unmanned aerial vehicle; b) glider.

First, experiment No. 1 was performed to determine the influence of the size of the mini-batch and the size of the input optical images on the accuracy of detection of FO using the YOLOv4 CNN with the Leaky ReLU activation function. The experimental results are shown in Table 1.

Table 1. Accuracy of detection of FO in optical images for different sizes of mini-batches and of input images

Mini-batch size	Image size	Using BoF/BoS	mAP, %
4	416×416	–	61,3
8	416×416	–	62,4
4	512×512	+	64,4
8	512×512	+	64,5

A set of techniques or methods that change the training strategy or the cost of training of the CNN to improve the accuracy of object detection is called BoF (Bag of Freebies). BoS (Bag of Specials) contains various plugins and post-processing modules that only slightly increase the cost of training of the CNN, but can significantly increase the accuracy of object detection [3]. It follows from Table 1 that the use of BoF/BoS in our case also increases the accuracy of detection, but the size of the mini-batch has practically no effect on it.

In experiment No. 2, the accuracy of detection of FO in optical images was determined using the YOLOv4 CNN for different activation functions and sizes of input optical images. The size of the mini-batch remained unchanged and was equal to 8. The experimental results are shown in Table 2.

Table 2. Accuracy of detection of FO in optical images for different activation functions and sizes of input images

Activation function	Image size	mAP, %
Leaky ReLU	416 × 416	62,4
Mish	416 × 416	62,8
Leaky ReLU	512 × 512	64,2
Mish	512 × 512	64,5
Leaky ReLU	608 × 608	65,2
Mish	608 × 608	65,7

In experiment No. 3, the rate of detection of FO was determined using the YOLOv4 CNN for different sizes of the input optical images. The size of the mini-batch remained unchanged and was equal to 8. The results of the experiment are shown in Table 3.

Table 3. Rate of detection of FO in optical images for different sizes of input images

Image size	Frames per second (FPS)	Average time of detection, ms
416 × 416	46	21,7
512 × 512	37	27,0
608 × 608	30	33,3

Here, the detection rate was defined as the average time of detection of FO per analysis of one image. It was calculated by averaging the results over the detection time of 1000 optical images.

In the following three experiments, only the initial data changed: instead of optical images at the input of the CNN images obtained in the IR wavelength range are used. The results of these experiments are shown in Table 4, Table 5 and Table 6.

Here, the detection rate was defined as the average time of detection of FO per analysis of one image. It was calculated by averaging the results over the detection time of 1000 images obtained in the IR wavelength range.

Table 4. Accuracy of detection of FO in images obtained in the IR wavelength range for different sizes of mini-batches and of input images

Mini-batch size	Image size	Using BoF/BoS	mAP, %
4	416×416	–	55,4
8	416×416	–	56,7
4	512×512	+	58,9
8	512×512	+	59,1

Table 5. Accuracy of detection of FO in images obtained in the IR wavelength range for different activation functions and sizes of input images

Activation function	Image size	mAP, %
Leaky ReLU	416×416	56,7
Mish	416×416	57,1
Leaky ReLU	512×512	58,6
Mish	512×512	59,1
Leaky ReLU	608×608	60,2
Mish	608×608	60,7

Table 6. Rate of detection of FO in images obtained in the IR wavelength range for different sizes of input images

Image size	FPS	Average time of detection, ms
416×416	42	23,8
512×512	36	27,7
608×608	27	37,0

4   Analysis of the Obtained Results

As follows from Table 1 and Table 4, the accuracy of detection of FO in images using the YOLOv4 CNN changes insignificantly when using BoF/BoS. Without using of such procedures, the mini-batch size significantly affects the accuracy: the higher its value, the more accurate the detection. This is consistent with the results obtained in the detection of various objects of a different physical nature [6].

The experimental results in Table 2 and Table 5 show that the accuracy of detection of FO in images using the YOLOv4 CNN is higher when using the Mish activation function for different sizes of input images. This function is smooth, monotonic, bounded from below and unbounded from above, so these properties of it allow us to obtain the best results compared to the Leaky ReLU activation function.

From the experimental results given in Table 3 and Table 6, it follows that the best rate of detection of FO in images using the YOLOv4 CNN can be obtained with the input image size of 416 × 416 pixels. As the size of the input images increases, the detection time for image increases and the number of frames processed per second (FPS) decreases. These results indicate that there are sizes of input images at which the YOLOv4 CNN-based computer vision system that performs detection of FO can function in real time.

Analysis of the experimental results shows that the accuracy of detection of FO using the YOLOv4 CNN in optical images is 5–6% (according to the mAP metric) higher than in images obtained in the IR wavelength range. This is explained by the fact that the YOLOv4 CNN takes into account the color characteristics of FO in the formation of feature maps that increases the detection results.

5   Conclusion

The most important task in airspace control is the task of localization and classification of various FO. To solve it, in recent years, images of FO obtained in the optical and IR wavelength ranges have been increasingly analyzed. For this, computer vision systems are being created based on modern CNN.

Large-scale studies of the efficiency of the YOLOv4 CNN were performed in detection of two classes of FO in images: helicopter-type unmanned aerial vehicles and gliders. It was found that the accuracy of detection of FO using the YOLOv4 CNN increases with increasing of the size of the input images and the best results were obtained using the Mish activation function. It is shown that the accuracy of detection of FO using the YOLOv4 CNN in optical images is higher than in images obtained in the IR wavelength range. The obtained estimates of the rate of detection of FO in images indicate the possibility of creating a computer vision system based on the YOLOv4 CNN that detects FO in real time.

References

1. Makarenko, S.I.: Counter Unmanned Aerial Vehicles. Science-Intensive Technologies, St. Petersburg (2020)
2. Tkachev, S.A.: Hardware Implementation Analysis of YOLO Convolutional Neural Networks. Scientific Session 2020, Collection of Selected Articles of TUSUR, vol. 2, pp. 82–84. TUSUR, Tomsk (2020)
3. Bochkovskiy, A., Wang, C.Y., Mark Liao, H.Y.: YOLOv4: optimal speed and accuracy of object detection. Journal arXiv, preprint arXiv:2004.10934v1 (2020)
4. Wang, C.Y., Mark Liao, H.Y., Yeh, I.H., Wu, Y.H., Chen, P.Y., Hsieh, J.W.: CSPNet: a new backbone that can enhance learning capability of CNN. Journal arXiv, preprint arXiv:1911.11929v1 (2019)
5. He, K., Zhang, X., Ren, S., Sun, J.: Spatial pyramid pooling in deep convolutional networks for visual recognition. Journal arXiv, preprint arXiv:1406.4729v4 (2015)
6. Zoev, I.V., Markov, N.G., Ryzhova, S.E.: Intelligent computer vision system for unmanned aerial vehicles for monitoring technological objects at oil and gas industry. In: Geo Assets Engineering 2019, Bulletin of Tomsk Polytechnic University, vol. 330, pp. 34–49. TPU, Tomsk (2019)

Modern Experiment Management Systems Architecture for Scientific Big Data

Anastasiia Kaida$^{(\boxtimes)}$ ⓘ and Aleksei Savelev ⓘ

National Research Tomsk Polytechnic University, Lenina Ave. 30, 634050 Tomsk, Russia
ayk13@tpu.ru

Abstract. Experiment management systems (EMS) have more than twenty-five years of history. From small desktop prototypes to large-scale distributed systems, they become more and more complicated. The new chapter of EMS was uncovered with the age of Big Data surrounded by a special ecosystem to extract, analyze and store data. The big data ecosystem considers new elements that must be taken into account to expand the functionality for EMS to support all data lifecycle stages.

One of the challenges is to highlight the key points of a huge variety of EMS evolving through time. Such systems do not usually follow a unified pattern because of special needs for each project. This paper introduces the conceptual high-level architecture as an example of a unified pattern of building EMS for big data ecosystems. The architecture does not consider to be used with the grid computing approach.

Keywords: Big Data · Experiment Management System · Data Lifecycle · Data Reprocessing · Knowledge Base

1 Introduction

1.1 Experiment Management System

Experiment Management System (EMS) [1] is a system that provides support to scientists throughout all stages of an experiment. It is a special software complex that connects the scientist conducting the experiment and the data. EMS allows to plan and organize an experiment, manage data and analyze the obtained results, in other words, it allows to ensure the complete life cycle of the data. The first scientific experiment control systems appeared before the age of big data, but still there are several challenges related to EMS and Big Data:

- Exponential growth of data.
- Growth the number of used formats (data heterogeneity).
- Usage of distributed heterogeneous computing systems.
- Expansion of cooperation through the creation of scientific collaborations and interdisciplinary research groups [2].

© Springer Nature Switzerland AG 2024
R. Yavorskiy et al. (Eds.): TMPA 2021, CCIS 1559, pp. 183–187, 2024.
https://doi.org/10.1007/978-3-031-50423-5_17

1.2 Data Lifecycle

When we are talking about data, we consider that data may be gathered in a huge variety of types. This is the source of information that is useless without a chain of processing steps, from data extracting to data storing/eliminating that forms the whole data lifecycle. There are five main stages:

Data Extraction. This is an initial stage of the data lifecycle. Data can be previously stored and retrieved by a request from a source in the digital infrastructure of an experiment or get from an external unsupervised source like web-source using crawlers [3], API, or web-scraping [4].

Data Pre-processing. Usually, we consider that the quality of raw data is unpleasantly poor. To increase the quality, we need to make an exploratory data analysis and prepare data for future use. Pre-processing is needed to eliminate mistakes, fill missing data (if possible) and eliminate doubles [5].

Data Analysis. Despite the fact that we included EDA in the previous stages, after making data exploration and data quality assessment, we need to make a particular data analysis (e.g. semantic or statistical analysis) according to data type to extract new information and send it to the next stage [6].

The Operational Stage. On this stage the extracted information may be applied as an input for other tasks (e.g. in applied AI tasks).

Data Storing/Eliminating. The last stage. The data lifecycle may be performed as a circle or a flat line. The answer what data should be stored in the end of data lifecycle depends on the experiment digital infrastructure and the goals of a research group [7].

1.3 Scientific Big Data Processing

In contradiction to building standard engineering solutions, making digital infrastructure around a new research group may have a stochastic nature. On the initial step or during a switch to a new concept there is a probability of understanding that expected amounts of operated data will increase rapidly and require new tools [8].

2 Generic Big Data EMS Components

2.1 Problem Statement

We propose the conceptual high-level big data EMS architecture for cases that do not require widely distributed computing systems. That class of scientific projects is usually related to so-called "mega-science" [9] projects with a unique hardware complex as well as specific digital infrastructure. We suppose that the need of searching the common pattern in such class of scientific facilities is still under the question.

2.2   Components Description

The proposed architecture was formed based on our previous experience and observations of how to perform dataflow in scientific experiments and avoid data overloading (see Fig. 1). We divided the whole set of mandatory components into two categories. Some of them are based on existing open-source solutions that require only a particular configuration. The others may be developed by research groups on their own.

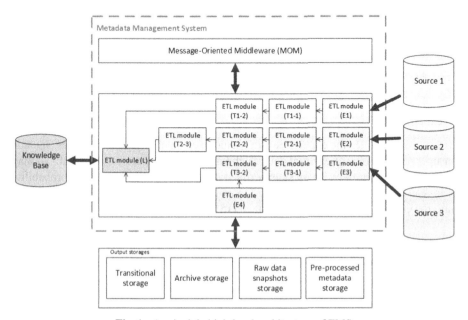

Fig. 1. A principle high-level architecture of EMS.

Knowledge Base. It is a key element that contains links to data sources and additional metadata. It provides a high-level management option for a huge variety of big data ecosystem configurations [10]. We consider that knowledge base may be performed based on non-relational document-oriented storage or ontological storage.

ETL Pipelines. As we discussed before, ETL pipelines allows to operate with heterogeneous data in a flexible form. This flexibility was gained because of logical separation between ETL-modules and its data-oriented structure. Changing the aim of a research will make less influence on dataflow rebuilding process than using a holistic solution [11].

Metadata Management System. The whole big data ecosystem built around scientific experiment consists of different separated items. Dataflow must be organized through each needed item including storages and processing modules. Maintenance the dataflow manually operating with amounts of heterogeneous complex data may cause data errors, imbalance of computational loads and memory overloads in processing "bottleneck" parts. Management system is aimed to link the components and control the dataflow in automated way [11, 12].

Supervising Tool. This is a high-level end-user tool to manage the data streams processing. Basically, the supervising tool allow to run, observe and stop the process.

Message-Oriented Middleware (MOM). The smallest dataflow item that contains data may be presented as a message, but data delivery can not be performed by the processing stage by itself. MOM is a middle layer between metadata management system and ETL modules that helps to deliver data and control processing state [13, 14].

Input/Output Data and Metadata Storages. Due to the fact that evolving of scientific project may cause appearing different storages during experiment lifetime, we deal with heterogeneous data sources and the request of metadata aggregation. Moreover, we need to collect data produced during processing stages: raw data snapshots, transitional data, pre-processed data and archived data that may be retrieved later by a request to reproduce an experiment [7].

External Sources. Some experiments (e.g. studying social media sources) may include unsupervised sources of external data. Such kind of data sources are essential, but may deny of service abruptly. To make experiments with a consideration of this probability of loss an essential data source, we need to make data snapshots and store them at least until the end of an active experiment stage [15].

3 Future Objectives

An implementation of the proposed architecture will let to organize experiment automation. It means that the dataflow inside big data experiments may be organized, managed, and even re-built with less cost of time and less manual interaction. In turn, that will reduce the probability of data overloading and the number of errors made because of human factors. This work relates to scientific experiments performed in the laboratory of unstructured information processing at Tomsk Polytechnic University. The next step is to build a test bench based on our proposed architecture as a PoC and run experiments using the deployed system.

Acknowledgement. The study is funded by the Science State Program as part of the project No. FSWW-2020-0014.

References

1. Ioannidis, Y., Livny, M., Haber, E., Miller, R., Tsatalos, O., Wiener, J.: Desktop experiment management. Technical report. Stanford InfoLab. Publication Note: Appeared in IEEE Data Engineering Bulletin, vol. 16, no. 1 (1993)
2. Ioannidis, Y., Livny, M., Gupta, S., Ponnekanti, N.: ZOO: a desktop experiment management environment. In: Proceedings of the 22nd International VLDB Conference, pp. 274–285 (1996)

3. Scrapy—A Fast and Powerful Scraping and Web Crawling Framework. https://scrapy.org/. Accessed 21 Sept 2021
4. Mitchell, R.: Web Scraping with Python, 2nd edn. O'Reilly Media Inc., CA (2018)
5. Kwak, S.K., Kim, J.H.: Statistical data preparation: management of missing values and outliers. Korean J. Anesthesiol. **70**(4), 407–411 (2017)
6. Bruce, P., Bruce, A.: Practical Statistics for Data Scientists. O'Reilly Media Inc., CA (2017)
7. Bengfort, B., Bilbro, R., Ojeda, T.: Applied Text Analysis with Python. O'Reilly Media Inc., CA (2018)
8. Ferreira D.R., Enterprise Systems Integration: A Process-Oriented Approach. Springer, Heidelberg (2013). https://doi.org/10.1007/978-3-642-40796-3
9. Megascience class installations. https://ckp-rf.ru/megaunu/. Accessed 21 Sept 2021
10. Golosova, M., Grigorieva, M., Aulov V., Kaida A., Borodin M.: Data knowledge base: metadata integration for HENP experiments. In: CEUR Workshop Proceedings, vol. 2507, pp. 200–205
11. What is ETL (Extract, Transform, Load)?—IBM. https://www.ibm.com/cloud/learn/etl. Accessed 21 Sept 2021
12. Buchert, T., Ruiz, C., Nussbaum, L., Richard, O.: A survey of general-purpose experiment management tools for distributed systems. Futur. Gener. Comput. Syst. **45**, 1–12 (2015)
13. Narkhede, N., Shapira, G., Palino, T.: Kafka: The Definitive Guide. O'Reilly Media Inc, CA (2017)
14. Active MQ. https://activemq.apache.org/. Accessed 21 Sept 2021
15. Karpova, A., Savelev, A.O., Vilnin, A.D., Chaykovskiy, D.V.: Studying online radicalization of youth through social media (interdisciplinary approach). Monit. Public Opinion: Econ. Soc. Changes J. **3**(157), 159–181 (2020)

An Approach to Modules Similarity Definition Based on System Trace Analysis

Ilya Samonenko[1]([✉])[ID], Tamara Voznesenskaya[1][ID], and Rostislav Yavorskiy[2][ID]

[1] Higher School of Economics, Moscow 101000, Russia
{isamonenko,tvoznesenskaya}@hse.ru
[2] Tomsk Polytechnic University, Tomsk 634050, Russia
ryavorsky@tpu.ru

Abstract. We study a distributed process organised as a sequence of somehow related modules. A token passes through different modules and leaves a digital trace in the log. Our goal is to design an optimal distance function between modules for clustering purposes, finding abnormal behaviour and predicting the digital trace of new coming tokens.

Keywords: log analysis · distributed system · similarity measure · educational data mining · machine learning

1 Introduction

Our research is motivated by the analysis of data produced by learning management systems, although the mathematical model we study is quite general and could be applied in a different context.

Typically, a university department suggests a collection of different courses to students. Some of the courses are mandatory, while others are optional. An individual educational trajectory is a sequence of courses, which is formed according to the personal preferences of students and the courses' prerequisites.

In literature, there are many approaches to using process mining for data analysis in education and modelling the educational processes [1–3,6,11].

In some works, approaches to measuring distances between courses have been proposed [7,9,12,13].

Our goal is to figure out the similarity between courses on the basis of available historical performance data. By similarity, we mean comparable resulting grades for different categories of students. Also, there are many different approaches to compute distance or similarity measures for vectors [4,5,8,10]. Our idea is to use machine learning algorithms in order to find the best optimal combination of them.

In Sect. 2, we provide all the necessary definitions of the general model. In Sect. 3, we describe our approach. The data and computational experiments are described in Sect. 4. The plan for the subsequent research is in Sect. 5.

ⓒ Springer Nature Switzerland AG 2024
R. Yavorskiy et al. (Eds.): TMPA 2021, CCIS 1559, pp. 188–195, 2024.
https://doi.org/10.1007/978-3-031-50423-5_18

2   Definitions

The generalised mathematical model is defined in this section.

2.1   The System Model

A **distributed modular system S** is a tuple

$$\mathbf{S} = (\mathbf{M}, \mathbf{T}, \mathbf{O}, \lambda),$$

where:

- $\mathbf{M} = \{m_1, m_2, \ldots, m_n\}$ is a finite set of **modules**;
- $\mathbf{T} = \{t_1, t_2, \ldots, t_k\}$ is a finite set of **tokens**;
- $\mathbf{O} = \{o_1, o_2, \ldots, o_r\}$ is a finite set of **outputs**;
- $\lambda : \mathbf{M} \times \mathbf{T} \to \mathbf{O} \cup \{\#\}$ is a **trace** function, where $\#$ is a special symbol that denotes an undefined value.

All tokens are processed by one or more modules. We say that if a token $t \in \mathbf{T}$ is processed by module $m \in \mathbf{M}$ then an outgoing symbol $o \in \mathbf{O}$ is generated and $\lambda(m, t) = o$. If the token $t \in \mathbf{T}$ is not processed by module $m \in \mathbf{M}$ then the outgoing symbol is not defended and $\lambda(m, t) = \#$.

Without loss of generality, the **trace** of a distributed modular system $\mathbf{S}$ is a matrix:

$$\lambda = \begin{pmatrix} \lambda(m_1, t_1) \ \ldots \ \lambda(m_1, t_k) \\ \vdots \qquad \vdots \qquad \vdots \\ \lambda(m_n, t_1) \ \ldots \ \lambda(m_n, t_k) \end{pmatrix}$$

A **trace of module** $m \in \mathbf{M}$ is a corresponding row of the matrix λ:

$$\lambda(m) = (\lambda(m, t_1), \ldots, \lambda(m, t_k)).$$

A **trace of token** $t \in \mathbf{T}$ is a corresponding column of the matrix λ:

$$\lambda(t) = (\lambda(m_1, t), \ldots, \lambda(m_n, t)).$$

Remark. For these definitions, the concepts of traces of modules and tokens are dual. Further, we will talk about the traces of modules, but our reasoning can be applied to traces of tokens.

2.2   A Distinction Function of Comparable Modules

Let s be some fixed natural number. We say that

$$f : \mathbf{O}^N \times \mathbf{O}^N \to \mathbb{R}$$

is a **distinction function** iff:

1. The function f is defended for any $N \geq s$,

2. $\exists c_1, c_2 \in \mathbb{R} : \forall N \geq s$ and $\forall x, y \in \mathbf{O}^N$ we have $c_1 \leq f(x, y) \leq c_2$,
3. $\forall x \in \mathbf{O}^N$ we have $f(x, x) = 0$,
4. $\forall x, y \in \mathbf{O}^N$ we have $f(x, y) = f(y, x)$.

Example 1. Let $\mathbf{O} = \{0, 1, \ldots, 10\}$ and

$$f((x_1, \ldots, x_N), (y_1, \ldots, y_N)) = \frac{1}{N} \sum_{i=1}^{N} |x_i - y_i|,$$

then

$$0 \leq f((x_1, \ldots, x_N), (y_1, \ldots, y_N)) \leq 10.$$

Example 2. Let $\mathbf{O} \subset \mathbb{R}$ and

$$f((x_1, \ldots, x_N), (y_1, \ldots, y_N)) = 1 - r((x_1, \ldots, x_N), (y_1, \ldots, y_N)),$$

where $r(\cdot, \cdot)$ is a Pearson correlation coefficient, then

$$0 \leq f((x_1, \ldots, x_N), (y_1, \ldots, y_N)) \leq 2.$$

We say that two modules a and b are **comparable** if, at least, s tokens exist, $t \in \mathbf{T}$, for which both $\lambda(a, t)$ and $\lambda(b, t)$ are defined. In other words, for two digital traces, $\lambda(a)$ and $\lambda(b)$ have at least s defined values at the same positions.

More formally, let $a, b \in M$, $\lambda(a) = (a_1, \ldots, a_n)$ and $\lambda(b) = (b_1, \ldots, b_n)$. Denote:

$$I_{a,b} = \{i | (a_i, b_i) \in \mathbf{O} \times \mathbf{O}\}.$$

If $|I_{a,b}| \geq s$ then a and b are comparable.

Further, we will consider only comparable pairs of modules unless otherwise specifically agreed.

Let f be a diversity function. We can apply the function f for any comparable pair of modules a and b in the following sense:

$$f(a, b) := f((a_{i_1}, \ldots, a_{i_s}), (b_{i_1}, \ldots, a_{i_s})),$$

where $\lambda(a) = (a_1, \ldots, a_n)$, $\lambda(b) = (b_1, \ldots, b_n)$ and $I_{a,b} = \{i_1, \ldots, i_s\}$.

Now we can explain the meaning of the definition of the diversity function.

The properties 1. and 2. are required because we want to use one function f for different pairs of comparable modules a and b with different $|I_{a,b}|$. We want to avoid the situation when the value of the function f grows in line with $|I_{a,b}|$.

The properties 3. and 4. are required because we will build a distance function based on functions with these properties.

2.3   The Modules' Similarity

Suppose we know that some modules are similar in some sense. To formalise this, we introduce an equivalence relation $\sim$ on $\mathbf{M}$ into the model. Informally, $a \sim b$ when a and b have very similar or identical properties. At the same time, we cannot say anything about a and b if $a \not\sim b$. Maybe they are similar, maybe not.

From a practical point of view, we can assume that we have expert knowledge that some modules are similar. However, there may be many other similar modules, but we don't know anything about it. Thus, this equivalent relation $<<\sim>>$ is our a priori partial knowledge about modules' similarity.

Our ultimate goal is to find a **distance** function ρ on M such that:

1. $\forall a, b, c \in \mathbf{M}$ $\rho(a, b) \leq \rho(a, c) + \rho(b, c)$
2. $\forall a, b, c \in \mathbf{M}$ $((a \sim b) \wedge (a \not\sim c)) \rightarrow (\rho(a, b) \leq \rho(a, c))$
3. $\rho(a, b) = R(f_1(a, b), \ldots, f_N(a, b))$, where f_i - are diversity functions.

The first property is the $<<$triangle inequality$>>$.

The second property means that the distance between a pair of similar modules must be smaller or equal to the distance between a pair of dissimilar modules.

The third property means that the value of the distance is determined only through the values of diversity functions. Remark, that $<<$identity of indiscernibles$>>$ and $<<$symmetry$>>$ of ρ follows from 3. and 4. properties of diversity functions.

If such a distance function ρ does not exist, our goal is to find the best approximation. Denote:

$$\psi(\rho) = \frac{|\{(a, b, c) | \rho(a, b) > \rho(a, c) + \rho(b, c)\}|}{|\{a, b, c - \text{pairwise comparable}\}|}$$

– the ratio of pairwise comparable modules on which the first property is incorrect.

$$\phi(\rho) = \frac{|\{(a, b, c) | (a \sim b) \wedge (a \not\sim c) \wedge (\rho(a, b) > \rho(a, c))\}|}{|\{(a, b, c) | (a \sim b) \wedge (a \not\sim c)\}|}$$

– the ratio of pairwise comparable modules on which the second property is incorrect.

We want to minimise the number of triples (a, b, c) for which properties 1. or 2. by minimising performance function:

$$\chi(\rho) = \lambda_1 \psi(\rho) + \lambda_2 \phi(\rho) \rightarrow \min,$$

where λ_1, λ_2 – some fixed parameters.

2.4   Motivation

As we said earlier, equivalence relations can contain expert knowledge about the similarity of some modules. Using the constructed distance function ρ, we can solve the following problems:

1. Initially, we have only a binary classification of a small number of modules pairs (similar or dissimilar). Now we can determine the value of similarity of all comparable pairs of modules.

2. Initially, we had no information about non-comparable models. Now we can estimate the value of similarity of some non-comparable modules.

   For example, suppose a and b is a pair of comparable modules; b and c is a pair comparable modules; but a and c is a pair of non-comparable modules. Then we can deduct that the distance between a and c does not exceed $\rho(a, b) + \rho(b, c)$.

3. We can search for the abnormal behaviour of modules. For example, suppose we have a set of equivalence modules $\{a_1, \ldots, a_k\}$, i.e. we assume that they should have the same behaviour. But for some a_q we have that the average distance from a_q to all other modules is bigger than the average distance between all pairs of modules. It means that module a_q is an outlier. And we need to check why this module a_q has such behaviour.

3   Approach Description

Our approach for finding the ρ distance function is as follows:

1. Choose some quality threshold χ_0.
2. Choose some set of diversity functions $\mathbf{F} = \{f_1, \ldots, f_N\}$.
3. Solve a positive-undefended classification problem to find pairs of equivalent modules.
4. Construct the ρ function based on the probabilities of equivalency of a pair of modules.
5. If $\chi(\rho) > \chi_0$, then change the set of diversity functions and hyperparameters of the classification model, and go to step 2.

Suppose we have a distributed modular system $\mathbf{S}$ and a set of diversity functions $\mathbf{F} = \{f_1, \ldots, f_N\}$. To solve practical problems, various sets of diversity functions can be used: normalised distance functions, correlations, etc. This set can include different functions that make at least some sense for comparing modules. This set $\mathbf{F}$ may be redundant, the further procedure will leave only the necessary functions.

Consider a **positive-undefended (PU) classification problem** for pairs of equivalence modules:

- An object: pairs of all comparable modules $(a, b) \in \mathbf{M} \times \mathbf{M}$;
- Features of an object (a, b): values of all diversity functions:

$$(f_1(a, b), \ldots, f_N(a, b)).$$

- A sample of positive (target) class: $\{(a, b) | a \sim b\}$.

Suppose we have built a classifier that solves the PU-classification problem. Let $P(a, b)$ be a probability, then $a \sim b$. Define the distance function ρ in the following way:

$$\rho(a, b) = 1 - P(a, b).$$

There may be other ways to define ρ, for example:

$$\rho(a, b) = -\ln(P(a, b)).$$

After receiving $\rho(a, b)$, it is necessary to estimate its performance $\chi(\rho)$. Note that this estimation can be statistical, i.e. it is enough to select a large number of triples of modules (a, b, c) for the calculations $\psi(\rho)$ and $\phi(\rho)$.

The proposed approach has a large variability:

- Choosing a threshold.
- Choosing diversity functions.
- Choosing a classification model and its hyperparameters.
- Choosing a definition $\rho(a, b)$.
- Choosing an estimation $\chi(\rho)$.
- Choosing a strategy of changing diversity functions and model hyperparameters.

Each time the choice is made for a specific problem. In the next section, we will show how we applied this approach to the analysis of disciplines of educational programs.

4   Data and Analysis

We analysed the HSE courses and students for the period 2017–2020. We wanted to build a metric **of thematic proximity** of courses based on students' grades. Courses with similar content should be close, courses with different content should be far away.

We have considered the following distributed modular model:

1. **M** - a set of all courses.
2. **T** - a set of all students.
3. **O** $= \{0, 1, 2, \ldots, 10\}$ - a set of possible grades.
4. $\lambda(m, t)$ - the grade of student t on course m.

Constant $s = 10$, it means that we compare two courses if at least 10 students have grades on both.

We choose diversity functions as follows: l_1 - metrics, l_2 - metrics, Hamming metrics, Pearson correlation coefficient, Spearman correlation coefficient, Kendall correlation coefficient.

If some course (for example, calculus) lasts for one academic year, but it included two exams (for example, in the winter and spring terms), then we consider that we have two proximal courses with the same name.

We assume that courses a and b are equivalent iff:

1. they have the same name;
2. they are implemented in the same educational program and the same academic year.

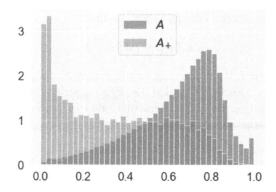

Fig. 1. Distribution of distances between all pairs of comparable disciplines and the proximal disciplines (Color figure online)

Our dataset contained $2,582,129$ grades for $|\mathbf{M}| = 54,652$ disciplines. Number of pairs of comparable disciplines is $959,201$ and the number of pairs of proximal disciplines is $12,179$.

We have received a classifier for which ROC-AUC is equal to 0.81 and distance function $\rho(a, b) = 1 - P(a, b)$ for which $\phi(\rho)$ is equal to 0.98.

In Fig. 1 the distribution of $\rho(a, b)$ values is presented separately for all pairs of comparable courses $\mathcal{A}$ (blue colour) and all pairs of proximal disciplines $\mathcal{A}_+$ (orange colour). By our expectations, we can see that the distances between the proximal disciplines are, on average, less than between arbitrary pairs of disciplines. The average distance between all pairs of disciplines is 0.64, while the average distance between obviously thematically-related disciplines is 0.34.

5   Conclusion

Although contemporary information systems produce a lot of data, analysing the digital trace is a complex task. The approach described above allows a combination of expert knowledge (when defining the proximity relation) and modern machine learning tools.

References

1. van der Aalst, W.M.P., Guo, S., Gorissen, P.: Comparative process mining in education: an approach based on process cubes. In: Ceravolo, P., Accorsi, R., Cudre-Mauroux, P. (eds.) SIMPDA 2013. LNBIP, vol. 203, pp. 110–134. Springer, Heidelberg (2015). https://doi.org/10.1007/978-3-662-46436-6_6
2. Bogarín, A., Romero, C., Cerezo, R., Sánchez-Santillán, M.: Clustering for improving educational process mining. In: Proceedings of the Fourth International Conference on Learning Analytics and Knowledge, pp. 11–15 (2014)
3. Cairns, A.H., Gueni, B., Fhima, M., Cairns, A., David, S., Khelifa, N.: Process mining in the education domain. Int. J. Adv. Intell. Syst. 8(1), 219–232 (2015)

4. Choi, S.S., Cha, S.H.: A survey of binary similarity and distance measures. J. Systemics Cybern. Informat. **8**, 43–48 (2010)
5. Egghe, L.: Good properties of similarity measures and their complementarity. J. Am. Soc. Inform. Sci. Technol. **61**(10), 2151–2160 (2010)
6. Juhaňák, L., Zounek, J., Rohlíková, L.: Using process mining to analyze students' quiz-taking behavior patterns in a learning management system. Comput. Hum. Behav. **92**, 496–506 (2019). https://doi.org/10.1016/j.chb.2017.12.015, https://www.sciencedirect.com/science/article/pii/S0747563217306957
7. Méndez, G., Ochoa, X., Chiluiza, K., De Wever, B.: Curricular design analysis: a data-driven perspective. J. Learn. Analyt. **1**, 84–119 (2014). https://doi.org/10.18608/jla.2014.13.6
8. Ochoa, X.: Simple metrics for curricular analytics. In: CEUR Workshop Proceedings, vol. 1590, pp. 20–26. CEUR-WS (2016)
9. Ren, Q., et al.: Network modelling and visualisation analysis of the undergraduate dental curriculum system in China. J. Comput. Commun. **09**, 38–51 (2021). https://doi.org/10.4236/jcc.2021.96003
10. Santini, S., Jain, R.: Similarity measures. IEEE Trans. Pattern Anal. Mach. Intell. **21**(9), 871–883 (1999). https://doi.org/10.1109/34.790428
11. dos Santos Garcia, C., et al.: Process mining techniques and applications - a systematic mapping study. Expert Syst. Appl. **133**, 260–295 (2019). https://doi.org/10.1016/j.eswa.2019.05.003, https://www.sciencedirect.com/science/article/pii/S0957417419303161
12. Sekiya, T., Yoshitatsu, M., Yamaguchi, K.: Analysis of curriculum structure based on LDA. In: Lecture Notes in Engineering and Computer Science, vol. 2178 (2009)
13. Johnson, T.: Applications of intuitionistic fuzzy sets in the academic career of the students. Indian J. Sci. Technol. **10**, 23–25 (2017). https://doi.org/10.17485/ijst/2017/v10i34/94944

Author Index

© Springer Nature Switzerland AG 2024
R. Yavorskiy et al. (Eds.): TMPA 2021, CCIS 1559, pp. 197–198, 2024.
https://doi.org/10.1007/978-3-031-50423-5

Printed in the United States
by Baker & Taylor Publisher Services